THE SMARTEST MAN IN HISTORY

DR AUGUSTO CURY

ISBN: 978-1-965965-12-2 (Paperback)

Table of Contents

PREFACE

I was probably more skeptical and critical than some of history's greatest atheists such as Marx, Nietzsche, Diderot, Freud, and Sartre. While I was working on one of the few theories of modern times about the works of the mind and the process of formation of thinkers, I became, for many years, a scientific atheist, while the majority of remarkable atheists was, in fact, composed by anti-religious people.

In spite of my limitations, I decided to conduct a thorough study on the mind of the most famous character in history, looking at him under psychological, psychiatric, psycho-pedagogical and sociological point of view. I was hoping, when studying Jesus' personality, to find an ordinary intelligence, not very creative, not very analytical or stimulating, with no emotional management, in other words, I thought I would look at a "hero" poorly constructed by the Galilean. However, I was baffled. I became a boundless human being.

The result of this extensive research, which took me over 15 years, composes this book. The Most Intelligent Man in History, which will be comprised of many volumes. I believe that, had I not have more than 30 years of experience as a researcher and mental health professional – with over 20 thousand services –, I would not be able to write it. In spite all of this, I preferred to write it as a novel.

I am happy to see that, now, some of my books are being adapted to the movie screens. Recently, a remarkable filmmaker caught me by the arm and confessed that shooting a series based on *The Most Intelligent Man in History* will be his most important life project!

The psychiatrist and scientist Marco Polo is the protagonist of this story. During a paramount conference promoted by the UN in Jerusalem for discussing Earth's future, he shakes the people present talking about the preservation of another planet, planet emotion: "Before Earth's resources extinguish, the human mind will die out", he declared.

Questioned about who, among the brightest thinkers, were good emotion managers, Marco Polo commented: "All whom I have studied failed: Freud, Einstein, Gandhi, Nietzsche…", leaving the audience in awe. But, right after, an American sociologist raised the ultimate question: "How about Jesus? Was he a good emotion manager?" Marco Polo was imperative: "As an atheist I will not discuss religion in my conferences."

However, the audience of intellectuals, knowing that he was studying the process of formation of thinkers, challenged him to study Jesus' mind in the light of human sciences. He resisted firmly, but eventually, arranged a discussing table of prominent personalities in order to reflect and analyze Jesus Christ's intelligence.

Perhaps for the first time in history, the intellect of Jesus will be studied under strict parameters as the ability to cope with loss and frustration, resilience, self-control, ability to protect emotions and the tools to form great minds.

Marco Polo will, little by little, find out for himself that all of human's sciences and religions, have made the dramatic mistake of not studying

Jesus in the light of science. The mind of the most famous character of all times remains unknown even by the billions of humans from different religious background who admire him....

With the avalanche of stressing stimuli that he has lived since his childhood, Jesus had many reasons to become depressed and anxious. But, did he manage his emotion? Did he develop a solid mental health? Did he show self-control in stressful situations? As an educator, he had everything to fail, for he chose a team of disturbed young men that would only give him headaches. But, did Jesus use modern psychological techniques to transform rough matter into a work of art? Did he succeed?

The world celebrates the birth of a boy whose personality they do not know, let alone, how it was formed. I was very surprised with this analysis and, probably, many will also be surprised or even shocked with The Most Intelligent Man in History.

See for yourselves!

Dr Augusto Cury

CHAPTER 1

THE EMOTIONAL BEGGARS' ERA

The United Nations Secretary-General started the emergency meeting about violence in the world. Political leaders and thinkers from different areas were present. The numbers showed an alarming increase in violence, not only in poor and emerging countries but also in the richest nations.

"Bullying at schools, violence against women and children, psychological harassment in companies, sexual assaults, political corruption, market sabotage, immigrant segregation, suicides, homicides, and terrorism; the level of violence in modern societies is enormous. We have been living at a peak in terms of material progress in the digital era, but we could not stop the open vein of violence bleeding all over the world. Quite the opposite, it has been increasing. It's unbelievable!" He concluded in a worried tone. "The debate to find sustained solutions is open."

Several Presidents, Ministers, and Congressmen talked about the subject. A few sociologists also mentioned population density, economic crisis, social exclusion and so many other serious problems.

When the conference was coming to an end, and the audience was tired of listening to the same topics of discussion, the Secretary-General took the floor.

The United Nations wishes to thank the world leaders for attending this great conference about causes and solutions to violence in the modern age. We will make a report and send it to all nations, although I sense that we do lack appropriate diagnosis on this matter."

"We sure do!" shouted Dr. Marco Polo, a psychiatrist who was in the audience.

The Secretary-General rolled his eyes and warned him,

"I am sorry, sir, but the debate is not open to the audience."

Dr. Polo responded, "Great ideas are not properties of the political leaderships."

Surprised, the Secretary-General changed his mind.

"I'll make an exception. What is your name?"

"Marco Polo."

"Please, be brief. It's late, and we are to finish this meeting shortly."

Marco Polo, a daring man, a teaser who seemed wonderfully comfortable speaking in public said,

"Ladies and gentlemen, we step not merely on the surface of Earth but further on the surface of planet Emotion. An eruption of psychological and social disorders is taking place. This eruption is mostly because traditional Education has become extremely Cartesian, logic driven, and linear, disregarding the socio-emotional skills which can protect the psyche. If we don't change the setting of educational paradigms, we will become an unfeasible species!" The audience reacted.

"Change educational standards? What do you propose, Mr. Polo?" asked the Canadian minister who was sitting in the front row.

"World Education calls for a change. It must end the information age and take in the Self, as the conductor of the human mind era! The former has produced giants of science, that are only children in the field of emotions; The subsequent, generates well resolved, coherent and selfless human beings."

The matter in hand was altogether new and disturbing. Authorities who had been yawning during the lectures were now very much awake.

"What is it to be 'the conductor of the human mind'?" an American senator asked. "I have never heard of such thesis."

"To be a conductor of the human mind, is to know how to manage thoughts, how to protect emotions, how to free creativity, and how grow into being the protagonist of your own story. The classic Education believes that the best way of creating brilliant minds is to bombard students' heads with a ton of data, forcing them to learn everything. This is a tremendous mistake!"

"Education has been this way for centuries. It has always been the container and conductor of the most significant knowledge in humanity." The Secretary of Education in France replied.

"Very well, sir, but such wisdom doesn't work anymore, at least not generally. Our pupils' minds have changed. It is not possible to give paint and paintbrushes to a machine and expect it to create masterpieces as Da Vinci, Van Gogh and Rafael did. Nor is it possible to create masterpieces on the canvas of human minds with this educational style. People must learn to think cooperatively, to be selfless and seeing themselves in other people's shoes. They need to learn to cope with frustration!"

Marco then asked permission to play some projections on the screen. He always had a flash drive with him, and it contained videos and animations that he would use in his talks. But, his request was denied.

"Not possible. It's late, sir," an arrogant Secretary-General assistant replied.

"If the audience is not willing to hear me, I will immediately sit down," Marco said.

The audience cheered. The crowd now seemed to be athirst for learning the ideas that the doctor wanted to share.

The Secretary-General reconsidered his appeal. After receiving permission, Marco handed the flash drive to the technician in charge.

The conference saw people driving cars at excessive speed, drivers disrespecting traffic laws and causing serious accidents.

He then stated,

"Our intellect is an intricate mental vehicle, and we drive it excessively. Why? Schools and universities don't educate the Self. They don't show what it means to 'be behind the wheel' in terms of decision-making skills, free will, and critical awareness."

"Are you suggesting that we are currently at the childhood-stage of the 'Self as the conductor of the human mind' Era?" - Asked outraged, the Canadian prime minister.

"Yes. That's exactly what I'm saying!" Marco answered.

Then, being careful to protect the identity of the people involved, he projected pictures portraying extreme cases of bothered young adults self-mutilating, and anorexic girls who stood only as skin and bones.

"Do you know why these girls are as thin as the starving children in the Sub-Saharan Africa?" Marco asked. "Because they think they're fat. The beauty dictatorship has been poisoning our children from within."

After that, he showed anonymous individuals in violent scenes, involving murder for petty disputes.

"Minor frustrations causing disproportional reactions; We are surrounded by untamed emotions"

It was clear to notice the astonishment, displayed by the audience, during Polo's presentation. A powerful politician who was sitting in the front row, was silently reminiscing about the way he had yelled at his wife the day before as if she was his servant. 'Get out of my way, you fool! This suit doesn't match this tie!'

Marco continued his presentation.

"Vaccines protect us against viruses, but what vaccines will protect us from violence and psychological disorders? This will not be done without a change in the Education. Which of those vaccines would you give to your loved ones? Normally Neither! We are used to scolding, pointing out flaws and criticizing."

"But aren't the ones who follow a behavior-rule's manual, and carry it within themselves, doing good job in terms of education?" Asked an Republican-American senator.

"Unfortunately, people who only have code manuals, can only fix machines. They cannot, by any means, train brilliant minds."

After this comment, Marco went even further and said,

"Loss of emotional stability is the biggest violence, and we commit it against our children!"

With wide eyes and raised eyebrows, the Secretary-General asked, "How can we change this, Dr. Polo?" "There are many tools at our disposal. We can react slower and think faster; we can be more empathetic, worry about other people's troubles and know that behind the one who hurts there's an injured person. We can think as mankind and not only as a social group; All of these tools are directly related with the conduction of our own minds."

Then, the researcher showed that we are driving our mental vehicle of thought construction at unprecedented speeds. That is the reason why it's so easy to lose selfcontrol.

"But… but… I've never heard of it," a German leader said.

"It's about time you hear about it! Today, a seven-year-old child has more data than the Roman Emperors ever did. A nine-year-old child has more information the Socrates or Plato, and this is unbearable. Such non-useful information overload becomes intellectual garbage. It exhausts the brain. On average, who had more information; Einstein or the engineers and physicists of today?" "Einstein?" a European secretary of education asked.

"Wrong, sir. The engineers and physicists of our time; however, why don't they build such complex theories as young Einstein produced at 27, inside the little patent office he used to work? What makes a man a good thinker is not how much data he has, but by the way it's organized."

Marco then projected revealing pictures of children and teenagers who were connected to their cell phones all day long, though not connected to themselves. He showed pictures of teenagers storming out at the slightest difficulties. He showed children with horrible sleeping habits, who would wake up in the middle of the night to access social networks. They looked like zombies.

"But the digital era has brought undeniable gains!" an Indian leader said.

"That's true. We have seen a cognitive progress and that the logical thinking and productivity have risen. But this era has brought great harm as well. We cannot close our eyes to that. Millions have been suffering from digital poisoning," Marco explained.

If we take away their cell phones, they will struggle with the same withdrawal symptoms as drug addicts! Anxiety, annoyance, impatience, low tolerance to frustrations, a dreadful boredom as soon as they see they have nothing to do."

"But we live in a democratic era; we are free to make our choices," a Swiss philosopher pointed out.

"Yet, sir, But I can assure you that inside of democratic societies, there has been a gigantic number of slaves in the only place where they should never have to be prisoners: their minds."

"Technological progress has prolonged life expectation. We cannot condemn it. We now live double the time the Romans used to live!" an Italian leader who was an expert in public health commented.

"Technology has brought extremely important additions. In the old times, a simple condition like tonsillitis would kill a person. However, it is essential to check both sides of the social coin. We live an average of 80 years, but the human mind is so stressed due to information overload that 80 years passes as if only 20 had passed."

"So, our policy has been producing crazy people. You are saying that we are living longer on biological terms, but dying earlier because of emotional issues, is that it?" a French leader asked.

"I remain sure that we've been living in this paradox, a subliminal violence against ourselves, not classified by the UN, nor addressed in this debate. Ladies and gentlemen, don't you feel as if we've fallen asleep and awoken at the age we are today?"

"Doctor Polo is right. Studies point out that this hectic pace makes us more selfish and unhappier. We are in the leisure industry era, but we've never had a sadder generation. This is another great paradox," said Michael, a neuroscientist who would wind up becoming friends with Marco Polo.

"We are in the emotional beggars' era." Marco concluded. "Many of you wear designer suits and ties but beg for the crumbs of joy. This is another aspect of selfviolence."

The audience was now humming.

"Are you implying that modern society has turned into a public asylum?" a Russian politician shouted.

People were shaking their heads and massaging their temples. They were there to look over the violence of others. They did not realize they had been violent with themselves. Marco mentioned the rise in the number of beggars in France in the eighteenth century. Due to the wars, the political corruption, and social conflicts, so many were poverty stricken that it was possible to stumble over the starving people surviving on the streets. He pointed to a shiny happy country:

Brazil.

"For example, in the city of São Paulo, between years 2002 and 2012, the suicide index among young people raised 42%."

"This is insane! If this is the scenario in Brazil, what will become of the rest of the world?" the people asked each other.

Marco continued.

"FAO, an office of the United Nations that draws international efforts to defeat hunger showed that 800 million people are starving in the world. This is an unacceptable problem."

Then he pointed out, staring at the Secretary-General, who was frowning at such exposure: "Statistics shows billions of emotional beggars, some even living in nice apartments and cozy houses."

The audience burst into cheers.

At this point, an Argentinian politician even made a sincere, though amusing, comment. Marco was about to end his lecture, but people asked him to carry on.

"Where is there an emotional restaurant, Doctor Polo? I'm thirsty: I like to complain, I resent it when it takes a long time for my laptop or cell phone to turn on. I'm emotionally starving." Many people laughed and cheered.

Marco said,

"The main feature of emotional beggars is to get little from much. For instance, parents are frightened that their children have become drug addicts, but, without knowing it, they have their children's brains addicted to excessive stimuli."

One of the largest contractors in Spain, who used to give her children everything they wanted, became deeply concerned.

"Can excessive presents harm our children?"

"It may be an attack against their emotional health, ma'am. It may cause them to demand more and more stimuli only to feel crumbs of pleasure. Not only drugs can lead to dependence," Marco warned.

The leaders were very much disturbed; many had sunk into that trap. Then, the psychiatrist projected the image of an African child flying a kite. He was thrilled. Next, he showed another image of a child running after another, smiling, as if they had been dropped into an oasis of pleasure.

After that, the scenery changed, it was a video of a boy throwing tantrums," I want more!" Then, he showed a child crying to his mother, "You've got to give me a new cell phone!" They acted as if they were little kings whose parents were their servants.

"My God, what have I been doing to my two kids?" The contractor said to herself. "I give them gifts every day and, the more I give, the less they appreciate me, the more they cry, and the more miserable they get."

"The risk of wealthy parents causing emotional malnutrition and anxiety is greater than the risk of poor parents doing so, "Marco added.

World leaders held their heads with their hands in their hands in dismay. They represented the establishment of their countries.

"You have shaken us awake, Dr. Polo. At this congress, we have examined violence, but not the one we apply to our very own children," the German Minister of Defense said. "That's enough for me. We need to change our violent frame of mind."

Marco could not stay quiet anymore, before the Minister of Defense left, he dropped another bombshell,

"Please, seek to give your children what money cannot buy: your presence and your story. Teach them how to contemplate beauty. This is the greatest present of all!" "Is contemplating beauty the same as admiring beauty?" The Minister of Defense, still standing, asked.

The answer caused him to sit.

"No! Even a psychopath, such as Adolf Hitler, admired beauty. He used to pet his dog Blondi with one had while the other was on the telephone calling his subordinates, giving orders. He was a vegetarian, he didn't want animals to bleed, but he did not care if children and women were bleeding to death in concentration camps. To admire beauty is a fleeting experience. Contemplating beauty is to fully and attentively surrender yourself to it." People looked at each other.

The United Nations Secretary-General asked,

"Did the great thinkers in history contemplate beauty?"

"Not really. Einstein was depressed; Kafka, pessimist: Van Gogh, hypersensitive; Nietzsche, morbid. Financial, political, and intellectual success, if not dealt with, bring emotional failure, leading to a psycho addiction to success. It makes them need 'too much' as they feel 'too little.' Celebrities suffocate the pleasure of living as they succeed in their careers."

He finished the presentation telling that many millionaires, as they get richer and richer, end of living miserably in castles.

"I'm shocked...I came to the United Nations headquarters rich, and I'm leaving as a beggar," joked a businessman from the Silicon Valley.

Everyone laughed.

"Emotion is democratic, ladies and gentlemen; it feeds from the simple and anonymous things in life."

Then an unexpected and very complicated question disturbed the atmosphere even more.

"What about Jesus Christ? Did Jesus know how to contemplate beauty?" a British Parliament leader asked.

Marco paused, took a deep, long breath and said,

"I respect those who follow a religion, but I am an atheist. God, to me, is an idea built by the human brain. Being so passionate about life, we can't stand the chaos in the solitude of a grave. So, I will not discuss religion here."

The British Parliament leader again confronted him.

"I didn't ask if you believe in God or not. I asked if Jesus was healthy, happy, and if he contemplated beauty!" he insisted.

Marco breathed out slowly. The atmosphere at the United Nations got tense.

"I have never studied his personality, but Christian religions sell a sad, intimate Jesus Christ; a man who carried the weight of the world on his shoulders, with little joy."

A listener who seemed to be in tune with the British politician stood up and challenged Marco,

"I know you study the formation of thinkers, doctor. You are bold, but you seem to be afraid to investigate Jesus' mind from the angle of the human sciences," the psychologist commented.

Everyone was amazed at the woman's courage.

"Afraid? Me?" he questioned, looking into her eyes.

"Yes, afraid. I sense fear, that old human prison. Why don't you accept the challenge of investigating the broad aspects of Jesus' intelligence?"

The silence in the audience was intense. "Is it right to pressure me in front of this noble audience of world leaders?" He spoke as if outraged.

"Of course!" she said.

A buzz took over the place. The UN Secretary-General stood up to control the situation. Then Marco asked more seriously than before,

"What is your name?"

"Anna."

He then smiled and said,

"I'll think about your question, Anna. But first, I want to say out loud that I love you."

No one understood what was happening. But, after a short silence, he explained, "Well, I do need to manage my mind, because even my wife is stressing me out."

When they learned that Anna was his wife, they all smiled, stood up and burst into applause. They understood they were an incredible, spontaneous and intelligent couple. That was how Marco ended his presentation.

Many left the UN meeting transformed; some were reflective; others were stunned. The attendees realized that they did not know how to drive their mental vehicles.

These were world leaders, but they were not leaders of themselves. They were emotional beggars only having crumbs of pleasure.

CHAPTER 2

EMOTIONAL EARTHQUAKES

Anna, Marco's wife, was a brilliant psychologist. Her mother had always been depressed and had taken her life when Anna was a child. She had to reinvent herself to survive. Her father, Dr. Amadeus, was a classic example of a man who became poorer as he grew richer. He was authoritarian, insensitive, controlling, demanding.

Her mother's illness encouraged Anna to become an expert in depression, the last level of human pain. Marco was a turning point in her story, a new chapter in her biography. He contributed greatly to her becoming a sweet, resolute, generous and determined woman. Her primary goal as a mental health professional was to assist her patients to be self-sufficient.

Her father tried every possible way to break up their relationship. Having a psychologist daughter was complicated for a mega-entrepreneur whose god was money. Now, having a psychiatrist son-in-law, one that was friends with 'schizophrenics,' was unbearable. This revealed Dr. Amadeus' own madness.

"My daughter, you live like a queen with this poor psychiatrist who's full of intellectual romanticism. Life will eventually make you step into reality. You two will certainly add to the statistics of failed relationships."

Marco arrived without being noticed and overheard his father-in-law talking to his daughter. He was always a very secure man, so he intervened with conviction,

"People, who love without risks, love without glories!"

Caught off guard, Dr. Amadeus did not apologize. In fact, the word sorry was not part of his vocabulary. He confronted Marco,

"But there are stupid and irrational risks. My daughter's social status will fall, and you will not be able to afford to keep it at its present level without my help."

"We will not need your help," Anna said.

"That's what rebellious children always say," her father snapped and then walked away.

Anna was a hostage of her past. In the beginning, she was possessive, jealous, hypersensitive, always seeking Marco's attention. His smallest distraction would trigger dramatic pleadings. The doctor urged her to practice critical thinking because he knew people don't marry just their partner, but also the ghosts of the person's past and their family.

"An unresolved person has insatiable love and always seeks in the other what she does not have within herself," he used to say.

Anna was shaken by her boyfriend's words, and she thought about these words night and day.

"Very well, Marco. What I want is not for your love to set me free, I have to learn to be free. But, what I want is for your love to give me wings to fly farther."

"Jealousy means lack of 'yourself' in the first place, not lack of others. If you abandon yourself, I cannot satisfy you," Marco would often say.

Anna gradually solved the difficult equation of possessiveness. They would nourish a rich relationship starting there. Finally, against all her father's attempts to break them up, they got married. Therefore, while the turbulent coexistence with Dr. Amadeus slowed down, it was never solved, even with the birth of their only son. Luke was a smart, sociable and good-humored boy.

* * *

Over the years, Marco had gained international fame. He was a daring yet calm, humble and remarkable professional. Above all, he was an astute researcher. He could keep serene even in times of crisis. But every human being has his limits. Keeping selfcontrol while facing other people's pain is one thing, but facing our own pain, especially when we lose someone we love the most, is something else. His moment of loss had arrived.

Marco sobbed. He was losing his eternal girlfriend, Anna.

"Why? Why?" he wondered.

He placed his hands on his head, wiped the tears from his face, and walked back and forth.

"I love you, honey. Don't leave us so soon," he said aloud to himself. "I've seen personalities destroyed due to irreparable losses. Now I'm being destroyed. What a terrible pain."

Mild solitude is creative; intense solitude is abortive. Marco sat on the armchair where he used to read the biographies of the great characters in history. There, where he'd write his texts, he could not think. Around the polished travertine marble table, the room had never felt so cold and lonely. In front of him, there was a pile of his books, some of them published in several countries. At that moment, Marco was not the famous psychiatrist, nor the scientist and fine writer, but a broken human being trying to assimilate his own chaos.

It was common to have pleasant surprises when he sat on that chair. Anna, generous as she always was, would bring him coffee, fruit or juice or she would caress his hair.

"You don't let me think," he teased.

She often asked him questions about the texts he wrote. Marco remembered her last questions.

"What thinker are you studying now?"

"Some existentialist philosophers: Nietzsche, Merleau-Ponty, Sartre."

"How did they leave their comfort zone to produce new ideas?"

Marco spoke enthusiastically about his notes. They had long, pleasant conversations. Studying the formation process of thinkers was exhausting, but having Anna by his side was like having a perfume to inspire his mind. On their last talk, he had produced a couple of conclusions that made her think a lot,

"Anna, what is the age of majority?"

"Sixteen or eighteen, depending on the society." "And what is the emotional majority?" he asked.

"I've never thought about that."

"Many in their fifties and sixties are still immature. They do not even know how to be contradicted or even acknowledge their smallest mistakes. They want the world to turn around them because they have the emotional age of ten or twelve years old."

"I wonder what emotional age my father is."

"He's a boy in the body of a middle-aged man."

Then, breathing slowly, he joked: "It was difficult to seduce you."

"It was me who seduced you, young man. Thank goodness you know how to make choices," she said, grabbing his shirt and kissing him.

That was the relationship Anna and Marco used to have, full of affection, serenity, and good humor. However, now he was experiencing the arid solitude of a desert. Anna was dying. His cell phone rang, bringing him back to the cold reality.

"Marco Polo?"

His heart pounded. He was about to receive the bitterest news a human being could hear.

"Yes."

"It's me ... Matheus." It was his pneumatology's friend.

"Matheus how is Anna?"

Matheus had a broken voice. He could not utter those words. He was close to Anna as well.

"I know, my friend. Anna has closed her eyes forever."

"Not yet, my friend," the pneumatologist commented in a choked voice.

"Oh, fortunately. How is she?" Marco asked, his eyes sparkling with tears.

"She's unconscious, in an induced coma. She had two cardiac arrests. We've been able to resuscitate her, but ... but ... she will hardly bear a third. She has multiple organ failures."

"Multiple organ failures?" Marco exclaimed, brokenhearted.

He was experiencing a real emotional earthquake.

"I'm sorry, my friend. You're losing your wife, and Claudia and I, a great friend." Dr. Matheus said, not holding back his tears either. "Well, you're better prepared to bear this loss. Now it's time to prepare Luke."

Telling his child, he would never hear his mother's voice again or hug her and kiss her is the last thing a parent wants to do. Marco sat back in his chair and thought about it. He missed her so much that he felt breathless due to the wave of emotions.

Luke was in Miami, on vacation at his grandfather's house. As soon as his son left, Anna began to show the symptoms of a rare and rapidly evolving autoimmune pulmonary disease, catching all doctors by surprise, including Marco. He expected her to recover on a daily basis, so he had not told Luke the severity of her illness. But Anna was getting worse.

When Marco picked up his cell phone to give him the sad news, another emotional earthquake shook him even more. He received a call from an American police officer.

"Doctor Marco Polo?"

"Yes."

"This is Miami police, 25th district." Marco froze.

"Has something happened to my son Luke?"

"Sadly, yes."

"An accident?" he asked, almost voiceless.

"No."

Marco was slightly relieved. The head of the district continued,

"Drug possession."

"Drugs? A sixteen-year-old boy using drugs? But he has never used drugs." In fact, Luke had never used drugs. Not until two weeks ago.

"Parents are always the last to know."

"What drugs?"

"Five grams of cocaine."

"Cocaine? He does not have the money to buy it."

"And he committed another violation. He was driving without a license."

"How is it possible? There is no car at his disposal. He's on vacation at his ..."

But then Marco pulled himself together and whispered, shaken,

"Doctor Amadeus." "What?" the head of the police district asked.

"I was thinking out loud. Can I talk to my son?"

"Yes." The police officer said and handed the phone to Luke.

"Luke?"

But Luke only cried.

"Talk to me, son."

"Sorry, Dad. I'm sorry," the boy said in tears.

"I have always encouraged you to value your life, son. Cocaine creates a severe dependence. What a terrible emotional prison."

"I know, Daddy. I was just trying ... I am the worst son in the world ..." Marco did not know which pain was bigger, losing his wife or his child.

"Don't say that, my son. I love you. When did you start using it? Be honest, please."

"It was here in Miami. I tried it on the second day after I arrived. Some friends I met here ..."

"They are not your friends, my son."

Luke was still much shaken, and he cried.

"Calm down, son. Some pains are worse than this."

"Worse, Dad? How? Grandpa is furious. He said I'm a piece of shit, that I am the family shame, that I will never make anything of my life."

"No, no, my son. You are a wonderful boy. Let's turn this mistake into something positive. Let me talk to your grandfather." Dr. Amadeus picked up the phone,

"What upbringing did you give your son? Aren't you a famous psychiatrist?"

"I'm a human being subject to mistakes. Do not humiliate your grandson, Dr. Amadeus. He needs you in this difficult time."

"I have to clean up after him and you still want to give me moral lessons?" his father-in-law said with no compassion at all.

He did not even ask about his daughter's health, even though he knew she was in the ICU.

Marco, who was hurt, raised his voice, "Did you give Luke unlimited money and leave a car at his disposal knowing he didn't have a driver's license?"

""Are you calling me irresponsible? You fail as an educator and you still blame me, you're...you're..."

"You didn't even ask about your daughter. You cannot be generous even when Anna is losing her life."

When Marco talked about Anna's condition, Dr. Amadeus saw reason and stopped talking for the first time. Trembling, he said,

"Is Anna ...?"

Luke heard his grandfather's words and panicked.

"What is it, Grandpa?"

"Unfortunately, Anna had two heart attacks," Marco reported. "She's breathing with the help of machines. I was about to call you."

"My daughter is dying," said Dr. Amadeus, who was silent and dropped the phone at that moment.

Desperate, the boy took the phone and spoke to his father,

"Dad ... Dad ... is Mommy dying?"

"Oh, my son, she's still alive."

"Is her illness serious?"

"Unfortunately, it is. She is breathing with the help of machines."
"No! No! Mommy can't die," Luke said in tears.

"Let us hope. We'd better be together. Come back home."

Luke hung up the phone and fortunately was released from the police district due to his mother's medical urgency. The boy would still have to report to a court and go through an educational corrective action at home. His grandfather was to show up again at the police department for further clarification. Although he hated hospitals, Dr. Amadeus could not refuse to visit his daughter at such delicate time.

CHAPTER 3

IRREPARABLE LOSSES

They took the first flight to Los Angeles. Dr. Amadeus's fourth wife was with them. When they arrived at the hospital, Marco soon spotted his son, and they ran to each other. They cried together. It was an emotional moment that touched everyone. Then he shook Dr. Amadeus's hand, who greeted him.

"How's Mommy?"

"I'm waiting for the latest news."

Dr. Matheus emerged from the ICU. He approached the boy with moist eyes. He brushed his hair and greeted him.

"Hello, Luke!" He said, letting out a tear.

"Did Mommy die?"

"I'm sorry." The pneumatologist took a deep breath and nodded. Then he asked for something impossible for a boy who had just lost one of his parents: "Be strong." "You have every right to cry, son. Cry without fear," Marco said, devastated.

"No! No! I want my Mom...!"

Anna's father, Dr. Amadeus, stumbled trembling. He went straight to a hotel and took a handful of tranquilizers as he always did in difficult times. He did not know to look inward. Thinking about his life made him panic. Marco took his son to see his mother's body. He hugged his mother.

"Mom ... Mom, why did you leave us?" Luke repeatedly muttered, kissing her.

The next day, the funeral took place. It was sunny, but a melancholic day. Luke was not weeping alone. Over two hundred children and teenagers who lived in one of the twenty orphanages that Anna took care of cried over her death.

Each group of abandoned boys and girls carried a poster. One said: 'You're gone, Mom, but you will forever live inside of us! - Saint Claire Orphanage.' Another said: 'Our parents abandoned us, but your heart welcomed us, Anna. You are unforgettable! - Los Angeles Orphanage." Another one said: 'Thank you for giving your best to those who had little. We love you - Hijos de Maria Orphanage - San Diego.'

Not only Luke, but all the 'foster children' hugged Marco. It was the most poignant funeral that the graveyard had ever seen. Despite the sad scenery, Marco honored his wife.

"Anna was my eternal girlfriend. Living by her side was a privilege. She was kind, generous, patient, and tolerant. She overcame the most important chapters of her life in the most desperate moments of her story.

Luke also said,

"Mom died so soon...but she will live forever inside me. She loved me welcomed me, she was patient, she was...was..." and he could no longer say any more words.

Then the priest paid his honors,

"Anna is like one of those rare flowers born in the garden of humanity, prematurely harvested. She pursued the signature of the Author of Life between the lines of existence. She was both a remarkable human being and a professional. She left us a written message a few days ago. It was to be read at her passing.

'As long as life is, it quickly fades in the parenthesis of time. Being dazzled by this should be the greatest responsibility of every mortal. Luke and Marco, my darlings, I will love you forever, even if my eyes are closed. My foster children at the orphanages and my dear friends do not weep for me. If I deserve to be honored by all of you, honor me by being happier, honor me by dazzling yourselves with existence, because life is a great theater and death is only an act. I will continue to play my role in eternity.'"

Beatrice, Julia, and Hillary couldn't stop crying. When they heard those words, they clapped for a long time in honor of Anna's wisdom, as did everyone present. They honored Anna by making a toast with an imaginary glass of joy.

At the end of the service, Dr. Amadeus approached Marco. It seemed that the old man would finally break his mask and bow down in generosity. It was a silly thought. Looking at the children in the orphanages, he raised his chin and said,

"You and my daughter have done interesting things. But do not forget Dr. Marco Polo: if life is a theater, you have shortened the play of my daughter's existence. You did not put Anna under the care of the finest doctors. I will investigate your conduct!"

Then he kissed his grandson on the forehead and left without a word. The multimillionaire went to his very own prison, a huge mansion in Miami. Surrounded by people paid to tell him what a great man he was. Financial sociopaths have no friends, except for sycophants.

* * *

One year later

Marco Polo was a professor at a medical school and also taught the psychology program at a university. Although he was a renowned intellectual, he did not hide his flaws under cover of intellectuality. Once, while he was in the teacher's lounge at the psychology department, Dr. Robert, a renowned psychologist and a professor at the same institution, asked him,

"How's Luke?"

"He's still using drugs," said Marco, holding his head with his hands.

"I'm sorry about that."

"I feel sad when I hear something along the lines of the famous saying 'Physician, heal thyself' to 'Psychiatrist, heal thy child'"

"Is he resistant to treatment?"

"Luke has been to five psychologists and three psychiatrists. But he always ends up giving up. I try to help him, but it's difficult. He seems to be a vault; he doesn't open up. He needs to reinvent himself, but he doesn't hold on to his motivation. When the traumatic windows are open, he closes his memory circuit, and prefers to punish himself, to feel powerless, to forget about everything."

Dr. Robert tried to bring hope to Marco, who was someone he admired and who had helped him in his training. However, it was difficult to help his master.

"You're an excellent psychiatrist who has trained so many of us. I'm sure you'll be able to help him get over this."

"I dream about that night and day. But I'm afraid of losing him."

Then he took a deep breath and said: "It's hard to accept that I, who've helped countless patients, and trained psychiatrists and psychologists, can't take care of the one person who I care about the most."

Dr. Robert said,

"You've developed a theory about how the mind works, so you know better than anyone that we have no control over the process that forms personality. Its psychiatrists, psychologists, leaders, and celebrities that make children sick. Don't blame yourself, Marco. You have always been a present and loving father."

"Present parents also fail. I did not fail in giving my son love or support. But I failed in offering him tools that could have helped him be the author of his story." "We all failed on this issue," Dr. Robert said regrettably.

"Unfortunately, I only developed these tools when he was already a teenager. My son does not know how to manage his anxiety or to protect his mind."

"Who knows, Marco? How many psychiatrists and psychologists can protect their emotions? They are good for others, but they forget about themselves. My children also grew up with difficulties. Laura is a consumerist and Pedro is restless."

"We teach values like ethics and honesty, and we are silly enough to think that this will do. We have thrown our children into the lions' den in this stressful society with no skills to survive whatsoever. Humanity has become a factory of madness, and we are its builders."

His cell phone rang. It was someone giving Luke's whereabouts. Marco had hired a detective to find out where and from whom his son was buying drugs.

"Excuse me? Where's Luke?"

Marco hurried out without even being able to say goodbye to his friend. He got into his car, drove quickly, and went to a dangerous area where the trafficking network was most powerful. The detective did not know his son had business with dangerous dealers. The region's chief of police talked to him during his journey.

"I know where my son is!"

Upon arriving, he entered a dimly lit house. There were prostitutes and several people were using drugs; some were lying on the floor, stoned. All of a sudden, he was in a room where some of the drug dealers were discussing their business. They got tense noticing the intruder's presence. Marco rushed in and closed the door; then he continued to look for his son. Marco found himself in a scene a father would never imagine witnessing: Luke was on the floor having convulsive seizures. His eyes were rolling, his mouth foamed and his limbs had spasms. He was overdosing.

"Son! Son!" he shouted in despair.

Luke was having a heart attack. He was dying.

"Luke, my son, don't die!" Marco begged as he started to cry.

He punched Luke in the chest to resuscitate his heart, but he was not responding. He increased the force of the cardiac massage, followed by mouth-tomouth resuscitation. He had tragically lost his wife; now he was losing his son in an even more tragic way.

Meanwhile, the police arrived at the scene and began to hunt down the drug dealers while Marco continued his maneuvers. Finally, Luke's heart started beating again. The boy coughed and Marco hugged him hard and once again began to shed tears.

"Dad ... what happened ...?" Luke asked in a low voice.

"You're back, my son ... You're back ..." he said, trying to wipe his tears as he held Luke's head to his chest.

He lifted him slowly and, with the help of a police officer, he took him to the car. The drug dealers in handcuffs were displaying their rage. The police found ten pounds of cocaine and thousands of crack stones. The gang leader, looking at Marco, said,

"Nowhere on this planet is too far for me to find you."

Marco continued to support Luke. He was fearful, but the chief of police, who was his friend, said,

"Don't worry, Doctor. They always say that."

Then, the cops pushed the drug dealers into their police cars. Luke was admitted to a general hospital. When he was finally better, he told his father,

"I want to go to rehab."

"You've already done that, my son. It is not enough to isolate yourself. You must want to treat yourself; you must want to locate the ghosts that haunt you."

"I have no control, Dad. This time I want it, I need it."

Luke was then sent to rehab for the second time. He would spend three months away from everything and everyone, but not from the emotional vampires in the basement of his mind. He would have to let the light of reason penetrate the grounds of his psyche so that he could write his own story.

CHAPTER 4

MANKIND ON FIRE

Deafening blasts were an invitation to panic. Men were shouting like crazy animals wielding bayonets against enemies created in the offices of governmental leaders. It was World War I. Then, the image changed. Trains crammed with children; women and other innocent people were stopping in Poland at the most morbid station ever created. Unutterable moans. Then, the goblet of death started to take shape in Hiroshima. Japan was burning in pain. Unimaginable fear!

Blasts of machine guns were destroying the forests in Vietnam. Men had become predators of themselves. And then, there were frightened beings looking up. The twin towers were collapsing. The bare reality was even more brutal than fiction. Terrorist attacks multiplied, the virus of corruption was infecting nations, immigrant flows, intolerance to frustrations, celebrity worship. Mankind was on fire.

At that moment, the flight attendant woke the passenger,

"Sir, sir ... wake up."

"What?" Marco asked, startled. "I was having a nightmare."

"Please, lock your table and return your seat to its original position. We're going to land in Jerusalem," the flight attendant said.

"Yes, of course."

As he had caused such impact on politicians at the UN conference, Marco Polo had become a consultant at the agency. He had been invited to give a lecture at the most important international congress for the preservation of natural resources on the planet, sponsored by the UN. The theme was 'Global Warming - The Future of Earth.' The nation's leading minds were to gather: lawyers, environmentalists, executives, political leaders, sociologists, psychologists, and educators. But, Marco would talk about the natural resources of another planet: planet emotion.

The past few years had been the hottest ever recorded, and the countries' responses to global warming were cautious. "We are creating dangerous traps for our children. Do you know the secrets of date palms? People who plant them do not harvest their fruits; instead, they plant it for the next generations. We are such an irresponsible species," Marco thought.

At the entrance to the great hall of the Congress, a French ecologist said to a German colleague,

"Strange. I'm leafing through the conference themes, and there's a researcher, Dr. Marco Polo, who will talk about 'sustainability of planet emotion.' I've never heard of this."

"Me neither. I don't understand how it may be related to global warming."

Several lectures were happening that day. Now, at the great hall, it was time for the main conference of the day. Right after being introduced, Marco picked up the microphone and shocked an audience of over 500 people,

"Homo Sapiens emotions will fail before the planet's resources end. It is no use talking about preserving the natural resources of this blue planet without first mentioning the preservation of the resources of planet emotion. Studies show that one in two people will develop a psychological disorder; anxiety, depression, panic disease, and psychosomatic diseases.

There are over three billion human beings. Every 40 seconds, a person takes their life. About 70 million people suffer from eating disorders, such as bulimia and anorexia. Only 3% of women consider themselves beautiful, which shows a collective death of self-esteem. That's the failure of emotion."

People looked at each other worried. Many considered his words. Then Marco said sharply,

"We have been living in the emotional waste era. We turn off our devices, but not our minds. Freud said that the first childhood traumas would determine adults' psychological illnesses, but we can get sick at any phase of our lives if our NEEE index is high."

When Marco talked about the NEEE index, psychologists, sociologists, and educators got puzzled. They had never heard about such an index.

Soon a sociologist, Dr. Michelle, who taught at a university in Paris and was sitting in the second row, stood up and interrupted him,

"I don't know what NEEE index is, Dr. Polo."

He was waiting for that question. He smiled and said,

"NEEE index means 'Negative Emotional Energy Expenditure.' We don't get sick only because of traumas or neurotransmitter deficits, but also due to an irresponsible expenditure of emotional energy."

"What are the behaviors that make up this index?" a Canadian environmentalist asked.

"If I told you, the global warming in your planet brain would skyrocket!" he joked. Everyone smiled. Then, he said, "Relax your legs and arms and, please, smile, because I'm talking about a situation about which we all should be crying."

Everyone smiled again at the humorous professor. He, however, was deadly serious.

"The first behavior that drains the natural resources of planet emotion is being a loan shark of emotion."

No one understood what he meant. Marco continued,

"The financial loan shark lends at high-interest rates, which at times are impossible to pay. Likewise, the loan shark of emotion gives himself to the ones he loves but charges excessive emotional interest. Those people are parents who cannot stand the slightest setback from their children, intolerant teachers unable to hug controversial students, partners who are experts in creating trouble, and business people unable to laugh at their stupidity. Let us be honest. Who here is an emotional loan shark deep inside?"

Many in the audience raised their hands.

"I start to see that I drain my brain and other people's brains easily," one lawyer said to another.

Marco then showed images that shook the audience. Executives were hitting the tables, treating their employees as if they were servants. One said:

'Incompetents!' Another shouted: 'Get out, you are fired!' The images also showed parents tearing up their kid's test while saying: 'What is wrong with you; in my day, I only had the highest grades!'

"There are other cruel types of demanding people, the ones who demand too much from themselves," he continued. "They are loan sharks of their own emotions. People who demand too much from themselves and others can work in the financial area, but aren't able to have a healthy relationship with their emotional health."

Many smiled though it was an occasion for crying. Marco continued,

"Deliberating losses, frustrations and suffering in advance are other behaviors that destroy planet emotion and infect the present which is the only time possible to be happy, fulfilled, and relaxed."

Dr. Moses, a Jewish lawyer who was a human rights activist, raised his hands and joked,

"Professor, when can I be hospitalized? My NEEE index is sky high." The audience laughed and clapped at his good mood. Then, he became serious and concluded,

"Many of us are ideal for society, but at the same time, we are executioners of ourselves. How are we going to take care of planet Earth if we are irresponsible with planet emotion?"

"You got my thesis," Marco said. Then he showed close-ups of people from many social statuses who were sweating, putting their hands on their heads, desperate, and panting. It was possible to imagine their hearts beating at an incredible pace. "They are the slaves of the modern age; handcuffed by their emotions."

A Chinese psychiatrist, Dr. Ma Tao, was so astonished by the presentation that he asked,

"So, tiredness while waking up, headaches, hair loss, and difficulty in living with people who are slow; can those be symptoms that show that the resources of planet emotion are drained?"

"They are more than symptoms; they are warning cries from the brain. But we are deaf," confirmed Dr. Polo. "Ladies and gentlemen, the 'deficits in everyday memory,' which almost everyone suffers, is the brain's plea to change the course of life. I dream that the NEEE index will decrease and become an index of positive energy instead, so we can call it PEEE, Positive Emotional Energy Expenditure, and we will give brave answers to mitigate global warming."

As the applause from the audience echoed, Dr. Polo continued.

"Mankind is on fire! There's no emotional management. Rich people become miserable; couples engage in romances as if they were in heaven and they end up living in hell; young people suffocate their creativity, and professionals sabotage their skills. Without emotional management, psychological heaven and hell coexist in the same mind."

Dr. Polo was launching the first emotional management world program. He dreamed of contributing to the future of mankind.

"One of the most violent and anti-management behaviors which drain planet emotion the most is the obsessive need to change others. No one can change anyone; we only have the power to make others worse, not to change them. Who here has ever tried to change a stubborn person?" Almost everyone raised their hands.

"I'm sorry, but you only made this person worse." Many laughed, but they should have been worried. Dr. Polo continued: "Only the person can change them self. There is a phenomenon that files all experiments in the cerebral cortex without the conscious authorization of the self."

He then projected videos on the screen representing the phenomenon AMR (automatic memory registration) acting on a large brain. Rejection, offense, high tone of voice, criticism, a disturbing thought; the brain recorded everything in a fraction of a second that formed files that changed the landscape of the memory. He used the metaphor of a city to illustrate the explanation. It was as if the squares were no longer full of trees and light as if the neighborhoods had lost their shine and the streets were full of holes.

"Beware, ladies and gentlemen, the techniques we use to change others generate traumatic windows that crystallize in them everything we hate the most: raising their voices, criticizing them, lecturing, comparing and pressuring."

Marco then made other important and complex comments. He discussed the nature of thoughts, stress management, autonomy, and memory reprint. Everything seemed to be going brilliantly at the conference.

Then an unexpected emotional storm took place, as the lecture came to its conclusion. George, an existentialist philosopher, expert in Sartre, asked permission to speak,

"I have always taught that the human being is condemned to be free, but, according to your explanation, Dr. Polo, without emotional management, we can be slaves living in democratic societies."

"That's right, Professor."

"My question is: isn't your program too utopian to be put into practice in a digital and logical society?"

"If we don't do that, we'll become an unfeasible species."

"Do you know of any intellectual who has shone in history as manager of their emotions? Thinker, artist, leader, or religious person?"

"I study the formation process of thinkers, but I don't know anyone who has been role models in emotional management," Marco commented.

"None?" the philosopher insisted.

Marco gave astonishing examples,

"Freud used to ban those who opposed his ideas from the psychoanalytic family. Einstein had depressive features and also, hospitalized one of his children in an asylum, never visiting him again. Gandhi was a pacifist, but he did not pacify the ghosts of one of his children, who was an alcoholic. Franz Kafka was a pessimist. Schopenhauer was witty, but he was wallowing in the mud of anguish. Kant hid in his castle in his hometown. Socrates was a master of the art of questioning, but he did not question other alternatives to hemlock, even after Plato's and other disciple's pleas. Finally, to answer your question, I do not know intelligent men who have been experts in managing their emotions during tense periods."

"And you? As the author of this emotional management program, are you an expert in the field?" a Japanese psychiatrist asked.

The audience was mute. Marco mentally left the auditorium, and his mind traveled, briefly remembering his story. Anna was breathless. He was desperate. Seconds later, she was no longer in her bed. Marco was crying at the foot of his bed. 'Anna, my dear, why did you leave me? It all happened so fast then, the mental scenery had changed again. He thought of his son. Luke was saying: 'Why are you so worried about me? Is the great Marco Polo afraid?' 'Yes, my son. I'm an average father, who's scared of losing you,' he answered.

All of a sudden, he turned to the audience who was waiting for an answer. Everyone wanted to know whether he was an emotional manager or not. Marco confessed with tears in his eyes,

"I suffer in advance; I'm afraid of losing someone I love. I also deliberate about the past, I revive the loss of someone I loved, and I feel distressed. When it comes to emotional management, I am still crawling. I'm a human being under construction." "How honest," people said because of his openness.

"If this person, so intelligent, is a human being under construction, I am an embryo," a man in the first row told his friend.

After a moment of reflection, when the emotional storm seemed to have left the premises, it came back even harder.

"What about Jesus Christ?" an American sociologist asked.

"Again?" Marco whispered, only to himself.

That reminded him of his wife Anna, who publicly urged him to answer a similar question. Now, they were questioning another psychological field of the same character. Once more he declared,

"Sorry, but I'm an atheist. I don't discuss religion in my lectures" he said, but that did not deter further questioning.

"But who said I'm discussing religion? I'm referring to the man Jesus Christ, the historical figure. I'm asking if he was an expert in emotional management or not." Marco took a deep breath and asked the sociologist's name.

"Anna," she answered.

"Anna? Amazing!"

"Yes, Anna. Why?"

With moist eyes, he said,

"Sorry, your question reminded me of a dear person. I have already been challenged to study Jesus' mind, but I only analyze reliable biographies. I have always considered his biographies, or gospels, an attempt by a group of Galileans to produce a hero to get rid of the yoke of Tiberius Caesar, the tyrannical Roman emperor."

There was uproar in the audience. Lightning struck in the middle of the emotional storm.

"Dr. Polo, your thesis on the NEEE index and the emotions is brilliant, but don't you think this behavior expands the index?" Dr. Sofia asked.

There was a general silence in the audience. Dr. Polo was serious for a moment, but then he grinned. Everyone laughed.

After a brief cough, he said: "I think I'm a good teacher, I even allow my assistant, Dr. Sofia, to put me up against the wall."

Everybody clapped. Then Marco spoke openly,

"Prejudice is undoubtedly a foolish way of wasting the energy of both the excluded person and the excluder. Prejudice nurtures the vampires that are in the dungeons of our emotions. One day I will have to analyze the character Jesus from the angle of the sciences. Does anybody else want to stress me?" he joked. Then, he ended the conference.

"Thank you very much for listening."

The inspiring thinker then finished his speech on 'sustainability of planet emotion.' He received a long-standing ovation. Soon after, several people surrounded him to greet him and ask for autographs for their books. Jerusalem was a magical city, producing unpredictable mental impacts on its visitors. Jerusalem would shake the foundations of Marco Polo.

CHAPTER 5

THE WESTERN WALL

After the conference, Marco and Sofia, his assistant, went to the hotel to rest. As the hotel was one mile from the event, they preferred to go on foot. They wanted to enjoy the beauty of the city. People from over a hundred nations visited Jerusalem every year.

Besides his love for producing knowledge about the human mind, Marco had a hobby: photography. With his increased sensibility, he liked to capture people's facial expressions, their joys, their sorrows, their successes, and dramas.

Suddenly, from out of nowhere, a man was pointing a gun at Marco.

"Careful, Marco!" Sofia shouted.

As the man was about to shoot, he was quickly restrained by undercover security guards. They knocked him down, arrested, and handcuffed him.

"What was that?"

"That man was pointing a gun at you!" Sofia said in a panic.

"At me? Why?"

"I don't know. He was in the middle of the crowd, about 30 feet away, when I saw the man pointing the gun at you. Let's get out of here!"

"Calm down, Sofia. Was he a terrorist? A sociopath? I have no enemies." At that very moment, the man who once held the gun stared at Marco.

"Can we go to the hotel now?" Sofia insisted.

"Hold on. Calm down. This man must have mistaken me for somebody. Remember the NEEE index. We will not suffer in advance. They've already arrested him. We will not let it steal our emotional health," he said.

She was surprised by Marco's resilience. A few minutes later, she had relaxed. She watched her boss taking pictures of people and was intrigued. "I'm amazed to see you, such a famous person, pay so much attention to simple, anonymous people."

"The secret of happiness is getting a lot from a little. Every human being is a more beautiful work of art than Da Vinci's Mona Lisa and more complex than Picasso's Guernica. And I also appreciate those with mental illnesses. The only ones who cannot see are the ones who don't have…"

Before he could complete the sentence, she said,

"...eyes to see. That's why you said in one of your classes that 'celebrity worship' is a symptom of a sick humanity."

"Exactly. Even a patient in a psychotic outbreak is as dense as or denser than the best actor in Hollywood. The patient lives a horror movie while the actor lives the character."

He was then surprised by his assistant, who said,

"The aversion to those who suffer and the applause to those who are in the gossip columns are typical of a sick society."

"Congratulations, Sofia."

Shortly afterward, they were standing in front of the famous Western Wall. Marco kept taking pictures of people praying, crying, and pleading for help with their problems. Marco was thinking about his own tears. He revived the image of Anna, his wife, and of Luke, his son. There was a thrilling moment. The three of them were running through the trees, trying to catch each other as if life were an endless game. The image disappeared, and Marco was slightly breathless.

Sofia, looking at him thoughtfully, said,

"I'm sorry if I put you in the middle of the debate, Professor. I did not mean to be impolite."

Sofia was 31 years old, and Marco was 47.

"I learn more from those who challenge me than from those who applaud."

"I've always been very timid; I don't know why I said that."

"Shy people are always in debt to spontaneity. They have a high NEEE index because they care too much about the opinions of others. If you silence your ideas, Sofia, you will have an unpayable debt to yourself."

Sofia was surprised by those words.

"As you urged me not to be quiet, what made you change your expression while taking those pictures?"

"I don't know how to define it; I photographed some strange characters that made me travel back in time."

"Was the trip pleasant?"

"Yes, but the return was cruel."

The Western Wall was an open-air museum; the remnant was a supporting structure for the main building, a place where the Temple of Jerusalem had been built. Kings, presidents, businessmen, celebrities, people from all countries and cultures have passed by it. These people withdrew their political makeup, crying about their losses and had made their requests. When they touched its huge stones, human beings stripped themselves of the robe of gods and wore the robe of their fragility and mortality.

They whispered inaudible words, wrote desires they had never expressed, and embedded them in the gaps of the wall. Given that Marco had experienced an avalanche of stressful stimuli, he should have leaned against the Western Wall, but he would not bow to the 'superhuman.' Watching the behavior of Asians, Americans,

Europeans, Africans, Latins, he said to himself,

"I do not understand why these people spend so much time wallowing in their sorrows and making requests. Aren't there any intelligent and productive methods to solve their conflicts?"

Sofia stared at him. He, in turn, grinned and explained,

"I'm prejudicial, I know. But I cannot accept this kind of behavior."

Dr. Sofia was a psychiatrist, both her parents were doctors. Her father was Catholic, and her mother was Protestant; they were both oncologists. She believed in God although she was not religious. After listening to Marco's question, she replied,

"Many of those people who weep on the Western Wall have already wept with oncologists, orthopedists, psychiatrists. They have already pursued science to solve their pressing problems."

Marco listened to his assistant's words.

"It is probable," he confirmed. "Socialism did not end religiosity, the theory of evolution did not stifle it, and the digital age did not silence it. It's interesting."

"Who satisfies the unstoppable desire of the human being to seek his origins and relieve his anguish?" Sofia asked.

"When I was young, I said that I was an atheist, but then I thought it over, and became a romantic person like you. I came to believe in God, Sofia. But finally, when I researched the most complex scientific frontier, that is, the construction of thoughts and the formation of consciousness, I became a scientific atheist."

Then, he paused for a long moment and questioned his assistant with arrogance and irony,

"Answer me sincerely; can the belief in God be the basis of an evolved brain?"

"Before I answer the question, tell me first, can arrogance result from an evolved brain?" she snapped, stabbing his pride.

"Hey, wait a minute. Did you just call me arrogant?" Marco asked surprised.

Unafraid of the consequences, she asked back,

"And did you just call me stupid? I am not religious, but I believe in God. Therefore, according to your diagnosis, my brain is not evolved."

"I'm sorry!"

"You were neither at the beginning of time created by the Big Bang nor took part in the millions of physical events that followed the birth of the universe. You affirm that in none of these events there was a Creator of Existence. Whoever he may be, how do I classify you? God, super genius or naïve?"

"How dare you!"

"You have encouraged me not to be quiet, remember."

Marco had high-level discussions when he was torpedoed with lucid arguments. Sofia messed up his thoughts so much that he began a rare and most interesting philosophical debate,

"Stephen Hawking, a physicist, once said that the search for God resulted from the fear of the dark. I think he was naive because the reasoning of religious people is more complex than a mere escape from any fear or phobia. Many evolutionists are also simplistic in believing that the theory of evolution excludes God. God could be both the trigger and the check of the random processes of evolution. Darwin, when he died, knew that, because, in the midst of vomiting and anguish, he cried for God."

"Interesting," Sofia said, impressed by his knowledge. "Please, go on."

Among so many bystanders who were passing by the Western Wall, the two scientists of the human mind continued their challenging debate.

There was nothing or no one in Jerusalem able to distract them. Marco completed his reasoning,

"I think differently from the classical atheists, Sofia. For me, the human being is a big question in search of insatiable answers. The eagerness to know his origins, along with the aversion to the intrinsic death of the human mind, is what fosters an unstoppable search for God. However, I am not a genius; I only serve science, science is my God."

"I am also a neuroscientist, although I do not have your international recognition, Dr. Polo. However, unlike you, science is my instrument of work, not my God. The same arguments that make you an atheist inspire me to believe in God. I'm sorry to say that rational extremism is as atrocious as religious fundamentalism."

Debating with Marco without experiencing the taste of ignorance, even if mild, was rare. But Sofia's intelligence disturbed his brain.

"I have to admit that your reasoning is romantic but brilliant," he said, smiling and added, "We have a draw."

However, Sofia was not satisfied with a draw. Thinking of terrorist attacks, masses of immigrants, and multiplying cultural conflicts, she added,

"I believe that today's science and universities are belittled when they refuse to debate God and spirituality, thinking that this has to do with adherence to religion. The philosophers of the past, such as Descartes, Spinoza, Augustine, and Kant, were bolder. These themes were the subjects of thinkers, not only in the hands of religious people."

Marco frowned and then smiled.

"What a daring woman."

When the debate was over, they found that dozens of people were intently listening to their discussion. Some applauded them. No one had won the debate, but they had at least defined their territories.

CHAPTER 6

DEAD SEA SCROLLS

Marco and Sofia arrived at the magnificent hotel. When they passed by the lobby, they were talking to each other sharing smiles. Then his eye was attracted by a brochure. He read that a conference would take place that night. The theme was: 'Dead Sea Scrolls - The Greatest Archaeological Finding in History.' "Interesting," he said to himself.

Marco paid attention to the speaker's name and the topic of the conference. His eyes flashed. He had the curiosity to expand his knowledge on the Manuscripts, but not from a religious viewpoint, and this made him think of Anna, his companion.

He exhaled and had a quiet moment of silence. Sofia watched him.

"Curious?"

"Yes."

He said farewell to his assistant, and the two agreed to have dinner together after a rest. He was worn out by the intellectual work. As delightful as it was it tended to exhaust him. After showering, he sat on the bedroom armchair. He picked up a newspaper but could not read it. His mind fixed on the conference he had seen on the leaflet. He thought long and hard. Feeling uneasy he decided to call Sofia.

"I'm thinking of attending the conference on the Dead Sea Scrolls. It starts in 30 minutes. I would like to invite you if you are willing to go. We'll have dinner after the event. What do you think?" She smiled.

"Invitation accepted." Ten minutes later, they were in a taxi on their way to the location on the leaflet. They arrived just in time. The lecturer, Professor Moses Abraham, was an archaeologist at the University of Jerusalem, a respected Ph.D. There were 70 people in the hall there to see him speak. Marco sat down in the last row, not wanting attention.

"The Dead Sea Scrolls are a collection of hundreds of texts embedded in the Qumran caves in the Dead Sea. They were found soon after World War II, between the late 1940s and the 1950s. They are strict copies of the Hebrew sacred texts by a cast of Jews, the Essenes, who lived over two thousand years ago in the 2nd century BC. The writings illustrate, therefore, the greatest archaeological findings in world literature," Dr. Moses said with authority.

The audience was impressed by the longevity of the texts and the obsession of the Essenes in making faithful copies of the Old Scriptures. Dr. Moses then explained,

"The Manuscripts are certainly the earliest versions of the Hebrew Bible. Only the books of Esther and Nehemiah are missing. Its copyists lived in the cloisters, and they discarded the versions with spelling errors because they were faithful to the original texts. They probably lived in absolute silence while preforming this noble task."

Marco was fascinated by what he had heard. After the exhibition, there was a public question session and after introducing himself briefly, he stated,

"Doctor Moses, I'm surprised by your disclosure. I have always criticized how translators manipulated the texts throughout the centuries. Those masters of language are vital in society, but I remember an Italian expression: 'Translators, traitors.' I have always thought copyists and pious people had changed the ecclesiastical texts over centuries, mindful of it or not."

Not only was Marco an investigator of old biographies but he was also a writer, hence these thoughts on translations. One or two of his books had not been translated correctly into other languages, generating confusion and inaccurate interpretations.

"I'm a writer; I know translations can distort the work," Marco said.

"Your astonishment, Dr. Polo, is equal to mine. It is natural to let in our colors and flavors while copying or translating texts. But, to the surprise of archaeologists, the earliest versions we had of the Old Testament date back to the 9th and 10th centuries BC.

These are the same versions made a millennium earlier by the Essenes, in the second century BC."

Such archaeological findings impressed Marco. As a researcher, he always used the art of questions as a scalpel to examine deeper understanding. He hated easy solutions. Under Sophia's awed gaze, he bombarded Dr. Moses with his inquiries,

"What is the story of the Essenes? What were their life projects? What conscious and unconscious motivations did they control? Who taught them to write? Were their interpersonal relationships generous or competitive? How was their social hierarchy made up?" Dr. Moses smiled.

"I've heard of you, Doctor Polo. Your questions express the mind of an insatiable, demanding scientist."

"I'm sorry, but I do not know how to learn differently," Marco joked.

"Unfortunately, I don't have many clues. For over twenty years I have been studying this strange Jewish caste, but the records on the Essenes are scarce. They were presumably educated, lived in the religious community and had extreme behavioral rigidity, which shows an uncontrollable motivation to live up to their life project. Preserving these writings for the next generations was their legacy to the world."

Alberto Mullen, a renowned Vatican theologian, was in the audience. He too had questions,

"Did the Essenes await the coming of the Messiah?"

"Some of the texts spoke of the Messiah; they waited for him to come," the archaeologist said.

At that point, Thomas Hilton, an American professor of theology, asked the last question,

"In the Gospel of Luke, in chapter 3:15, we see the Jews of that time holding high expectations for the coming of the Messiah. Maybe this religious phenomenon, associated with the political and economic tensions of the time, had motivated the Essenes to carve several copies of the scrolls in the mountains."

"Your thesis is interesting. Powerful phenomena were the basis of the interest of the caste. They abandoned all of their secular life to consecrate themselves to this reclusive endeavor."

Marco found the interruptions of Dr. Thomas and Dr. Alberto clever. But then again, he showed the sparks of his skepticism,

"When tyranny prevails at any time or era, people pursue a savior. Moreover, how did they call for the coming of the Messiah if they made numerous copies to be dug up by other generations? It does not seem rational."

The theologians looked at each other. Dr. Thomas defended himself,

"But what is rational?" The hope, the motivation, the transcendence, the faith of the caste; The Essenes, fearful of political persecutions, could have made copies for themselves or their children."

"Fear is an old excuse," Marco pointed out.

"The Dead Sea Scrolls are a list of answers tempered with many doubts," Dr. Moses noted, to soften the moods.

Soon after, the conversation ended. Marco loved being challenged. It was a brilliant night. He and Sofia were looking for a restaurant where they could have dinner. During the meal, he said,

"In philosophy, doubt is the principle of wisdom. It draws out the human spirit and brings us to see the world from other outlooks. Without it, we are wearing blinders."

"A thinker is quick to ask but slow to answer. He asks as if he was firing a machine gun and this frightens people," Sofia noticed.

Marco smiled and added,

"The dictatorship of answers is evil. Scientists, educators, and church people are often addicted to answering with questioning first. They do not form thinkers."

They had a pleasant chat and, after dinner, they went back to the hotel. They would spend a few more days in Jerusalem. They wanted to explore that magnificent, mystical city, which was the stage of dreams and nightmares, of peace and wars. Marco often called his son. He wanted to know how the treatment was progressing.

"How are you, son?"

"Rethinking myself."

"Do you like the psychologists there?"

"They are interesting. But I feel no joy."

"The abstention from the drug generates a depressive reaction. Fight for your life, Luke! It is your greatest treasure. Are there teachers in the therapeutic community?"

"Yes. They all went through the same chaos. They give me strength."

"Never forget that the biggest prisons are not in jails, but in our minds."

That's how the conversation went on.

"Are you enjoying Jerusalem, Dad?"

"A lot."

The question made Luke think of his mother.

"Mom would have loved to be there."

Luke began to cry, and this shook Marco. His eyes dampened.

"Don't be afraid to remember or to speak of your mother. Don't be afraid to cry; great men cry."

Next, they ended up saying they loved each other.

The next day, when they came back from a walk, Sofia saw a leaflet where she learned that another conference of renowned theologians was going to take place. The theme was 'The biographies of Jesus, reality or fantasy?' she was seduced.

"Look, Marco, what an interesting theme."

He looked into her eyes and doused her enthusiasm.

"I'm sorry, I'm not interested in going," he asserted.

"Remember the UN conference. You were challenged to search the mind of Jesus."

"Challenged even by you. But I have no interest at the moment."

Sofia did not like his refusal, especially since on the day before she had accepted his invitation. He could have been more delicate. Rethinking his indelicacy as they were heading to the elevator, Marco said,

"Okay. I'll wait for you at 7:00 pm in the hotel lobby."

"Do not feel forced to go."

"I will, but my presence may not be welcomed," he said.

"Why?"

"Machine gun questions," he reminded her. She understood the message.

Marco would not stop; he would have a great chance to question the speakers and disturb the event. Shaking stubborn minds was one of his specialties. Sofia admired her teacher, but she was worried. He seemed uncontrollable when he questioned everything and everyone. It was as if Socrates and Marco had drunk from the same fountain. Although,

Socrates was not an atheist. When he was condemned to take hemlock, the poison that would kill him, he protested that he would continue to philosophize in eternity. Marco did not want to know about the future. He wanted to debate the present.

CHAPTER 7

AN INQUISITIVE MAN

When they arrived at their destination, they took a seat in the last row as they had done the day before. Sofia breathed calmly. She peeked at Marco and saw him drumming his fingers. There were 55 people there, and they soon recognized the speakers. The first was Professor Alberto Mullen, a Vatican theologian. He was so regarded that some wished he would one day be the Pope. The other speaker was Thomas Hilton, a Protestant, Doctor of Theology at Harvard, and a renowned writer.

"Weren't they speaking at the conference on the Dead Sea Scrolls?"
"Yes," said Marco who was rather serious.

They learned many things about paleographic, archaeological, and geographic findings. The lectures added much to their knowledge of the gospels. Sofia thought Marco would enjoy it, but the stubborn genius remained silent, and his expression conveyed nothing.

Dr. Thomas finished his speech addressing a sensitive subject for both psychiatrists,

"The biographies of Jesus Christ spoke to overcoming death, hope for mortals, and a topic that outrages medicine and other sciences."

Soon after the lecture, they opened a space for questions and debates. Dr. Sofia exclaimed,

"The purpose of existence lies in the essence of the human mind. It permeates most psychological illnesses. Panic Syndrome, paranoia, stalking ideas, and phobias exist because we are mortals."

Marco stared at his colleague, stood up and said,

"A subtle and intelligent remark, Dr. Sofia." And he completed her ideas:

"It is the frail and mortal condition of human beings which keep the insurance industry, the military forces, medical science, safety devices, and Hollywood movies moving. Anyway, they answer, either directly or indirectly, for over two-thirds of the world's GDP."

The audience observed the two scientists with full attention. Doctor Thomas Hilton, impressed, went on,

"All these questions are fascinating. In fact, Hollywood's history would be rewritten if there wasn't death; the weapons, persecution, terror, action, superheroes who feed on our existential fragility."

Sofia, agitated, replied,

"Over 10 trillion cells make up the human body, and neither of them is scheduled to die. Brain mechanisms are triggered by a hormone wave in the bloodstream, leading to tachycardia and elevated pulmonary ventilation, all so that human beings can operate in risky situations."

The debate appeared to be flowing well when Marco stated,

"Religions are also a runaway mechanism for risky situations."

There was a general silence in the audience. His statement shocked some people. To Marco's amazement, Dr. Alberto said,

"Thank you for your honesty. However, not every escape is dangerous. When one faces the inevitability of death, religion is an active source of hope."

"It depends. Religion can be a source of mental illness if there is extremism, intolerance, and it can cause a generosity deficit," Marco said.

"We agree!" both speakers confirmed.

"Agreeing does not satisfy my question."

"Is the dream of overcoming death a virtue of the weak or an intelligent quest to continuous existence, Dr. Polo?" Sofia asked. "Isn't this quest for eternity the same as the atheists' when they argue for the right to freedom of expression?"

The perceptive questioning made Marco rethink,

"Your questions are sound. Perhaps, at the unconscious level, both lucid and brilliant atheists seek freedom in its broad aspects." Again, he turned to the speakers, "If freedom is so precious, then we have to be true on its grounds. Although you speakers are remarkably intelligent people, you haven't convinced me that the gospels are not biographies arranged by men with political interest."

Dr. Thomas Hilton replied,

"Men wrote it indeed, though inspired by God. Over two billion human beings regard it."

Marco refuted,

"Divine inspiration pervades the realm of faith. When faith whispers, reason shuts up. But, being a man of science, I cannot shut up. That's why I ask you: how was Jesus' personality shaped? Did he have depressive and/or anxious reactions? Did he know how to manage them? Was he resilient? Did he have self-control during tension peaks? Did he go through stress tests? Did he know how to filter stressful stimuli? Was his intelligence brilliant or obscure? Did he train thinkers or blindly repeat information? What was his main psychological thesis?" After verbally shooting both lecturers with those questions, he concluded: "I will leave here a little more literate, but still an atheist and with more doubts."

Dr. Thomas and Dr. Alberto were stunned by that course of questions. They had never studied those measures of Jesus' personality. Marco shocked the audience.

"I'm sorry," he claimed to everyone. Then, he looked at Sofia, who gasped as he said, "I told you I'd better not come." He left the room, leaving her behind. She stood up to leave with him. Dr. Alberto, seeing him heading for the door, declared,

"Newton and Einstein believed in God."

Turning to him, Marco reported again,

"Physicists are more emotional, more dramatic, while doctors like me, with emphasis on neuroscientists, are more rational."

He took a few more steps, stopped again, looked at both lecturers and uttered his last words to a startled audience,

"Every day children die of hunger; young people waste their lives with drugs, parents give in to cancer. If there is a God, what is the reason for his silence? My skepticism goes beyond this silence. However, I have no claim to deconstruct what you believe. I'm better left alone with my ghosts."

Sofia was standing. She didn't know what to say or how to proceed. After speaking, Marco continued to head for the door.

It was then that Dr. Thomas teased him,

"Not all biographies of Christ were written by Jews. Why don't you investigate a biography written by a Greek scholar?"

Marco stopped. Then Dr. Alberto provoked him even more,

"We went to your UN-sponsored conference on emotional management." Marco turned to him.

"You were urged to study the mind of Jesus from the perspective of the human sciences. As you are a neuroscientist, why don't you study the only biography of Jesus produced by a physician?"

Marco took a deep breath. Taken aback, he asked,

"A doctor? Who is the author?"

"Dr. Luke." The Harvard theologian said, referring to the gospel written by Paul's partner.

Marco thought of Anna once again. At that moment, he snapped,

"If you give me the writings of Dr. Luke in several versions, I will study them." Sofia relaxed and smiled.

After the event, only four people remained: Marco Polo, Sofia, Thomas, and Alberto. Marco said,

"As you have challenged me, I propose we have a round table to study Jesus' mind. Sofia will be the moderator, Dr. Alberto and Dr. Thomas will be the two theologians. Two atheist neuroscientists, a friend and I, will be in the opposite position."

"Two atheists against two theologians?" Dr. Thomas asked.

"Against is not the right word. We will be debating. I suggest we study the main texts of Jesus' biography, written by Dr. Luke in a disciplined way, so that the content is not weak and counterproductive. We will meet to discuss our conclusions every night."

The two renowned theologians felt both honored and challenged. They chose a calm place to take the most incredible trip: the study of some intelligence layers of history's most extraordinary character. They scheduled the debates at the University of Jerusalem.

Feeling thrilled, the Vatican theologian said,

"We know that you research the formation process of thoughts and thinkers. We are honored to study the gospel of St. Luke with you."

"Excuse me, Dr. Alberto. I do not feel honored to explore the gospel of St. Luke, but of the man Luke, with his possible madness and sanity, serenity and superficiality. You, Dr. Alberto, represent Catholicism, and you, Dr. Thomas, Protestantism, right? Well, I will only accept this debate if it is free. I mean, without religion, without spotlights, without brakes, without fear of discussing and checkmating ideas, dogmas or concepts. Let us discuss Jesus under the cloak of psychology, sociology, and psychopedagogy."

Dr. Alberto and Dr. Thomas looked at each other, swallowed and confirmed,

"We accept the conditions."

Marco honestly commented,

"However, there is a risk that, after this debate, you may discover that Jesus' intelligence is deprived of depth and complexity."

"But the opposite may be true. Your skepticism may implode." Dr. Thomas challenged.

Marco shook his head as if he was feeling compassionate for both debaters' misconceptions. Sofia agreed to be the moderator. She would stimulate the debate, reduce tensions, draw conclusions and guarantee the right of expression of each debater.

"And who is the other atheist?" she asked curiously.

"Michael Herman, doctor of neuroscience, who lives in Jerusalem. We are friends, but I don't know whether he will accept the challenge or will be available at the moment."

"Doctor Michael Herman? I've read some of his articles. He is a famous neuroscientist whose thesis criticizes religions and their inconsistencies." Dr. Thomas commented.

Having fascinating synthesis ability, Marco said he would analyze Jesus' mind under defined parameters:

"I will analyze ten basic skills of Jesus:

1. Emotional management skills;
2. Ability to filter stressful stimuli;
3. Capability to overcome tensions and reinvent himself in chaos;
4. Ability to free his imagination and develop creativity;
5. Resilience and threshold to deal with frustrations;
6. Sustainable pleasure and ability to contemplate the beauty;

7. Ability to think before responding and self-control;
8. Ability to be empathic and build interpersonal bridges;
9. Ability to train brilliant thinkers and minds;
10. Ability to be the author of his own history and critical awareness."

The Theologians were impressed by the ten themes and understood they would go on an epic journey where everyone would be extremely focused and objective. They were excited at the possibility of getting to know Jesus under probable unique angles and areas. They couldn't help feeling shivers down their spine though. The results would be unpredictable.

Sofia knew that Marco had a great ability to analyze subliminal details that few could see. He was a detailed-driven thinker, and that is how he became the first neuroscientist and psychiatrist to attempt such ventures. He had no idea what was yet to come.

On their way to the hotel, they took a taxi. The driver was serious; he didn't smile and barely spoke. Marco gave him the address, and the man began to drive. Halfway to the hotel, something unpredictable happened. A car passed them in the opposite direction, and the taxi driver got worried because the other driver seemed to be wielding a machine gun. Both Marco and Sofia were distracted and noticed nothing. Then, the suspicious car made a U-turn, 100 feet behind them, and began to chase their taxi. The driver immediately sped up.

"What's going on?" Marco asked.

"We're being followed!"

"What? This is not Hollywood, sir," Sophia said, worried.

"Unfortunately, ma'am we are being followed."

The pursuit was relentless around one curve and another. Marco asked,

"Who are they chasing? You or us?"

"I don't know. More than ten years ago I worked for the intelligence service," the breathless taxi driver said, making a fast turn. "And you?"

"We're scientists. We're harmless!"

"Harmless? Scientists are at the center of global conspiracies!" he said.

Sofia looked worriedly at Marco. She was frowning. Her heart was pounding. She was breathing fast. She squeezed her hands as if she was going to fall off a cliff.

At that very moment, the driver lost control of the car and hit another car. Moments later, several police cars arrived. Noticing the commotion, the stalkers drove away without a trace. Marco injured his right thigh, Sofia her forehead. They were taken to a local emergency room but were soon released.

"Who was following us?" Sofia asked.

"It's disturbing, but we have to stay calm. Either the chasers wanted to rob us, or they were after the driver. We don't know who he is or what he has done."

They hugged each other affectionately and took another taxi to the hotel. Sofia was quiet; trying to understand what no one else could. Her story had never been a calm one, and Sofia dreamed of having quiet days in Jerusalem. However, everything was buzzing. The taxi driver was hospitalized with fractured ribs.

When they finally arrived at the hotel, Marco received a call from Luke. He told him about the accident, but, before he did it, his son increased the tension.

"Dad, it is difficult to put up with this loneliness. This clinic is like a prison," Luke, who was feeling very discouraged, said,

"Be patient, my son. Follow all the treatments."

"I sleep little, have no appetite. It seems to me that I am only here physically. Life has no color for me anymore."

"You're depressed. Within a month you'll be back, my son. We will be together.

Your Self must write your biography, don't let that addiction of yours write it. Open your mind and try to develop the pleasure of living and be sure to take your anti-depressant."

"Ok. How are you?" Luke asked, trying to change the subject.

"I was in an accident, but it was nothing serious. I am staying here in Israel for a few more days. But I promise I'll be home before you leave the clinic."

"I still haven't overcome mom's loss, I'm sorry," Luke said, thrilled to have thought of his mother.

"She is unforgettable, don't punish yourself," after a pause, Marco said, "I think she would have liked to have known what I'm about to do."

"What is it?"

"Study the personality of Jesus in the light of the human sciences."

"I can't believe it."

"Believe it. I will study a writer who is your namesake: Luke."

"Luke? The one who wrote the Gospel?"

"Yes. I'll tell you the results later."

Then, father and son said goodbye. The next day, Marco phoned Michael to talk about the project.

"Would you agree to be part of this debate, my friend?"

"I admire you, Marco. I am grateful for the help I received from you in the past, but stepping into such an arena is a dead end."

"Why, Michael?"

"We are rational, while these religious people ..." He wasn't able to complete his thought.

"It could be an interesting intellectual experience. A break from our tiring academic and research activity."

"Studying Jesus' mind? Can his intelligence contribute to universities and science? I don't think so. Are there any interesting ideas? It's hard to say," he said, full of prejudice, and then added: "Furthermore, your studies on the human mind, associated with mine may mislead those religious men. The Pope won't be pleased," he teased.

"Dr. Thomas and Dr. Alberto are unique; they are brilliant theologians," Marco insisted.

"Well, it will be interesting to knock them out in this debate. I accept."

They said goodbye soon after. Marco received the book of Luke, the third Gospel, in several versions. There were so many texts that the hotel room desk was too small to accommodate them all.

In the days that followed, he would get up in the morning and study. He only stopped at dusk. Never were the foundations of an intellectual so shaken. Likewise, the renowned theologians had never realized that they knew so little about the texts in which they had sworn to be experts.

CHAPTER 8

A WINDSTORM IN PAUL'S AND LUKE'S MINDS

Marco knew the pitfalls of the process of interpretation, and every interpretation might contaminate an observation: a cockroach, to some, resembles a dinosaur; an elevator, a stifling box; an audience a threat.

"The human being is the creator of the monsters who terrify him," he said while guiding Sofia. "Who am I? How am I? Where am I? Where am I going?

What infects the mind?"

These are some of the unconscious phenomena that induce psychologists, parents, magistrates, and business people to misjudge their patients, children, defendants and collaborators, she recalled.

"Study the texts of Dr. Luke transparently. Your atheism, your personality, your emotional and motivational status cannot influence your reading, not excessively," she claimed.

Marco knew that. Otherwise, he would fail the complex task of studying Jesus' mind. He did not want to play God; he just wanted to be a serious and exempt scientist.

Bearing in mind such critical awareness, he read the introduction to the first chapter of the book of Luke. He thought it over, compared, and analyzed it. He did not expect big surprises; what to expect from the first paragraphs of a book?

However, the narrative puzzled him.

"It's not possible! Who is this writer?" he asked.

He was disturbed by the interpretations. He realized that he could not continue the analysis of Jesus' biography without first studying his biographer, the man Luke. As a researcher, he tried to use more than the Socratic Method to deepen his analysis. He tried to question the questions and to ask what was behind the Greek physician's first words.

"Who is Luke? What is the basic structure of his personality? Was he a shallow or a balanced man? Was he a healer or a sensible physician? What conscious motivations controlled him? Were there unconscious motivations behind the biography he wrote? Was his text long-winded and detailed, long-winded and evasive, synthetic and superficial, or synthetic and deep?"

While analyzing the first few chapters, he became convinced that the last option was correct. Luke writes synthetically, trying to say a lot with only a few words. He summarizes one day in a few dense words. Marco studied the biographer and his subject with such concentration that he seemed to move back into the past, observing historical events as if he had experienced them himself.

After hours of study, he rubbed his eyes. Feeling the need to rest, he slept a short, yet deep sleep. Oddly enough, something strange happened. He dreamed about the facts of his reading.

Two thousand years ago

A young doctor was sitting on a wooden bench in the central square of Antioch, an ancient Syrian city. It was evening. The day had been strenuous.

Many patients, much suffering. Then, a man about his age invaded the public environment. He walked restlessly around the square, speaking to anyone who wanted to listen to him. He was so motivated that he seemed delusional. But only the camels paid attention to him. Still, his conviction was unshakable,

"This man whose followers I imprisoned made me fall from my pride and kiss the ground of my insignificance!"

"Another religious madman," Luke thought aloud and turned his head away to avoid listening to him.

However, the man saw him and approached Luke. Without apologizing, he began to speak of the character that had imploded his prejudices and calibrated his concepts. Luke did not care. The man, who spoke three languages, addressed him in Greek.

Luke was impressed and asked politely,

"What is your name, sir?"

"Saul from the city of Tarsus," the speaker said.

"I'm sorry, Mr. Saul, but I'm not interested in your preaching."

"You must listen…"

"I do not have time for such things; I'm a doctor."

"Excellent. Jesus is the doctor of the doctors."

"Did he take the Hippocratic oath?"

"Oath?"

"Don't you know the oath which the great Greek physician taught his disciples?" Luke asked, quoting the words of this oath: "I swear I will neither give a deadly drug to anyone who asks for it nor will I make a suggestion to this effect. Into whatever house I enter, I will abstain from every voluntary act of mischief and corruption and, further, from its seduction. Whatever I see or hear ought not to be spoken of abroad. I will not divulge as reckoning all that should be kept secret. While I continue to keep this Oath unviolated, may it be granted to me to enjoy life and the practice of the art."

"Interesting," Saul said. "Unlike this oath, it's my duty to spread what I have seen and heard."

Then, Saul told of his experience on the road to Damascus and all the physical, social, and emotional damage it had caused to those who followed Jesus. Luke was astonished by his account.

"Mr. Saul, you had unrestrained wrath! Being contrary to your thoughts was an invitation to be your enemy. How could it have changed so much?"

Saul of Tarsus gave a long account of the crucified man and his project.

"Mr. Saul, what you are telling me about this man is crazy."

"I am amazed at what happened to me. I was pursued, pressured, punished, induced blasphemy, arrested and testified against the murders of those who 'walked that way.'"

"What harm had those miserable people done to you that you wanted to hurt and imprison them?"

"Nothing except they hurt my prejudices. I confess: I was very disappointed in myself," and then he reported his violence.

"The death of a man on the cross is the height of fragility, the greatest of all social vexations. I deal with death night and day; any death is better than crucifixion," Luke emphasized.

"I agree, but his death was part of God's plan," Saul said.

"When did this Jesus die?" Luke asked.

"Eight years ago."

The conversation went on. Little by little, the Greek doctor became involved with the accounts of Saul. Dialogues, exchanges, and experiences would come later. Luke had been moved in such a way that he could not be what he had once been. Within a few weeks, the big day of his decision would come. He would give up his medical profession, a solid career, to follow a dazzled man with a sense of brutal guilt. It was a high risk for those who had much to lose, especially for a rational person.

Great decisions are always solitary. Luke had decided to make the second journey, the journey of the heart, the journey that does not bring financial profit to one's pocket, but to one's emotion. He had chosen the journey in which he would do the best he could to make others happy. He restarted his story with Saul of Tarsus, who was then named Paul. Thus, Paul and Luke became inseparable friends for decades.

Jerusalem, fifteen years later

Paul and Luke were so successful that they had impacted nations. While Paul was acting on the stage of the social theater, Luke was working behind the scenes. The man from Tarsus, educated and eloquent, convinced the audience; Luke, generous and meticulous, healed the wounds. Paul spoke to the masses, while Luke acted with the people, touching the bystanders he met, whether they were Roman officers or miserable people excluded from society.

Paul made Luke feel safe, and the latter gave Paul all the medical and emotional support. They were charming men. None of them had any salaries, but they felt rich. They had no food security, but they ate enough. The bed was not always comfortable, but they slept satisfied. The stones were their pillows and the starry nights were their sheets.

"Get out. You are disturbing the peace," a Roman officer, Lucius Extilo, once said, accompanied by an escort.

"If we say anything, we die," Paul said.

Fearless of the sword that might pierce his abdomen and expose his bowels, the brave Paul spoke once more of the 'path.'

Not far from them, the Roman officer had set up camp. One night, they heard that he had become ill. Thus, Luke was willing to treat him. The officer initially rejected him, but the high fever, diarrhea, and vomiting forced him to change his mind. He eventually accepted the visit of the Greek physician. After medicating him, Luke, as usual, left in silence charging nothing. The next day, he returned to see if the patient was recovering.

"That's absurd, Dr. Luke!" the officer said when the doctor spoke of Jesus. "How can you believe in a man we have crucified? It amazes me that a man may believe in such fantasies!"

"We are amazed, Theophilus Lucius Extilo. The one who went to the solitude of a tomb overcame what the doctors have always imagined overcoming."

"Dr. Luke, we die every day. Political leaders, generals, rich people. We all fight death, and we all lose."

"I know, death humbles all doctors. Humans are born champions and die losers. When they are born, they weep for joy; when they die, others weep in sorrow for them. But ..."

Luke had long conversations with the Roman officer. The intelligent conversation with Lucius Extilo, his few questions, and his doubts moved the Greek physician to such an extent that he dreamed one day of writing an orderly historical narrative with detailed analysis and evaluations of the man who had fascinated him.

"I intend to write a synthesis of Jesus' story. What do you think, Paul?"

"Excellent idea. You can pick up facts that I did not learn themes I did not know. But how will you do it, Luke?"

"You know, I'm a perfectionist. I will only be able to carry out this project if I can interview the characters who have lived with the Master."

"We're going to Jerusalem in the spring. This journey will be our great opportunity."

Luke and his mission

Luke watched the old city, the how the people walked, the worn-out stones on the streets, the scars on the walls, and the old roofs. It seemed that the story penetrated his soul. He interviewed Mary for a long time, talked to the disciples of the crucified man, to eyewitnesses who had seen the events. These events stimulated his intellect as he made a psychosocial inventory of the facts that had touched these people.

At night, he would return to his quarters in a small lodge on the east side of Jerusalem. His pockets were full of historical fragments. He kept them as a priceless treasure.

'How will I organize all the material? Performing this task and writing such narrative is a great responsibility. Am I able to do it?'

Dr. Luke would sit on a hard chair with asymmetrical legs, which generated an uncomfortable position. However, Dr. Luke was excited and did not care. He leaned over a table made of the olive tree trunk that contained protrusions and some holes and was the fruit of the relentless work of fungi and termites. The light was not good, the place was not airy, but he had the best space in the world to free his thoughts.

Dr. Luke was now a doctor of languages, an obsessive writer, arranging the narrative and trying to synthesize the interviews.

"I have seen many sicknesses, I have seen tremors and feverish attacks, but now I am trembling, almost feverish myself. It is very challenging to write the biography of the man who has shaken our convictions," he said to Paul.

"I know how complex it is. This work is your life, your most important project," his partner said, giving him extraordinary support.

Luke would go out for the interviews and return. He wrote in detail, dripping with emotion. He had no idea that his book would be one of the greatest bestsellers of all time.

CHAPTER 9

ROUND TABLE IMPACTS

The first Round Table had finally started. Marco Polo had entered the building holding a cane due to the thigh injury. The doctor didn't to want to force his right leg, and he didn't want to think about the accident. He was focused on his reading and the analysis; he had done on Dr. Luke's writings. Marco greeted Sofia, kissing her on the cheek. She had a slight bruise on her forehead. He held out his hands to Dr. Alberto and Dr. Thomas. He then greeted his fellow neuroscientist, Michael, who soon teased the theologians.

"Are you worried about the accident, Marco? I'm sorry," Michael said.

"I'm not worried about the accident. I'm concerned about the reading," he said.

"I sense you're already disappointed at the texts. I know you," the neuroscientist said.

Despite feeling uncomfortable around Michael, Dr. Alberto, the Vatican theologian, tried to lighten the mood, but it didn't work out.

"We are excited to discuss the texts of Luke, one of the most remarkable saints of the Church."

"Wait! I am not here to study saints and dogmas." Dr. Michael retorted, standing up to leave. "I'm a scientist. I will not waste my time with questionable beliefs."

"Wait, Michael. The debate has not even begun, and you are giving up already?" Marco said.

"But your face says it all."

"Are you able to read minds now, Michael?" asked Sofia, the moderator.

Michael sat down, but he was still feeling uncomfortable.

"Before studying Jesus' mind, we must explore the mind of his biographer. Calm down, Michael. We will not study the beatified Luke, but the real, tangible man, who shouts through his writings," Dr. Polo reaffirmed.

"Excuse me; we're so addicted to religious talk that it is hard for us to change our language," Dr. Alberto said, feeling embarrassed, and he added: "But we know almost nothing about Luke. His origin, where he was born, who his parents were, his education, how he became Christian or when he died ..."

"It is strange. I studied so much about the first texts of Luke that I ended up sleeping and dreaming of him. His first texts had no scientific validity. But silence can report more than words," Marco said.

"Marco is right. Although the findings are narrow, we need to discuss the writer behind the book, even if this makes us go deeper in the sea of doubts than in the sea of answers," Sofia said.

Marco grinned and then asked the participants,

"Don't you find it strange that a Greek doctor, a follower of Hippocrates, followed a crucified person? Doesn't it surprise you that a human being decided to quit medicine, his security and his hometown to travel the world?"

"In fact, these are strange behaviors, strange to human eyes, particularly at the birth of Christianity," Dr. Alberto agreed.

Marco continued, showing his sharp ability to ask probing questions,

"What do you think of Luke, a logical and supposedly generous man, having a mentor who showed irrationality and revealed clear traces of sociopathy?"

"What do you mean? Are you referring to the Apostle Paul?" Dr. Thomas asked, trembling.

"Exactly!" Marco replied, waiting for the theologian's reaction, which was immediate.

Dr. Thomas and Dr. Alberto stood up to close the debate, while Dr. Thomas said,

"This Round Table is doomed to failure. I will not be part of it. Extreme interpretations make me sick."

"I agree," the Vatican theologian said. "Being an atheist, Dr. Polo, is something respectable, making severe prejudgments like this is inadmissible."

"Congratulations, Marco, we won!" Michael said.

"Michael, this is not a ring," Marco pondered.

"If it were, we'd have a knockout in the first round."

Sensing that the two theologians would leave, Dr. Sofia tried to calm everybody down,

"Calm down, gentlemen. Wait for Dr. Polo to explain his thesis. We barely sat around this table and already we've broken it in half."

Without the debater's acknowledgment, some people had installed hidden cameras to film the debate. The idea was to make the content available live on the internet. They did not know that, in a short time, there would be a crowd watching them:

'Atheist intellectuals debate the intelligence of Jesus with religious intellectuals.'

The content was so exciting that, in less than a week, the videos would go viral and would be watched in several languages. Although the discussion was in English, there was a translated program for spectators.

Parallel to this, the debates would also be on-site. Some students and professors, as they passed through the half-open door, were interested in the discussions. Eager for knowledge, they entered quietly, sat down and were impressed. At first, none of the debaters noticed their presence. Little by little, the audience increased. Those who attended the debates made their impressions known and promoted the event.

On that first day, Marco remained silent due to the tense situation. He waited for them to calm down. The theologians sat down again and gave him an opportunity to explain himself.

The psychiatrist didn't apologize and triggered other questions instead,

"What do you think of a man who punishes the innocent? For instance, chasing them relentlessly; taking them to jail; pressuring them to go against their conscience and beliefs. What do you make of the man who allowed the murder of these same people without a fair trial? Even worse, my friends, with nothing to justify such a severe sentence? What can you say about this behavior registered by Luke in his Book of Acts, gentlemen?"

"Well ..." Dr. Thomas began.

Dr. Michael interrupted the Harvard theologian,

"What? Paul, Luke's mentor, the biographer we're studying, had such a background? Luke was crazy to follow such a violent man."

"That was before he converted to Christianity," the Vatican man said.

"Regardless, he had traits of sociopathy, which differs from being a psychopath," Marco said.

"What do you mean?" Dr. Thomas asked who, like most people, didn't know the difference between the concepts.

"Psychopaths kill, hurt and do not feel the pain of others, however,

Psychopaths can be well-behaved. Sociopaths, on the other hand, have social disorders, are violent, authoritarian, controlling, do not follow the rules, but this does not mean that they are cold and do not have feelings. Paul had traits of sociopathy, but he was not a psychopath."

"Wow, now I'm relieved," Dr. Thomas said feeling satisfied.

"Paul was violent but not because he was a Jew or because he was in favor of his religion, Judaism. It was because he had personality disorders. He was a slave to the need for power." Then, he explained the concept of negative emotional energy expenditure. "He had no emotional protection. His NEEE index was high. Any setback could take over him."

"But how did he change?" Michael asked.

"That's the point. It is possible that something had happened in Paul's mind; something much stronger than a psychotherapeutic insight or critical awareness generated by self-knowledge."

"I don't understand," Sofia said.

"Me neither," Dr. Michael said.

"As a psychiatrist, I dealt with many complex cases; there were thousands of appointments and sessions. Nevertheless, what happened to Paul's personality seems to be very difficult to explain. It is as if his mind had suffered an altruistic revolution capable of imploding his egocentrism," Marco said, breathing slowly.

"You are not implying that Paul quit being a wolf and became a lamb overnight," Michael said, not believing his ears. "According to psychiatry, such a thing does not exist, Marco."

"I'm still evaluating, Michael. It seems that Paul continued to have a strong personality, but he focused his energy on building instead of destroying. He reallocated his mental energy."

"You're right, Dr. Polo," Dr. Alberto said, and he continued: "Paul relentlessly persecuted the followers of Jesus, but something happened on his way to Damascus that turned him into a man stripped of vanities and makeup. He was enlightened."

"Once again I repeat: we will not study superhuman facts. What is important to us is the psychological and social phenomena. I confess I was surprised while analyzing this passage. The emotional storm seems to have been so serious that Paul confessed his madness publicly."

"I cannot follow your line of thought," Michael confessed.

"Michael, would you dare to vent your mistakes, your stupidity, your aggressive reactions and weak behaviors to a journalist? Would you allow him to post all that on the university board?" Marco asked, sending a message to his friend.

"Of course not!"

"Paul did much more than that. He dissected his violent behaviors and allowed Luke to publish them. His craziness was known throughout generations. Perhaps, because he had opened up to a friend, Paul had a shoulder to cry on and another one to support him. We all need a shoulder."

"That's amazing, Marco! I had never seen this perspective of Paul," the Harvard theologian said.

Everyone was impressed by the description. Sofia was also very convincing while speaking,

"Men announce their deeds and hide their faults. They hide their stupidity under political, financial and social statements. I have never seen a politician, a businessman, or a thinker reporting his degrading behavior so spontaneously and publicly."

Suddenly, three spectators started talking to each other. They said that they were also experts at hiding their flaws. At that moment, the debaters noticed them.

Michael intervened,

"Sorry, but this debate is private."

James, a student, disagreed,

"Excuse me, who does knowledge belong to; to a small, remarkable group or mankind?" After his questioning, Marco and the others agreed that the audience could stay. Then, turning to the noted theologians, he asked,

"Catholics and Protestants love the Apostle Paul, but are they as straightforward as he was? Are they able to expose their emotional earthquakes?"

"Well, honestly...no," Dr. Alberto said.

"If there were an open and welcoming atmosphere in the religious circles, depression would be treated; suicides would be prevented; interpersonal conflicts would be solved, and pedophilia would be avoided. There would be management instead of an emotional implosion!" Marco remarked.

"The religious varnish is despicable. Paul tried to eliminate most of it," the Vatican theologian admitted.

In the following debate, Marco prepared to give very specific examples of what happens in the world's two major religions: Catholicism and Protestantism.

"I remember a Catholic bishop and professor of theology who used to have panic attacks. He was intelligent, sweet, kind, but every time in his homily, he had the sudden feeling that he would die. He felt that his heart would jump through his mouth, and his lungs were about to explode. It was a horrible experience. And do you know how many people this distinguished educator had the courage to talk about his panic, Dr. Alberto?"

"I have no idea."

"No one. It was only after his emotional disorder became very serious, with several social sequels, that he came to me in search of treatment."

At that moment, there were many religious people watching the intense debate on the internet. They all cried. Some cried for joy because they felt that they finally had someone who understood them; others for sadness because, all of a sudden, they felt dramatically alone.

"And you, Dr. Thomas, do you think that Protestants are emotionally more open, more welcoming than Catholics?"

"I think we all relate to the example of Paul and Luke."

"Indeed. The culture of religious people, in spite of some exceptions, is the culture of producing superheroes. Psychological disorders are not allowed. Showing any sign of them is a sign of fragility, an invitation to guilt. These people should be caressed, taken care of, and welcomed. This is not Paul's culture. How many people have been exhausted, suffering in advance, deliberating losses and sorrows, feeling distressed, with planet emotion completely dried up?"

"I don't know..."

"Neither do I, since there's no research on this. I remember assisting a Baptist leader who was remarkable among his peers. He was depressed, anxious, feeling no enjoyment for life. He thought of giving everything up. Do you know how many people he spoke to about his chaos, Dr. Thomas?"

"I suppose nobody."

"Not even his wife. That fine man, in a burst of despair, got his car and went on a road thinking of taking his life. He wanted to throw himself off a cliff. Then he got a phone call from his wife: 'Where are you? What are you doing?' He burst into tears. After that episode, he came to me for treatment. But many people keep this to themselves. Silence nurtures emotional vampires."

Then, the psychiatrist said that Paul's example was extreme, that no one should announce their deeds publicly, but we should always look for someone and open up. It can be a Luke, a doctor, a friend, or a therapist.

"Judging less and hugging more is one tool of emotional management. I believe that is what Dr. Luke wanted to scream in his texts. But who hears his voice? We see dead letters, not a living example," Sofia pointed out.

"Generals who don't value their wounded soldiers on the battle front don't deserve to win the war," the Vatican theologian concluded cleverly.

"Religions can be sources of mental illnesses if we use them to disguise our emotional ghosts and our mental health," the American theologian said in turn.

"Teachers hide behind chalk, intellectuals behind titles, spectators behind a movie, leaders behind power," Sofia said breathing deeply.

"Are you being straightforward, Sofia?" Michael asked.

Sofia had tears in her eyes.

"My ex-husband had a severe personality disorder."

"You do not have to get into details," Marco said.

"But I want to. My case has become public."

At that moment, Sofia, an intelligent and delicate woman, relived her past. She remembered the sad days when her husband humiliated her. *'I am as handsome as a model; many women fall at my feet,'* he would say. 'Then why don't you leave?' Sofia would ask. *'Because I feel sorry for you,'* he justified. 'I don't want you to stay with me out of compassion.' *'You have no one, you fool. Your parents died. Your brothers are broke.'* 'But I have my dignity. I'll go away!' He would then throw her on the bed, shouting and threatening, *'What do you mean go away? Leave me, and I'll kill you! You are more mentally ill than your patients. You are more dependent on me than drug addicts.'*

While recalling that brief scene of terror, Sofia dared to say,

"He pressured me every possible way. That killed me from the inside, but I was afraid of losing him. He was right; I was addicted to him. When

I dared to break up with him, he became a stalker. It was the birth of a monster."

"Stalker? What does that word mean?" Dr. Alberto asked.

"Stalker means a pursuer. It is used when a tormentor goes after his victim. He becomes a predator, and she becomes prey. In the United States alone, 500,000 women are victims of these offenders. My ex-husband started stalking me at work, on the streets, on the phone, and on social networks. He pressured me, blackmailed me, and threatened me. I was a victim of that man for five years," she said through tears.

"If you, a lucid psychiatrist, were submitted to such an outrage, how many women suffer without saying a word?" Marco questioned.

"Many. I feel like lecturing to help educate women."

Everyone at the Round Table applauded her courage. Without her knowledge, everything she said was broadcast via the internet, impacting thousands and thousands of women. Her privacy had been violated, but countless women decided to report their predators.

"What about you, Michael? What vampires haunt you?" Dr. Alberto asked.

"I'm not ready."

"And you, Dr. Alberto?"

"I'm not ready either."

"Same here," Dr. Thomas said.

"People who don't map out their mental ghosts will be haunted by them to the last existential sigh," Marco said. "It is late now, but one day I will tell you about my ghosts."

When that sentence hit the internet, it went viral. Millions of people shared the video. Soon after that debate, table members heard from some of their friends, students, and coworkers who said they were following them in real time. Before the next debate, the participants gathered and thought about prohibiting the broadcast.

"Our privacy is at stake. Everything Sofia said has leaked. We don't know how many people from how many countries have been watching. I received information even from Singapore," Michael said.

"I think we have to forbid the internet broadcast," Dr. Alberto said firmly.

Sofia was very mature in giving her opinion,

"It's obvious that no one should expose intimate and embarrassing situations on the internet. If we mirror Dr. Luke's mentor, the Apostle Paul, who had the courage to talk about his errors, we would be less hypocritical in our universities, institutions and even in our religion. We will help many people. I received several messages from people thanking me for telling my story."

"I think using the internet wisely is healthy. I am in favor of the broadcast," Marco said.

The others agreed with Marco and Sophia. Thus, the debate gained international reach. The most remarkable Round Table installed to study Jesus' mind was also exposing the personality of the debaters and internet users of all cultures. Taking part in it, even as a spectator, was an invitation to mine the emotional scars, a danger for those who loved to hide from themselves.

CHAPTER 10

LUKE, A LOGIC, AND DETAILED BIOGRAPHER

The round table continued. After briefly discussing the character of the mysterious Greek physician and his mentor Paul, it was time for Marco to reveal the details of the first analysis of the writings of Dr. Luke. His expression changed.

"We have considered the biographer's phenomena. Now, we will go on to the introduction or preface of his book. A preface, when profound, reveals a map of what will be found throughout a work."

"But what part of the text of Luke's gospel do you consider the preface?" Dr. Thomas asked.

"The first four verses."

"And what analysis have you done?" Sofia was eager to know.

"I'm astonished so far," Marco said, giving a long, enigmatic silence.

Michael, who knew his friend well, got ahead of himself and said,

"Apparently, he has condemned Dr. Luke as a writer. Does he write badly? Is he shallow? Let us wait for your next bombastic statement."

"Dr. Luke writes like a madman," Marco commented.

"I knew it," Michael said.

Sofia intervened, discouraged.

"Explain yourself better. This affirmation is not much of an answer, but a rather dictatorial opinion."

The two theologians were upset. Once again, they were gazing into the abyss. They wanted reasonable explanations.

"Looking at these verses, I see no reason for this madness. Calling Dr. Luke insane without plausible arguments is even greater insanity," Dr. Alberto said in tune with Sofia.

"You misunderstood me. I did not say that Dr. Luke is 'crazy,' but that he 'writes like a madman.'"

"What do you mean?" Michael asked, startled.

"Dr. Luke comments, 'many have tried to elaborate a historical narrative on the facts that occurred at the time, according to what eyewitnesses and leaders dedicated to the Word have described.' They say that 'he investigated everything in detail from its origin.' Then, he directs his book to a specific person: 'I decided to write an account, most excellent Theophilus, so that you may know...'"

Marco knew that the art of questioning forged thinkers. Asking and questioning were what opened the range of the mind for valuable answers. He was teasing the round table members every minute.

"What do you see in these first texts? What was the subliminal intention?"

"I see a writer who is worried about historical facts. Not a mere biographer, but an investigative author, as if he was defending a thesis," the Vatican theologian replied.

"Yes, he looks at facts like a doctor while diagnosing a disease. When Dr. Luke says he had investigated, interviewed, and organized the data, he is showing that he valued more the natural than the supernatural, the schematic reasoning over the superstitious narrative."

"Interesting," Sofia remarked. "He was a refined writer."

"But if he writes passionately about the biography subject, wouldn't there be an emotional involvement? One that would make the necessary detachment of a proper researcher more difficult?" Michael, the neuroscientist, asked.

"Yes, Michael, he gets emotionally involved, but he has a remarkable discernment. I would like to say that the original texts are insignificant, but I have to acknowledge that I am impressed."

"Why, Marco?" His friend asked.

"Let's see. Dr. Luke made a broad investigation about the genealogy of Jesus' family. He said: 'Jesus, son of Joseph, who was the son of Eli, who was the son of Matate ...' However, the accuracy of such data and pointing them out is essential. He conducted extensive interviews with people who lived with Jesus. I will not go into detail now, but he was the biographer who got closest to Mary, and she disclosed to him a couple of intimate facts about her son. I believe that, as a writer, Dr. Luke was fundamentally rational."

Marco's honesty disconcerted the two theologians and Sofia. He continued,

"Deductive thinking is the intellect's most logical thinking; few people develop it entirely. Let us exercise it. Dr. Luke wrote: 'Many have undertaken to draw up an account of the things that have been fulfilled among us, just as they were handed down to us by those who from the first were eyewitnesses and servants of the word.' What do you deduce from this passage?"

"That Dr. Luke wrote an intelligent narrative based on research," Dr. Thomas said.

"That is the obvious inference, but set your imagination free and go deeper into deduction, Dr. Thomas," Marco insisted.

However, nothing else came to his mind, or to the others.

"Luke wrote about 55 A.D., before John's biography or gospel, correct?" "Yes," the two theologians conceded.

"Therefore, Matthew and Mark had probably written their books before Dr. Luke wrote his. So, why does Dr. Luke say that many have tried to write?"

"Wait a minute. He should have said 'two' at most, but the expression 'many' has a significant meaning. It points out that, in addition to the ones we know, there were probably many biographers of Jesus whose writings were lost," Dr. Alberto said.

"It's a deeper deduction," Marco commented.

"Either that or Christians did not validate these writings," Dr. Thomas said.

"That makes sense," Sofia agreed.

"The deductive thinking that goes deeper into the facts is that the 'Jesus phenomenon' was contagious. It provoked the minds and the imagination of the characters of the time so much that it triggered an avalanche of dreams, expectations, and affections, urging people to speak and write about it."

"Was it collective delusion?" Michael asked.

"Collective delusion only happens when political and social tension peaks, as, for example, when a dictator is in power or a great social event is afoot. In this case, the Self is held hostage to the irrational imaginary."

"And the book of Luke was written more than two decades after Jesus was crucified."

"That's right, Dr. Thomas."

"Besides, if there were religious delusion, Dr. Luke would not talk about 'logical narrative,' let alone would his mentor, Paul, recognize his own madness," Marco pointed.

"I believe his critical awareness," Michael said, refining his deductive thinking. "Unlike Nazi Germany where leaders were 'unquestionable,' where they considered Jews the enemies merely because they were different."

"That's right and Dr. Luke, despite his passion for the biography subject, employed the assumptions of an exceptional analyst: focus on details, observation skills, interviews, data organization ..." Dr. Alberto concluded.

At that moment, Sofia decided to challenge Marco. Smiling at him, she said,

"At a time when illiteracy struck the masses, the fact that many were driven to record Jesus' behavior reinforces the thesis of a real rather than a fictional character," she pondered, staring at Marco.

Marco smiled. Sofia had just added fuel to the fire that he had already lit.

"I think Jesus had been a character built by a group of Galileans to free them from the tyranny of the Roman emperor, Tiberius Caesar. However, philosophical and literary criticism have yielded that Jesus could not have been a fictitious figure, a work of imagination, regardless of archaeological findings. He was the agent of a real 'emotional earthquake,' though we have not judged his intelligence so far," Marco acknowledged, disturbed.

"Amazing!" Dr. Alberto said. "We are always talking about the divine inspiration of this book, but we forgot that Dr. Luke also demonstrated remarkable intelligence."

"The human being rarely charms, inspires or impacts his students, co-workers or relatives. Unlike Jesus, we are too rough," Marco said, disappointed at himself, thinking of his son, Luke. "However, what shook my prejudice the most was not Dr. Luke's reasoning, but his purpose in writing the book."

"I don't understand. Dr. Luke wrote to mankind," Dr. Alberto exclaimed.

"No. His book was used by mankind, but that was not why he wrote it."

"To the Jews, then?" Dr. Alberto asked.

"No."

"To the Greeks?" Michael asked.

"Again, no," said Marco. "Take another look at the preface and try to find a detail overlooked by countless scholars."

"Amazing! That's crazy but it is true. Dr. Luke wrote to one man only!" Dr. Thomas cried. He said, 'I have decided to write you an orderly account, most excellent Theophilus, so that you may know ..."

"Exactly. Luke's introduction has baffled me and my prejudice once again," Marco said, remaining silent soon after.

"I don't understand what shook you so much," Michael said.

"Let's think further. Would you spend months or years preparing a book for only one person?"

"It would be a waste of time," Michael considered.

"We are Cartesian, logical, and belittled. We appraise time, and we do not waste it. Not even with our loved ones. We do not ask them what nightmares haunt them, nor what tears have they hidden under the mask on their faces," Marco continued.

Michael was speechless. His daughter had Down syndrome, but he was not the kind of person who would explore the treasures in her emotional grounds. A movie played in his mind. His daughter was saying, *'Daddy, Daddy, come and play with me.'* 'I can't now, honey,' he would reply and walk away. He had time for science, but not for those he claimed to love.

The audience in the debate room was growing. The people who were present, as well as the thousands watching live on the internet, were touched by the superficiality of the interpersonal relationships that they lived.

A fifteen-year-old Japanese girl, who was watching the debate, told her father,

"You never have time for me, Dad. You are connected to the world, but not to me."

A twenty-year-old from Shanghai said,

"Dad, you know I'm the best student in my class. You know my grades, but you never ask me anything about my feelings, not even about my tears. I'm depressed, on the verge of suicide."

A French doctor apologized to his wife for being dry and cold in the house. He muttered shyly, "What can I do to make you happier? Where was I wrong, and didn't realize?"

Many were being transformed as they watched the debates and saw how much Dr. Luke valued his friend.

Sofia completed Marco's reasoning,

"We don't even have time to ourselves. We betray our quality of life; we are machines working and performing tasks. The book of Luke rescues what money can never conquer."

Marco clapped softly and added,

"Did Dr. Luke write to a Roman officer in a period when time was scarce, and the average life span was not more than 40? It's almost unbelievable."

"Such behavior, of writing a book to one person, is a psychotic outbreak," Michael said.

"Or a love outbreak," Dr. Thomas commented. "We deduce that the book of Luke, being addressed to a single man, was not a political advertisement or a marketing piece of some religion, but it was a solemn act of love."

"Without love, there is no sustainable social inclusion. Europe, the stage of the First and Second World Wars, needs to rediscover a non-religious Jesus, a love that transcends cultural barriers, that embraces more and judges less, that wastes time with those excluded from society," the Vatican theologian concluded, thinking about immigrant inclusion, terrorist attacks, and economic conflicts.

They were all silent in honor of the innocent victims of the latest terrorist attacks. After that, Marco concluded the debate for that day.

"I don't know whether we will be disappointed at Jesus' intelligence, whether he will pass the stress and emotional management tests or not; however, he went about his life and undoubtedly caused an emotional windstorm that broke self-centeredness."

Another of Marco's round tables ended. The other debates would remain at the same level. Their minds and the minds of those who watched them would begin to experience an emotional revolution. Incredible surprises were yet to come.

CHAPTER 11

MARY, A DARING EDUCATOR

With respect and enthusiasm, fearing nothing and without restraints, the five members discussed, from the perspective of the human sciences, Jesus' behavior and the characters around him, such as Luke, Paul, and Mary. Without further delay, Marco resumed the debates,

"I know you're excited to start studying Jesus' personality, but this moment hasn't arrived yet."

"Why not?" Michael asked.

"We have studied, yet minimally, some characteristics of Dr. Luke's mind, Jesus' biographer. Now, we need to study essential characteristics of his educator: Mary."

Dr. Alberto cracked a smile and said,

"After the character of the Holy Trinity, Mary is the most beloved to the Roman Catholic Church."

"Do you think you know her?" Marco Polo asked.

"Of course," Dr. Alberto burst out. Then, he collected himself: "At least I think we do."

It is likely that the works of Mary's mind; Mary, history's most famous woman remains unknown to the ones who admire her.

Sofia started to think about her mentor's words and braced herself for the bomb which was about to detonate. Without further ado, the moderator of the round table asked,

"Could you explain yourself?"

"What characteristics of Mary's personality are most relevant?"

"She was sweet, kind, self-sacrificing. She gave herself to others," the Vatican theologian testified.

Marco confronted him,

"This is not the Mary that Dr. Luke pointed out. She may be kind and generous, but the most relevant features described by the Greek physician are: 1) great courage; 2) sheer thinking; 3) an amazing skill to think synthetically; and 4) extraordinary selfesteem."

Dr. Alberto pondered,

"I'm a theologian and have also graduated in psychology. I've presented countless conferences about Mary, but these characteristics were not on my radar. 'Extreme courage and extraordinary self-esteem'...aren't you mistaken, Dr. Polo?"

"These traits of Mary's personality are also new to me," Sofia, who also admired the mother of Jesus, said. "I have always seen Mary sad, suffering, as The Pieta, the famous work of Michelangelo in St. Peter's Cathedral. In what analytical basis do these four traits stand?"

"Think about it, Sofia. Who would believe the baby was a divine project? How would you think that a young woman, a 16-year-old, would turn out to be the ultimate missionary? How would you convince intelligent men, the scribes, and Pharisees, who determined what was right in spiritual terms or heresy? She accepted her pregnancy without hesitation in a land where adulterers were condemned to death. How would she explain this to her parents, her future husband and friends?"

"It would take a resolute spirit," Dr. Thomas acquiesced.

"Beyond that, an unprecedented, daring one."

"Those of us, who see the facts from the spiritual bias, gather that everything happened perfectly, harmoniously, but we neglect the anguish of these characters," the theologian of the Vatican said.

"Sure!" Marco, an expert on critical analysis, cheered.

"Interpreting one's behavior is something serious, especially when you describe it as cut and dried. We have to question our truths, think of other possibilities. We live in a violent world because people think poorly. Put yourselves in Mary's shoes and try to feel her emotions."

While doing the exercise, Dr. Thomas commented,

"Imagine the sleepless nights, the risk of being socially banned, the mockery, the criticism of those who disregarded her."

"Here she is seen as the 'Blessed woman'; there she was the most persecuted mother ever," Sofia said.

Marco was glad to see that his friends were leaving the surface of the debate and descending to deeper layers of deductive, inductive and reflective reasoning. Sofia, looking back to her brief and hard experience as a mother, sighed,

"The only son I had, was born two months premature, and my husband and I were fighting a lot back then. Unfortunately, my son had cardiorespiratory problems."

Sofia's eyes were dark as she told her story. She remembered the scene: 'Where is my son?' she asked. 'Calm down, Sofia. He's in the neonatal intensive care unit,' the nurse said.

"My maternal instinct spoke louder." She told the members of the table. "No one could stop me. I went to the ICU desperate. I reached the door, and they tried to stop me, but I shouted, 'I want to see my son!' The doctor looked in my eyes and uttered the final sentence, which pierced me like a dagger, 'I'm sorry, he has just died.' I got in the ICU and started caressing my baby. I wanted to see him playing, growing; to feel his kisses, but his mouth was closed, and his eyes were forever shut."

The members of the round table took turns placing their hands over hers.

"I'm sorry."

"You are amazing and strong, Sofia," Marco consoled.

Many in the audience and others who were watching via the internet cried. Sofia added,

"If I were in Mary's shoes and had to flee desperately so that my son would not be killed, maybe I would go mad or would feel completely deceived, not privileged," she said, still frantic.

After a brief pause, the Harvard theologian asked Marco:

"I understood that Mary needed extreme courage, but what elements lead you to see Mary as reflective?"

"In the first place, Dr. Luke comments that an outsider barged in her chambers, an 'extraterrestrial' named Gabriel. Instead of succumbing to fear, Mary got intrigued and asked about the reason for his greeting. Secondly, when the stranger proposed the divine project, she again pondered and wondered 'how would the events come true?'"

"In fact, your deduction is surprising. Who would debate with a ghost? Mary argued with the stranger, and she asked, 'How will this happen if I don't know any man?'" Dr. Alberto wisely pointed out. "She was a reflective and not an impulsive young woman."

"Dr. Luke said in the preface to Jesus' biography that he would give a first-hand account of the facts. It is likely that the Mary herself had told her thoughts to him," Dr. Thomas concluded.

"Most likely," Sofia granted.

Michael had a question stuck in his mind while Marco was presenting his ideas.

"Wait a minute! Do you believe in Mary's miraculous conception? How can you believe such absurdity is possible? It is the 21st century."

Marco asserted,

"As we know, Jesus would need to have 23 chromosomes from a spermatozoon and 23 chromosomes of an ovule. Thus, an egg would form, which would multiply rapidly in millions of cells, creating an embryo, and from the second quarter forward have billions of cells and would form a fetus, resulting in an organism with over 10 trillion cells. As you point out, Michael, the biological equation of Jesus does not equate."

"But we must not forget that the person who is giving us an account of the conception of Jesus is not a writer at all, but a clear-sighted physician, Dr. Luke," Sofia warned, assuming the role of the psychiatrist that she was. "The Author of Life could have picked up all of Mary's chromosomes, cloned and modified only one of the X chromosomes, turning it into a Y."

"Impossible!" Michael stormed.

"What is impossible for men is possible for God," Dr. Alberto effused.

"We said we would not discuss religion in this debate. In my opinion, God is fiction," Michael said, standing up sharply.

"If you're not fiction, how can you claim that God is fiction?" Dr. Alberto ranted.

The debate was hot. Marco tried to calm his friend down,

"When faith speaks, science is silent. This is our deal. Think a little further, Michael, let's make an exception and discuss the hypothesis of Jesus' conception philosophically."

At that moment, Marco went into such deep layers that all at the round table were shaken,

"Assuming God exists, let's put him at the center of our debate. I want honest and quick answers from both theologians. Who is he? What is his identity?"

"We do not know accurately. God is a mystery," Dr. Thomas said.

"Thank you for your honesty. Isn't it strange to love and follow the unknown?"

"Jesus Christ revealed some of his aspects," Dr. Alberto said.

"What's his origin?" Michael asked with a subtle giggle.

"He has no origin," Dr. Thomas said and completed, "He self-exists. He is, was and will always be. Jesus exists from eternity to eternity."

"How is that possible? If God is so great and powerful then he is mocking our debate right now," Marco said. The audience laughed.

"Maybe he's having fun," Dr. Alberto smiled. More laughs.

"Isn't he scared of my atheism or Marco's?" Michael teased.

"I think he's a father who sees children running up and down and says, 'What an interesting game!'" Dr. Thomas speculated.

"That's what I needed to hear. I'm a toy of God now," Michael said sarcastically.

The audience and now Sofia too burst into laughter. Then Dr. Thomas interjected,

"However, this debate is very serious and has significant consequences for us and perhaps for all mankind."

They recorded the debate, and afterwards, they would write a book.

"Ah, well, much better," Michael humorously said.

Marco raised the temperature of the waters,

"Why does God remain anonymous?" "I don't know," Dr. Alberto said.

"Why doesn't he intervene directly in this species?"

"I don't know."

"How do you say 'I don't know?' Aren't you remarkable theologians?" Marco wanted to know.

"No answer would be satisfying for this question. Especially after we started a debate about Jesus' mind," Dr. Thomas acquiesced maturely.

"Let's turn to Voltaire's thinking: Does God decide not to act because he is neglectful or because he considers mankind a failed project?" Marco teased.

"Good, Marco. You just hit the bull's eye," Michael cheered.

Dr. Thomas' answer poured cold water on them,

"The Author of Existence is so great and bet so much on mankind that he gave them an unreachable treasure: freedom of choice. Choices are the real reasons why mankind's biography is tainted with violence."

"Like the violence caused by Christian mistakes such as The Crusades, The Inquisition, and the segregation of minorities," Michael snorted.

"Absolutely!" the Vatican theologian said acutely. "Crimes committed by children cannot be attributed to their parents."

"Children make mistakes when parents don't teach them well," Michael said.

"Not always. You are a neuroscientist, and as you are aware, you cannot create a personality. What are we doing at this round table? Aren't we studying Jesus' intelligence? Aren't we going to analyze it as emotional managers? We don't intend to evaluate him as a Master. Shall we see whether he is a superb educator for mankind?" Dr. Alberto asked.

"Excellent challenge. But, let's also see whether Christians are good students, shall we?" Michael teased once more.

"Outstanding challenge! This is the reason we are here!" Dr. Thomas cut to the chase. "And we shall even map our emotional vampires."

The round table revealed strong debaters who were gradually losing the fear of looking within. The audience found these questions fascinating.

"Smart answer," Marco said. "In this debate, we will study the mind of Jesus and even check his skills to train thinkers. Now, let us continue exercising our complex reasoning. Imagine that God is hiding behind the curtain of time and space. In this case, he would be everlasting, above quantum physics and the special theory of relativity. How can such a great person send his child, who he loves so much, to his death? Wasn't God cruel?"

"What you call cruelty, we call love," Dr. Thomas affirmed.

Marco swallowed, sighed, and continued to bombard the theologians with his questions, some of these questions never before asked.

"Would it be possible that his super powerful, timeless son went through the embarrassment of being an embryo, a fetus, a baby, a child, a teenager, to become an adult later and act in the social scene?"

Michael stepped into that field, smiled victoriously, and added,

"Congratulations, Marco, I am a fan of your reasoning. If I were God, I would be smarter. I would have sent either a general with a mighty army or a superhero."

Once again, the audience laughed. Sofia did not like the way he mocked, and confronted him,

"Superheroes, like Superman and Batman, are brainless. They fight enemies without worrying about their opponent's socio-emotional history!" Everyone laughed. Sofia pointed, "But now some writers are trying to humanize them."

"Whoa! Dr. Sofia is no longer a moderator and is taking sides," Michael said wryly.

In the meantime, a few more spectators entered the conference room. Dr. Alberto admired Marco's reasoning and spoke,

"In fact, God's project is complex. It demanded a costly emotional investment. He cast his messenger, his son, to acquire full biological, psychological, human form. So that to understand the 'human madness', he could rescue the 'human being.'"

"The baby, the boy and the man Jesus needed to have physical and emotional pains, experience loneliness, contempt, the valleys of anguish and anxieties," Dr. Thomas added.

Marco paused to think; he did not expect that answer. However, he insisted,

"For you, then, Jesus was aware of whom he was in the maternal womb?"

"You are exploring a field I've never seen exploring. I don't know," Dr. Alberto admitted.

"If Jesus was the son of God, as you believe, Mary's womb could have been an unbearable prison," Michael said.

"Nine months could feel longer than eternity. An unimaginable jail," Marco said and speculated. "Unless his preexisting memory was suppressed during his fetal formation and during his childhood."

"I am dazzled by your questions, Dr. Polo. I have never imagined that, at this age, my mind would be so full of inquiries," Dr. Thomas exclaimed. "Maybe Jesus' memory was suppressed during his personality formation and brought back at the age of 30 when he began to spread his message. But that is a mystery."

"I started this inquiry, as a scientist, I have to think further about it. Was it temporary amnesia or an autistic attitude to his timeless past? It's hard to say. Moreover, how could Jesus have suppressed his preexisting past if, when he was 12, he debated with the doctors of law and said things beyond the teaching of his parents?" Marco pondered.

"I don't know; I don't know ... I'd never thought about it. If Jesus' memory was preserved, his suffering and sacrifice for humanity were greater than what religions that admire him imagine. His formation was as dramatic as his crucifixion. An unbearable jail," Dr. Thomas was perplexed.

"My God, the crucifixion would only be a figment of his pain," Sofia muttered.

"We read the Gospels with such superficiality that we silenced our ability to think," Dr. Alberto agreed.

Before finishing another round table, Michael got up and tried to summarize this sea of questions,

"Don't you find it absurd that an alleged Prince, sent by the most powerful King, was born in a manager? This is crazy!"

"Crazy in love," Dr. Alberto confronted him once more.

"Love, love, love ... You, religious men, are infected with romanticism!" Michael said.

"In fact, any baby in the slums of Rio de Janeiro, India and Bangladesh is born in a more dignified environment than that boy. If the possible prison of his mother's womb was not enough, the baby barely had time to play because he had to flee to another country, so he wasn't killed. This boy had plenty of reasons to be depressed and anxious. If he didn't know how to filter stressful stimuli out and manage his emotions, he would have sunk," Marco said.

"This is an unprecedented story," Dr. Thomas said.

"Even the creative Nietzsche in all his deliriums could not have imagined a story like that child," Michael said.

"I don't know whether Jesus would pass the social-emotional intelligence tests, which are far more complex than the logical intelligence of IQ tests, but I have no doubt his story is revolutionary," Marco asserted.

Everyone agreed. During those heated debates, countless Christians, Buddhists, Jews, and atheists began to follow them on the Internet. Even the Islamists, for Jesus, was one of the most quoted characters in the Koran.

Secrets and more secrets; the members of the round table had never imagined that the biography of Jesus, written by Dr. Luke, was such an unfathomable source of mysteries. They were just at the beginning of the debates. They did not know where it would eventually go.

CHAPTER 12

MARY, A DARING AND ANALYTICAL WOMAN

The beginning of this era

That sunny afternoon, the wind brushed the dry dirt road, raising a curtain of dust that blurred people's eyes and refreshed their skins. Three great friends who had just turned 15 were at a square sitting together, they were under an olive tree, its crooked trunk hid centuries of existence. The girls were not celebrating their birthday because their life was hard and having something to eat was their reason for celebration. Seated on old and irregular wooden benches, they contemplated the grape plantations and the barren soil on the horizon. Sparrows were singing, their symphony was always confused, rejoicing the young in the land of scarcity.

The friends shared pieces of bread made of flour mixed with olive oil and salt.

They had to chew repeatedly to moisten the food so it wouldn't get stuck. One of them stood out for being more sociable, eloquent and good-humored. She was enthusiastic and excited because she had been promised to a man. Her joy was contagious.

"Are you getting married soon, Mary?" Rebecca asked.

"In one year."

"The day I get married, I'll be happy too," Ruth said.

"Don't ever think of getting married to be happy, Ruth, but to be happier. Happy is something you should already be," Mary coached.

Ruth thought of what Mary had said, and exclaimed,

"You say odd things. It's difficult to follow your thinking."

"What is 'to be happy'?" Rebecca asked expressed an eternal question of humanity, the one that the wise men of all cultures and all times could not fully answer.

However, for Mary, the answer was quite simple,

"To be happy is to contemplate the significance of the Author of Existence in the simple to straightforward things. It is to be dazzled by the rain and the sun. It is to start all over again whenever necessary."

"You look so strong. Don't you get depressed on this dry land?" Rebecca asked.

"I'm happy to be alive, and for breathing, loving, dreaming, and having friendships. Have you ever stopped to think how amazing it is to be alive?" Mary asked. "You're so bold, Mary," Rebecca exclaimed.

"My boldness comes from knowing how small I am, Rebecca." "Don't you have any fear?" Rebecca was curious.

"I do have my fears. And the greatest is having no control over myself, especially over my superb negative thoughts," the young woman, who had the most singular reasoning, said.

"Where does your intelligence come from?" Ruth asked disturbed.

"We are all intelligent," Mary pointed.

Suddenly, a beggar showed up asking for bread. His face was deformed by leprosy-causing Rebecca and Ruth to step away, while Mary went to meet him, giving him a piece. Some scribes, educated men, were passing by, and they warned her,

"Be careful, young lady. It can be dangerous."

She surprised them,

"The greatest danger is to be indifferent to the pain of others."

"Who do you think you are to teach us?"

"Excuse me. I do not seek to teach you, I just said what I feel."

"Don't you realize leper contaminates the world? Also, he is stinking."

"Who exhales a good scent from their soul?" she asked. "Doesn't God glorify the humble, casting down the proud from thrones?"

The girls were amazed at her boldness. Rebecca pulled her arm and whispered,

"Mary, be careful. You are a woman."

"You are strange, young lady," one of the men said.

Thus, Mary expressed the relevant thoughts she would one day declare in her thesis known as *Magnificat*. She had an intellectual ability that was beyond her age. The friends decided to go home. On their way, Rebecca asked,

"Mary, can you teach me to read?" "I would like it, too," Ruth said.

"Are you willing to overcome men's prejudices?"

"I have doubts," Ruth said sincerely. "I know that reading is a privilege of a few men, especially the scribes."

"Knowing the letters is one thing, reading papyri in the light of lanterns is certainly another. That requires perseverance to cope with fatigue."

Rebecca frowned and confessed,

"I do not have all this motivation."

"I'm eager to read, and I want to know things. I didn't learn to read because my father taught me. I did it because I fought for this dream. I was quite disciplined."

A few minutes later, she said goodbye to her friends. The sun was preparing to say farewell to the farmers. Mary kissed her parents when she arrived home and said,

"It's good to see you excited, Dad!"

"Your love for existence fascinates me, my child," her father said cheerfully.

"In a land where we lack the bread made of wheat, we cannot lack the bread of joy," the young Mary said wisely. "How was your day?"

"We picked olives and squeezed them. We'll have a good crop."

Mary said goodbye to her parents and went to her chambers. Her straw bed had undesirable bumps. But for her, it was her emotion that gave density to the mattress and rocked her sleep at quiet nights.

She sat down on the bed and began to meditate. After raising her eyes to the bleak roof, she was preparing to recover the vital energy spent on another daily journey. Still, she felt something odd in the room. It seemed someone was watching. She should be trembling with fear. Substantial waves of adrenaline should be flowing through her bloodstream, making her lungs and heart pound to escape danger.

Mary was the kind of person who faced her problems instead of running away from them. Suddenly, she realized that a stranger had entered her room. To make matters worse, the stranger cried out to her,

"Hail Mary, full of grace. The Lord is with thee!"

Who would be happy facing an invader? What mind would remain calm having a stranger in such an intimate place? Instead of being dominated by fear and shock, the young woman went deep into herself and began to think about the meaning of the message. The stranger was surprised by her attitude.

"Don't be afraid, Mary. You have found favor with God. You will become pregnant, give birth to a son, and name him Jesus. He will be a great man and will be called the Son of the Highest and his kingdom will never end."

Mary, instead of being quiet, running away or calling her parents, began a conversation with the 'ghost' in her room,

"You broke into my chambers and asked me not to be afraid. Then you gave me such astonishing news saying that I will have a son. You also told me that the child would be called the Son of the Highest. Who are you?"

"I am Gabriel."

To his astonishment, instead of dismissing the shocking offer, taking it as the delusion of her mind, the young woman began to wonder how that unimaginable phenomenon would happen.

"How will it happen?" I have never been intimate with a man."

Then the angel clarified the plan and ended up saying,

"But nothing is impossible for God."

Gabriel was expecting many other questions, doubts, uncertainties about the future, especially because Mary was very young. However, to his amazement, she had accepted that hard quest. She did not think about the serious consequences she would have to face.

"Let everything you said happen to me."

The next morning, at dawn, she tried very carefully to tell her parents what had happened. She felt the drama she would have to face.

"What do you mean? Was there a stranger in your room? Mary, you have such a fertile imagination."

"But, father, the angel spoke to me!"

"Angels speak to men, to priests."

"But he spoke to me!" she said.

"And what did he say?" her mother asked concerned.

"That I was in favor with God."

"But all young girls are."

"He said one more thing."

There was a moment of silence, which disturbed her mother.

"Speak, child!"

"That I will get pregnant, actually that I am pregnant."

"Pregnant? But you're not yet married!"

She went quiet again. Her father panicked.

"Are you telling me you're pregnant from another man?"

It was a dramatic situation. If Mary's parents had reacted like that, how would she explain herself to others? What words would she say? Who would believe her? Her father loved her so much, but he was so shocked that he stood up and raised his voice.

"Mary, you always gave us many joys, your sensitivity is contagious. But you went too far." Wiping the sweat from his face, he said: "My daughter, do you know the consequences? They will stone you. You will bleed in a public square."

"Honey, if you are not pregnant with Joseph, you have committed adultery," her mother cried, her voice trembling.

"We will sink in disgrace. You will be disowned. Oh, my God ..." her father said, putting his hands on his head.

Her parents wiped the tears from their faces. They were in panic.

For the first time, Mary realized the responsibility she had accepted.

"Father, believe me, I'm not pregnant with a man."

"Are you crazy?" her mother said in anguish."

"What actually happened in your room?" her father asked, trying to be lucid in that tense emotional mood.

"My body was invaded by an unusual force. It felt like I was floating in the clouds.

God begot the child I carry."

"What do you mean? Mary, this is heresy! If you say so publicly, you will sign your death sentence."

Thus, Mary began to cross the long valleys of stress. She would have to be very strong. From that moment on, her quiet days would be over. She would no longer run in the squares nor have long pleasant conversations with her friends. She was a mother who would have to explain the inexplicable, who was at imminent risk of losing her life and losing her child. She would travel through social deserts, would be a companion of loneliness, migrating to Bethlehem, fleeing to Egypt, having to hide a special son. A decision that took her seconds to make would bring unpredictable hardships to her life. Mary, the Blessed Woman, wept.

"My husband, please stop talking about death. You have already murdered Mary three times." Her mother said, watching her daughter's despair.

"Angel Gabriel said that my son is to be the Messiah, the Son of the Highest. I was so happy about having the child, but now you're scaring me."

"Oh! My daughter, my daughter, my daughter." Her father said hugging the lovely Mary and placing her head on his right shoulder. "We are miserable, living in a tragic city, in a region despised by the leaders of Jerusalem. How can you say that you were chosen to bear the Messiah? Will he be my God?"

"Father, I only believed, and something happened. Angel Gabriel also said that Elizabeth, my cousin, is also pregnant."

"How can it be? She is old," her mother said, feeling so confused.

"But he said so."

Then her father had an idea, one that could save his daughter from becoming the target of the townsmen's righteous fury.

"Heroes always die sooner. Be discreet, dear. Go to the mountains where your cousin is. Let us wait for this troubled time to pass."

Mary sighed deeply, kissed her father and accepted his proposal. "I was actually thinking about visiting Elizabeth."

It was then that the young woman prepared to go to Zechariah and Elizabeth's home in the mountains. The Blessed Woman, chosen among so many young women, should travel in a luxurious carriage; have an escort of soldiers and assistants to meet her personal needs. But this never happened. Humanity did not smile at her, the same way it did not smile at her son. She would have a long and strenuous journey on foot. Solitude was her convoy and her belief, her protection.

Mary packed simply, put her bag on her back and said goodbye to her two great friends early in the morning. She decided to whisper the truth only to them. Once again, Mary tried to explain the inexplicable. She was expecting a triumphant farewell, but then again, she began to feel the pain of contempt.

"My friend, this is crazy," Ruth said.

"Mary, this is very serious," Rebecca said, questioning her sanity. "Let us talk to a Pharisee and ask for his opinion."

"No, no! They will not understand this for now."

"What about Joseph, did you tell him?"

"Not yet. I'm telling you. I believe in God's plan. I believe in the Messiah!" She stood firmly.

"But why would you be the chosen one and not me or any other girl?" Rebecca asked. "You are showing too much pride. Who says the Messiah is to be born as a frail and poor child?" Rebecca turned her back to Mary. Being close friends with her was getting dangerous.

"Mind your words and care for your safety," Ruth said, and along with Rebecca, she turned her back on her friend.

Human beings make their most important decisions in loneliness. She made her decision alone and went on the solitary road. She passed by a couple of evil-looking men on her way. She wondered whether those men could tell she was pregnant, but not pregnant with her partner. When she saw stones in their hands, she thought they were meant to hit her. The angel told her not to be afraid, but it was impossible to ask that from that frightened creature at that moment. She kept repeating to herself: "A person who wins without risks wins without glories." But her risks were unimaginable.

Suddenly, a gust of wind hit Marco's hotel, causing the bedroom door to open and hit hard, frightening him. Once again, he realized he had been dreaming about the facts from the past. He went so deep in Luke's text that it set his imagination free. He went to close the window. He looked at the horizon and saw the city of Jerusalem, the old part too, lit. It was a heavenly landscape.

At once, he saw nothing else; a curtain of smoke blindfolded his eyes. He looked down and struggled to see the flaming floors. Sirens sounded, fire engines began to arrive. He quickly left the apartment and banged on Sofia's door, which was next to his.

"Sofia! Sofia!"

She woke up dizzy.

"What is it?"

"The hotel is on fire! Let's go!"

Though frightened, she managed to say,

"Wait."

"Leave it all behind!"

Women have a different instinct. She had time to grab a bag of clothes and her purse and quickly set off towards the stairs. They could not use the elevator. As they were going down, they saw people screaming and crying. Some of them were coughing with the smoke.

When they arrived at the lobby, they were safe. The people who had inhaled smoke were taken to the hospital. Those in good health were referred to other hotels.

No one knew if anyone was sleeping on the upper floors. As Marco had woken up, he and Sofia were unharmed, but they were not emotionally well.

CHAPTER 13

AN AMAZING BOY

It was two in the morning when Marco and Sofia arrived at the new hotel, American Colony. She was still very terrified and asked to stay on a lower floor, lower than the high one she was in the previous hotel. She checked in quickly.

"I'm shaken. If you hadn't woken up, we would not be here."

"But we are here, alive and healthy. Try to rest, Sofia."

"How? I am restless. My nerves are on edge."

"Don't ruminate the past or suffer in advance. Try to challenge your fear as much as possible."

"I'll try," she said. She was still feeling tense while looking around for security guards.

Trying to distract her from her tension, Marco consoled,

"Sofia, you're smarter than me. I brought my documents and nothing else, while you also brought some clothes."

"I don't know if women are smarter or sillier."

"You are smarter. And don't forget our project."

"Yes, I'm excited. We'll have the round table tonight."

"I had incredible dreams of past events."

"Again?" she asked curiously.

"Yes; this time about the boy's mother. Mary must have crossed unthinkable emotional and social tornados, worse than the one we had today."

"Interesting ... I believe Dr. Luke did a good job as a biographer, challenging you this much." After a brief reflection, she kissed his face and said, "Good night, my guardian."

Happy with her gesture, he said nothing, just shook his head. Sofia went to bed, but anxiety is the enemy of sleep. Her hyperactive mind led her Self to be stuck in the conscious state. It took her a long time to fall asleep, but when her mind finally slowed down; she was plunged into the dense waters of the unconscious and had a deep sleep. As striking as it may seem, this time it was she who freed her imagination and penetrated the incredible story of the character they had been studying.

Year 55 A.D.

Fifty-five years after those events, a woman with gray hair, who was lucid, quiet, welcoming, and had a soft voice, was sitting on the small porch of a clay house. Her skin, just like the walls of the residence, showed the scars of time. She was 70 years old, and a man in his mid-40s was looking for her. He knocked on doors trying to find her.

Then, the man, after a relentless pursuit, approached the woman and looked into her eyes. His heart raced. He was a doctor and had treated so many old people he should have been impressed. However, the character he wanted to find was breathtaking.

"I'm looking for Mary. Is it you, by any chance?"

"And I'm looking for Dr. Luke. Is it you, sir?"

"How do you know my name?" he asked, intrigued.

"They said that the friend of the man who used to persecute the ones who loved Jesus, my son, wanted to interview me."

Luke's lips trembled.

"I will be honored. May I take a seat?"

"What's stopping you? My heart is yours, and so is my story. Did he impact you?"

"Touched, fascinated, enchanted. I do not even know how to describe it."

"I understand. I've felt that way since his birth."

Mary then began to tell her story to an interviewer who was eager for details. As a doctor, he had already heard many excellent stories, but that woman's path amazed him.

"Why are you conducting these interviews?"

"I need to write to a great friend."

"The writers are the first to savor their work. You write for yourself."

Luke said nothing, thinking it over. Mary's wisdom and her stories made Luke take a break from time to time. He lifted his eyes and set them on the horizon as if seeking for himself.

"Mary, your voice is slow, and your gestures are like music to my ears. We Greeks, love sculptures but the largest statue is the personality of a human being. Yours is carved with unimaginable pains, inexpressible joys, and unexpected adventures," the biographer of Jesus observed.

"I have lived many adventures, but I ask you, my good doctor, summarize what I am going to tell you. Do not talk too much about me. I prefer discretion."

"Why, ma'am?" Luke asked.

"I am privileged to have participated in the story of the Son of the Highest God. That is enough for me, my son. Being backstage is my specialty."

"Humbleness is an excellent quality," he acquiesced.

"Beyond that, humbleness is the foundation of wisdom and nobody was humbler than the boy I carried in my arms and saw growing up."

"Can I hear the entire story from the beginning? Was Joseph surprised?"

"How couldn't he be? However, he was an unusual man. I tried to explain to him, but he did not understand. How could he? He didn't shout, didn't shun nor accuse me. If he had been another man, he might have acted differently. Preserving me from social judgment, he secretly walked away. Then he was enlightened and, eventually, welcomed me, hugged me, wept and together we kept God's project."

Luke swallowed hard. Knowing all the injustices that Jesus and his disciples had suffered and still faced, he thought to himself 'How brave.' After that, Mary commented that her presence in her hometown had become unbearable. Many speculated about her pregnancy. Fortunately, there was the decree of Caesar Augustus, the Roman emperor, to make the first census of all the inhabitants under the empire's ruling. Joseph should enlist in the city where he was born, Bethlehem.

"I was feeling the pains of labor. I was suffering greatly, but at least I was far from prejudicial looks. We were looking for a hostel, but they were all full. No one welcomed us."

"You carried the most incredible boy ever conceived, and there was simply no place to give birth? You were unable to explain your pregnancy. Weren't you disturbed?" Luke wanted to know.

"Joseph would ask at times: 'Isn't he the chosen one? Why is he neglected? Why is he being born in such miserable conditions? My child should be born in a comfortable house or hostel, but with so many unanswered questions, I just accepted the inevitable." "Accept that the sour smell of fermented manure was his perfume; and that the warmth of the animals was his blanket. Then, there he was, being exalted by Wise men of the East. These are the paradoxes that would leave one in shock!" Luke said.

Mary was delighted.

"Imagine, Luke, that a few months later, the baby, who had not harmed anyone, was persecuted as the most miserable man. We had to run away day after day. The desert and the oasis have always been on the pages of our history."

"Did you cry many times?"

"Countless times; But God wiped away my tears."

"Has the Blessed Woman ever felt betrayed or abandoned by God?"

Mary took a deep breath. Luke was a man who did not waste questions.

"No. Never. Sometimes I felt I was the unhappiest woman in the world. Imagine the pain I felt when I knew that, because of my son, mothers wept desperately, for Herod had killed their children."

"But you were not to blame."

"Who could say? Neither the angels nor friends nor even my parents; But my boy comforted me. He kept smiling at me. He seemed to be saying, 'Be brave.' If I hadn't talked to God, I would have gone mad."

"Was the escape to Egypt difficult?"

"We traveled miles on the back of a donkey. We had to relieve ourselves in the open. There was a scalding sun. The winds were sharp and bitter; it was very cold at night. We were living in the land of strangers. What do you think?"

"Did you ever regret accepting the mission?"

"No, I never did. I'm privileged. I learned to be happy in chaos. Losers see the storms and retreat; I tried to see the opportunity to cultivate."

Luke was impressed by Mary's intelligence. Suddenly, he got curious about Jesus' childhood,

"How was the mother-child relationship with such a special son? Did he often surprise you?"

"My son's intelligence and behavior were incredible challenges. He was a baby who grew up physically like any other baby, but on the inside, I can't explain ... He was different, singular."

"What do you mean?" Luke asked.

"He was happy with everything. He would fall, hurt himself, weep, but he smiled and kept playing right away. He lived every minute with such intensity that sleeping was his biggest problem. It seemed that sleeping was a waste of time for him," she said, thinking in retrospect.

"Fascinating. Was your son sociable?"

"Very much so; my son was an extroverted child. He threw himself into everyone's arms; it seemed he didn't even have a mother. Older children were passive, quiet, but he, even as a baby, wanted to communicate anyway. 'Blah, blah, blah!' It was funny." Mary said, smiling.

"And fears, did he have many?"

"Fears? No. Fear was not in his vocabulary. That worried me very much. He played with wild dogs, approached horses. The amazing thing was; the animals calmed down before him. Wherever he went, he appeased the moods, people's feelings included."

"Interesting."

Mary paused to tell him something. She said that when the boy was three years old and they were in Egypt because of Herod's persecution, Jesus saw an elderly couple walking and he immediately let go of her. They had never met, but nobody was strange to him. He ran to the couple, took their hands and kept walking along with them. He was very happy.

"I rushed to them and took him from their hands. I then tried to warn him, but he just smiled. It was always fun for him."

"Amazing! Had he always been a detached boy?" Luke asked.

"Always, always...and later he proved to be more than just my son: he was the son of mankind, son of the Author of Life. He was Jewish, but he belonged to the human species. He loved the scent of humanity since he was little."

"Remarkable!" Luke exclaimed. "I've never heard of a child like yours."

"He grew up, but everything he had, was not his. His salary was not his; the time was not his; not even his clothes. One day, watching him once more giving away his clothes, Joseph, in spite of being a good man, said, 'my son, you worry too much about the poor'!"

"What was his reaction?" Luke wanted to know.

"He put either hand gently on Joseph's shoulders and told him, 'Father, I have to love people as I love myself and you. Being happy is making other people happy. I will work, and I will buy other clothes.' His love was bigger than himself."

"Was he eager to learn?"

"Yes. My son watched people's behavior and discussed it with me every day. I do not know who taught more if it was I who taught him or him who taught me. Deep inside, I don't know who the teacher was; him or me."

"Did he ever get angry?"

"He rarely lost his temper, even when he saw injustice. He was as calm as a breeze and as resilient as the leaves of date palms, which, humble as they are, bend before the storms, but do not break."

"Did he ever complain?"

"He would thank even the ones who hurt him."

"Was he happy?"

"He was full of unfathomable optimism and joy. He used to say something that I could not understand, 'Mother, I love you intensely, but I unimaginably love mankind. One day, I will cease to be your son and I will be the Son of Men, the son of humankind. On that day, remember to claim that you're the chosen one, the Blessed Woman."

The Greek physician was never the same after interviewing Mary and the witnesses who walked and breathed the same air as Jesus.

"I write the biography of someone who was hung on a tree and died as the most miserable man. I know the biggest favor done to this seed was to bury it. When buried, the tree grew, and then a forest was formed," Luke said to himself in tears.

* * *

Soon after they sat down for another debate, the members at the round table mentioned the subject of the day in Jerusalem: the hotel fire.

"You were in the hotel while it was on fire. What a horrible thing," Dr. Thomas commented. "There are still several people hospitalized; some with severe smoke inhalation.

"It was scary," Sofia said. "I've never felt such a terrible fear."

Then Michael said with concern,

"What's happening to Marco and Sofia is strange; First the accident, now a hotel on fire. Tourists in Jerusalem are usually very safe."

"Not to mention the man with a gun!" Sofia said anxiously.

"A gun?" Dr. Thomas asked. "We didn't know about that."

Marco had decided not to tell them in order not to cause alarm. To preserve the NEEE index, he didn't disclose his problems. It was Sofia, who told them,

"The shooter almost fired!"

"But it was accidental. The victim could have been anyone."

"How disturbing!" Dr. Alberto exclaimed.

"We have to warn the intelligence service in the country," Michael said.

"We can't be paranoid, thinking there's a conspiracy. If we do, we won't be able to live our lives. Who would want to silence us; and more importantly why? It doesn't make sense." Marco said. "Without managing our emotions, we are mentally kidnapped, though still free on the outside."

"I agree," Sofia said.

Dr. Alberto also commented on an unusual fact,

"I'm not paranoid, but yesterday I was followed by three evil looking men. I tried to lose them, but they kept stalking me. I know Jerusalem very well, so I mingled with the people who were on the Western Wall then I went through a portal and entered a friend's store. Finally, I got rid of them." "That's peculiar!" Michael said.

"I had a strange dream. I dreamed about Luke interviewing Mary," Sofia said.

They looked at each other.

"You too, Sofia? When?" Marco asked.

"In this new hotel; the debate, the fire, my reflections, all these things have intrigued my unconscious."

"Let's not talk about dreams in this intelligent debate. Dreams do not serve as material for critical analysis in history, except to analyze the dreamer's personality," Michael said.

"Of course, Michael. Like Voltaire, I hate superstition," Marco said. "In dreams, the Self's critical awareness stops anchoring in the thousands of windows or files that sponsor our autonomy and identity."

He also commented that during sleep, an unconscious phenomenon called selfflowing is active and goes either through relevant recently recorded files or to past events, especially the traumatic ones. Thus, it promoted a creative explosion with characters, scenes, environments.

Sofia watched her boss and admired him. She felt that he was sailing on to the fascinating seas of the human mind. After giving that synthetic explanation, Marco looked around the room used to hold the debates and was surprised to realize that it was almost full. Word of mouth on the debates increased, generating a network of interests, as the round table sessions were held. The audience was eager to learn.

Then, suddenly, a Capuchin friar stood up and made a request,

"You gave a logical explanation to dreams. But could you tell us your dream, Dr. Polo?"

"It is not relevant to this debate," he replied, not to give emphasis to his imagination.

Some other people, including two university professors, also asked him to tell them the dream. They were curious.

"Please," they said.

"I'll tell mine," Sofia said, much more detached than Marco.

Marco also gave in, and they both asked for a break in the debate to tell the fascinating movies that had passed through their minds. After the dream reports, people were even more impressed. Millions of internet users were following them closely without taking their eyes off laptops, phones, tablets, and TVs.

"I've never seen such creative dreams, with so much detail about facts that have never been written," Dr. Thomas said, intrigued.

"The content of these dreams is extraordinary. It's as if you have traveled in time." Dr. Alberto commented, looking at Marco and then at Sofia.

"I woke up feeling peaceful like no anxiolytic could make me feel; everything seemed so concrete," Sofia said with pleasure. "It is evident that they are phenomena that happen in the grounds of my unconscious, but, when I saw the face of baby Jesus, I was touched. His expression was beautiful. When he took the hands of the elderly couple and walked along with them, the couple was transformed by joy."

"It is funny. Unlike Sofia, I felt scared when I woke up, what made me notice the hotel was on fire," Marco said. "I was tense with the significant risks Mary would run. I rarely remember my dreams, but these have been magnificent."

Wiping his hands on his face, Michael took a deep breath. He wanted to say something but felt reluctant. However, he could not control himself anymore.

"My wife never had a lot of interest in my things, but she pressures me to know the content of what has been discussed here every single day. I haven't been dreaming of anything we have discussed, but I've never slept so poorly. This round table is a source of mysteries. Accidents and dreams; what else will happen?"

"You're not saying you're superstitious," Marco said to the Michael.

"I'm not! But I am saying that these things are very, very strange."

The whole room relaxed and smiled. Michael was a serious yet funny man. He struggled to be untouchable, but his mood overflowed even when he was uptight. However, he was right. No one could imagine the secrets that awaited them.

CHAPTER 14

MAGNIFICAT
A SOCIOLOGICAL THESIS

Mary's face perspired in her walk to the mountains where Elizabeth, the future mother of John the Baptist, lived. The muscles in her legs trembled with exhaustion. Dehydrated, her tongue clung to her palate. Her heart pounded, pumping blood with intense force, and her lungs needed more oxygen. She was eager to speak with from Elizabeth.

Mary should have taken a break to rest under the shadow of an olive tree before entering the small town set high in the mountain. While her body screamed 'Stop,' her mind begged 'Continue.' The quest for hope is uncontrollable.

As soon as she entered Zechariah's house, she saw Elizabeth. It was an unexpected visit, but she was surprised by her cousin's attitude. The host broke protocol twice. She greeted the visitor in a more solemn style and considered the teenager, superior to her. Though she was older than Mary, she placed her cousin in the highest regard. As incredible as it may seem, she proclaimed her son as Lord of the World.

"Blessed art thou among women and blessed is the fruit of thy womb. My body shakes with joy. Happy is the one who believes. What is the reason for the privilege of receiving the mother of my Lord?"

Surprised, Mary left the valleys of fatigue to enter the meadows of rest; she left the desert of tensions to walk in the oasis of joy. Mild stress irritates thought; intense stress aborts rationality. Mary was supposed to be mentally blocked and creatively sterile, but, to the astonishment of those who watched her, she opened the windows of her memory, set her imagination free, and produced a sophisticated psychosocial thesis. At that very moment, she began to recite her famous yet poorly understood poem known as *Magnificat.*

"My soul magnifies the Lord, and my spirit rejoices in God my Savior; because He has regarded the lowliness of His handmaid; for behold, henceforth all generations shall call me blessed; because He who is mighty has done great things for me, and holy is His name; and His mercy is from generation to generation on those who fear Him. He has shown might with His arm, and He has scattered the proud in the conceit of their heart. He has put down the mighty from their thrones and has exalted the lowly. He has filled the hungry with good things and the rich He has sent away empty ..."

Her poem was not a supernatural speech, but it was a portrait of the miracle of knowledge. It had as many subterranean elements as soil hiding gold nuggets, leaving them far from the eyes of the gold prospectors. Years earlier, her eagerness for learning had not only made her literate but also made her read with a critical mind and yield ideas just like a chef who, with simple ingredients, can make tasty dishes.

The days became months. Mary had a risky pregnancy, marked by rejections, long journeys on foot and the birth of her baby in the most inhospitable of places, a nest of bacteria and viruses, a stable. After the child was born, she received some relief. Eastern shepherds came to welcome her singing *Gloria in Excelsis Deo*! Mary and Joseph felt as if they were in heaven with the gifts they received. They did, however, make one mistake. Since Bethlehem was 8 kilometers away from Jerusalem, the couple set off to the old city to introduce their baby at the temple.

While they were performing the consecration rite, they had another pleasant surprise. Simeon, an old and righteous elder, took the boy in his arms and expressed the *Nunc Dimittis*. Full of joy, he proclaimed,

"Now, Lord, you let your servant go in peace; your word has been fulfilled. My own eyes have seen the salvation, the light to enlighten the Gentiles and give glory to Israel, and your people."

The facts surrounding the mysterious boy were staggering. Joseph and Mary confirmed that their son would be remarkably great. They held on to each other, cheered, and gently pinching the baby's cheeks. They relaxed without being aware of the mishaps that awaited them. However, it didn't take them long to realize how winding their road would be. Simeon, the same man who brought them the glass of joy, also gave them the glass of affliction. While continuing his proclamation, he dissected the spectacular events that Jesus would live.

"This child is destined to cause many in Israel to fall, and many others to rise. But many will oppose to him. So, the intimacy of the thoughts of many hearts will be revealed."

In the future, the boy would become a remarkable physician of minds. He would be able to dissect disturbing thoughts, subliminal vanities, obscure intentions, and veiled anxieties. Simeon declared the greatness and the risks of Jesus. In the land of the blind, the one-eyed man will never be king, but he will be wounded, execrated, banished. To see the invisible and reveal the intangible would be a danger to the social system. Old Simeon could have stopped there, he could have spared Mary, but he looked into her eyes and left her shaken when he declared,

"And a sword will pierce your very soul."

Mary would be the most privileged mother in the world, would drink from the fountain of delights, discover a fascinating baby, a bubbly boy, a spectacular teenager day by day, but eventually, she would suffer irreparable losses. She unquestionably loved, but she would lose him slowly, and end up seeing him perish on the cross.

* * *

"If she didn't learn how to protect even her most subtle emotion, Mary would not survive in an environment without the oxygen of generosity," Marco concluded.

The researcher and psychiatrist deeply and poetically described the events that occurred with Jesus' teacher; the encounter with Elizabeth, the *Magnificat*, the birth of the baby, the encounter with the shepherds and the terrifying words of Simeon. His narrative impressed everyone at the round table and in the audience.

Sofia looked at him once more in admiration. "How could an atheist go so deep into the details of Jesus' story?" she asked herself in astonishment. She had forgotten that he pursued his subject as a gold digger who refuses to stay on the surface.

After such description, Marco revealed his analysis. He said that Mary produced the famous *Magnificat* when she met Elizabeth in 4 A.D., the time of Jesus' birth – we now know he was not born in the first year of this age, but four years later.

"But how did Luke record Mary's poem uttered more than half a century before?" Marco asked. He suggested the answer: "Mary was literate. She must have written it down and kept it as a treasure. She waited for decades until someone special came along to reveal it."

"Life is a great book. For some, we reveal the cover; for others, the preface, and for others, the intimate secrets of the story," Sofia said, expressing unique sensibility.

"Many couples sleep together but don't share their dreams and nightmares. The relationship is a theater. From the perspective of emotional management, we only open ourselves up to the people we trust and believe only those we admire," Marco added masterfully.

"Indeed, Luke must have been special to Mary. He was the only one who recorded the *Magnificat*, the *Nunc Dimittis*, and many other parts of the story that only Mary could have known. She was charmed by the Greek doctor to the point of giving him her pearls," Dr. Alberto said.

Inquisitive as she was, Sofia wanted to understand the hidden pearls in Mary's *Magnificat*.

"What can be deduced and induced from the first sentences of Mary to Elizabeth: *'My soul magnifies the Lord and my spirit rejoices in God my Savior'?"* she asked.

Marco did not disclose his point-of-view. As a teacher who teases the minds of his students, he said,

"Take the risk, Sofia. Set your imagination free."

"She exalts the God in whom she believes."

"Sofia, that's on the surface of the sentence. What is underneath?" Marco teased again. "There is a revolutionary content in these words. Doctor Alberto and Dr. Thomas?" he asked.

Dr. Alberto analyzed it, but could not reach the reasoning of the man who was researching the formation process of thinkers.

"What do you mean, Dr. Polo?" Dr. Alberto asked.

"I'm sorry, but rituals overpower religious people. They have a cold and dry relationship with the God they believe in," Marco accused.

"You cannot say that!" the Harvard theologian said outraged.

"You're prejudging us," Dr. Alberto commented.

"It is not me who am standing by such thesis, but the very Mary that you value and do not know."

"I don't understand," the Vatican theologian said.

"Suppose God is real and has a concrete personality, why did he choose Mary? What were the criteria for his selection? Was it her kindness, gentleness or ethics? Thousands of young people were gentle and ethical. Was it her culture and her fast thinking? There were many educated and witty young women in their time." "What were the criteria, then?" Sofia asked anxiously.

"I don't have many answers, but the analysis of the *Magnificent* poem is astounding. What made Mary so different from all other human beings was her great intimacy with the God she believed. She was different from the religious people of her time, perhaps from all people, even people in the most varied ages."

"I'm sorry. I still don't understand," Sofia whispered, still, confused.

"Notice what she said, Sofia. *'My soul magnifies the Lord and my spirit rejoices in God'*. From the perspective of sociology and psychology, this statement in Mary's Magnificat reveals a non-ritualistic relationship, without barriers or gaps," Then, Marco went on: "In order to better explain it, let me ask you this. Are conscious thoughts real or virtual?"

"Real," Dr. Thomas said.

"Of course, they're real," Michael, the neuroscientist, said.

"Wrong. They are virtual. Does a father incorporate the reality of his child, his anguish, losses, frustration, or does a father just interpret them?" Marco asked again.

"He interprets it," Michael said.

"Can a psychiatrist experience the panic attacks of a patient?" Marco asked again.

"No, he can only interpret the reality of the other person, but never essentially assimilates it," Sofia concluded, as she started to see Marco's point.

"Of course, Sofia. Between a psychiatrist and the panic attacks, or the depressive crises of a patient, there is an infinite abyss. Why? Simply because of the 'thought', with which we understand the other, as well as the world around us, is virtual. Parents and children, teachers and students, couples; in short, all relationships occur within a virtual bubble. That is why over 90% of our judgments are wrong or contaminated. Judging the other without putting yourself in their shoes has led to many misunderstandings."

"I'm confused," Michael said honestly.

It always took some time for the members of the round table to understand Marco's point of view, but then their minds were suddenly lit. Thus, he completed his reasoning,

"Think along, Michael. Thought, is virtual; it sets our imagination free. So we think about the future, which is nonexistent, or revives the past, which is irrecoverable. However, at the same time, it imprisons us in dramatic solitude. Once again: we live on a virtual island. We are close, but at the same time infinitely distant from everything, even the people we love."

"What does this have to do with Mary?" Dr. Thomas asked.

"Mary's relationship with her God was so intimate and full of exchanges that somehow she broke this virtual barrier. She said *'My soul magnifies the Lord and my spirit rejoices in God my Savior.'* I am not religious, but critical analysis shows that Mary's God was not only in heaven, but he was also in the intimacy of her mind instead.

To make him bigger, she talked to him spontaneously night and day."

"Amazing! That's a bombastic conclusion!" Dr. Alberto said, and he was the expert on Mary.

"What a woman!" Sofia said, dazzled by this reading. Mary's God was more than a formal Jewish religion; instead her God was based on a close relationship between a daughter and a father.

"The most striking fact is that Mary said: *'My spirit rejoices in God, my Savior'*" suggesting pleasure instead of guilt; enchantment instead of fear," Marco added.

"From the psychological; is it possible to infer that Mary's spirituality was different from the hundreds of millions of religious people today?" Dr. Alberto asked.

"According to Dr. Luke's description, I have no doubt," Marco said. "She had an intelligent spirituality that was a source of emotional health and that must have made her into an empathic, determined, resilient human being, who was able to manage her own emotions."

"Religion becomes a source of mental illness when self-punishment. Fear, cold slavery, judgment, and exclusion dominate the minds of the religious people. Using Marco's lingo, we can say that all these facts only increase the NEEE index," Sofia hypothesized.

"I have never seen Mary from those angles," he Vatican theologian sincerely confessed.

"Although I lack many elements of her personality, Mary had the healthiest mind I have ever analyzed," Marco said excitedly.

"That's absurd, Marco." Michael said annoyed. "You're changing sides. Aren't you one of the most famous atheists of our time?"

"Michael, I'm not here to defend my atheism, let alone defend religions. I'm here to be impartial. It would be easy to say that it is all silly, that Dr. Luke is a weak writer, that Mary is a shallow woman and that the facts that involve the boy Jesus are banal.

However, I have to be honest; the analysis has shocked me!"

"Many religious people are stupid and shallow!" Michael ranted.

"I'm not analyzing them! Many have banished God due to the behaviors of Christians. For me, it is an invitation to superficiality. I decided to go deeper in the evaluation of Jesus' mind. I do not care about the consequences."

Sofia looked at Marco and took a deep, slow breath. She was impressed by his authenticity.

"What other elements do you have to support that Mary was mentally healthy?" she asked.

Marco answered with a question.

"Who was the woman with the strongest self-esteem in history?"

"I have no idea. I think it's impossible to know," Sofia said.

"It was probably Mary," Marco said.

"Mary? How?" The two theologians asked.

"Oh boy..." Michael muttered.

"Was she in danger of being stoned?"

"Yes," they answered in unison.

"Was there a risk of people considering her heretical or insane?"

"Yes," they said again.

"Would it be possible, amid all that emotional hell, to preserve a solid selfesteem?"

"It would be almost impossible," Sofia said.

"However, Sofia, Mary dared to proclaim: *'For* behold, *from now on all generations will call me blessed'*. She announced that all human generations to date would call her the Cause of Our Joy, Blessed Woman, while the ground at her feet was falling. Who could have had such solid self-esteem?"

Sofia smiled and said,

"I have to admit that this conclusion is incredible. Today, women look in the mirror and see a wrinkle, a scar, and there goes their self-esteem. Despite being a psychiatrist, my self-image needs calibration."

"I expect too much from myself and I'm hypersensitive to insults and criticism," Dr. Alberto confessed.

"Great professionals who don't manage their emotion are bullies of themselves. You have to reinvent yourself." The psychiatrist said, warning them. He then commented that self-esteem is a simple word but conveys harsh consequences. It is impossible to have emotional health without sustainable self-esteem.

"Why?" Michael uneasily asked.

"Because those who have low self-esteem are intolerant to frustrations, have low levels of pleasure, don't take risks, complain a lot and have great difficulty in reinventing themselves. They beg for the bread of joy, even being financially well-off. Unfortunately, as I said at the UN conference recently, we are in the 'emotional beggars' era."

"So, I'm an emotional beggar," a thirty-year-old girl in the audience shouted. "I am socially and financially privileged, but I am an expert in complaining and punishing myself."

"So am I. I'm a photographic model, but I'm always pressuring myself," a twenty-five-year-old said. "I hate to see my pictures in magazines and commercials. I've already cut myself twice, punishing myself."

All were shocked by those testimonies.

"But you are so beautiful," Dr. Alberto said, not understanding the reasons for those people, who all had reasons to be happy, to be sad.

"The mirror does not show the beauty. It lies in the eyes of the beholder. It is not the softness of the bed that makes for a good sleep, but the mind of the sleeper," Marco said with propriety.

Sofia took the opportunity to say,

"The world was falling apart on Mary, but her 'Self' did not succumb to fear or to pressures!"

"Perhaps she would shout night and day in the silence of her mind, 'The best days are yet to come'!" Then Marco warned those who were listening to him.

"Be careful! If you want to be emotionally healthy, there is a place where you should never be shy; within yourselves."

With these words, Marco closed another roundtable. Many people, who had been watching the debate, whether live or online, discovered that they were emotional beggars who needed much from little, whose emotion had no stability. They were happy one moment and distressed and discouraged the next.

They understood that they did not have to watch a horror movie to feel haunted. They had built their own monsters. They were part of the miserable statistics of the modern era. The full round table organized by Marco Polo had encouraged them to leave the audience, enter the stage of their own minds and start to write a new script. Jerusalem had once again influenced the world...

CHAPTER 15

STRANGE FACTS ON THE DEBATE BACKSTAGE

Michael was upset about Marco's explanation of the 'emotional beggars' era. Marco's comments had hit close to home. Michael was dissatisfied, cranky, was not very contemplative, and he was pessimistic. His NEEE index was very high. While Michael looked like an untouchable, tough man, deep down his self-esteem was fragile. He had been bullied during his childhood. He used to be fat, therefore was a target of terrible jokes. Losing weight had been hard work.

During the next debate, he brought back up the subject. However, instead of talking about himself, he attacked Mary's excessive optimism, questioning her sanity.

"Marco, in the last debate, you said that Mary had one of the most stable selfesteem in history and considering some aspects, maybe even the highest. She was brave to say that every generation would consider her the happiest woman or the most blissful. Nevertheless, as a scientist, I have seen many madmen suffering from delusions of grandeur. Wasn't Mary a victim of a psychotic outbreak? Or maybe wasn't she experiencing a state of euphoria? Perhaps even a form of bipolar depression?" Dr. Alberto was uneasy, and so were Sofia and Dr. Thomas.

"Michael is an expert at sabotaging the things we believe in," the Vatican theologian said, exasperated.

"Relax, Dr. Alberto, you accepted me at this round table; you will have to put up with me."

Marco, in turn, softly intervened.

"Michael's questions are pertinent, Dr. Alberto."

Then, smiling, he said,

"I've thought a lot about it. To psychiatry and psychology astonishment, in the same poem in which Mary says she is the blessed woman, the happiest one, she exalts deeply and poetically her own limitations. She says clearly *'For He has looked with favor on the humble state of His servant.'* Therefore, at the same time that her selfesteem was in the clouds, her critical awareness had roots stuck in the earth. Mary's self-awareness doesn't happen in a psychotic outbreak or the manic state of bipolar depression."

"Remarkable self-esteem and extraordinary humility inhabited the same mind," Dr. Alberto said with satisfaction.

"And at the same time!" Marco exclaimed.

"The Mary we analyze and describe in this round table may be a lot greater than the one Catholics have discovered and Protestants have imagined," the Harvard theologian commented.

"Perhaps Mary is even greater than the Islamists understood. She is the only woman mentioned in the Koran," Marco remembered.

"I didn't know that," Sofia said.

Michael rubbed his face, relaxed and then drew a conclusion, perplexed.

"Many psychiatrists and psychologists turn their noses up at Jewish-Christian religion saying that it promotes guilt and self-punishment. But I have to admit that Dr. Luke describes characters that lived with remarkable maturity and delicacy."

"Mary's God was a poet of generosity, his pleasure in giving himself away, embracing and giving as many opportunities as necessary, seems to consume him. It is the only thing that explains the expression in her *Magnificat*: '*His mercy is from generation to generation,*'" Sofia concluded.

After that, Marco asked an intriguing question.

"Congratulations, Sofia. Now I ask you; is judging mistakes a complicated or simple reasoning?"

She and the others said,

"It's complex."

"Wrong. It is a simple, linear, logical reasoning. Any miserable computer could be an expert at pointing out mistakes."

Everyone was thoughtful. Marco then asked,

"What about compassion?"

"That is difficult to answer," Michael said.

"Well, I assure you that compassion, tolerance, and respect for the differences are such complex skills that go beyond the limits of logic, and computers will never have that capacity."

"Honestly, I'm shaken. I have always considered that the *Magnificat* had been planted in Mary's brain, like a miracle, but it reflects a synthetic thought of a unique mind," Dr. Alberto said. "I have to review my beliefs and my classes."

Marco continued,

"And there's more Dr. Alberto. Mary had keen political awareness and dreamed of a fair society: '*He has exalted the lowly. He has filled the hungry with good things and the rich He has sent away empty …*' looking at these texts, I ask, did Mary speak only about material goods? Who are the rich ones?"

"Those who are infected with pride, envy, revenge, a neurotic need for power …" Sofia answered. Then she asked, fascinated,

"How many generations have passed until this Mary appeared? Possibly countless; how many young ladies were evaluated in transparency, critical awareness, boldness, humility, self-esteem? Maybe…millions"

Touched by that explanation, Michael couldn't bear it anymore, and he decided to open his mind's vault.

"Humility is not in my dictionary; low self-esteem and pride are. My NEEE index is high: an exhausted brain, tiredness in waking up, impatience...I need to look at myself," he confessed.

"I congratulate you for setting your limits, my friends. We are long-life learners; otherwise, we would be dead," Marco said.

"Congratulations, Michael! The more academic and social success people have, the more they play a role and stop being themselves, and seek to hide their worries," Sofia commented, feeling it under her skin.

"What about you, Dr. Thomas? You always seem to look so perfect," Michael teased.

At that moment, Dr. Thomas broke down. He would no longer be able to hide a conflict that had been disturbing him.

"I agree. It's harder to deal with success than it is with failure. The more theologians ascend in their spiritual career, the more they increase the chances of not recognizing their frustrations and human weaknesses or their depressive mood. They take on the role of superheroes. They are lonely, not able to open up to anyone. I'm like this, but I can't remain quiet any longer."

So, he told a touching story that was very much disturbing him.

"My oldest son, Peter, is depressive. I've never taken his disease seriously, but two months ago something happened. He didn't get up from the bed. He slept until one in the afternoon. 'It's 1 p.m., Peter! You seem alienated from everything! You live in a cocoon.' *'Leave me alone. I don't want to talk!'* he answered. 'You used to be a brilliant student; now you are isolated from the world.' I tried to persuade him. *'I'm not bright anymore.'* 'Wake up to life, boy. Get out of this marasmus!' I said.

Peter didn't answer. He pretended he didn't hear my voice anymore. I got angry. 'You only disappoint me.' I accused him. *'I know that.'* Peter said, raising his head. Full of pain, he added; *'The worst part is that I disappoint myself too. Forget that I exist.'* I tried to answer back. 'How can I forget that you exist? I pay your bills, give you food, buy your clothes, and pay for your cell phone and the college where you refuse to go.' At that moment, Peter sat on the bed and began to sob. *'I don't need a bank. I need a father...'*"

That touched Dr. Thomas deeply. He continued,

"Then Peter said: *'It's not because I'm irresponsible otherwise I wouldn't have been the best student in Law class. I don't go out because I'm dying inside! Don't you see? I have no reasons to live...'* I told him softly: 'Trust God, my son.' To which he replied: *'I trust God, but I don't trust life, people, or even you, father. You never talk about yourself and never ask me how I am, what I'm feeling, which nightmares are haunting me!'* Regretful, I apologized to him. Then, I hugged him, and we cried together."

After telling this story, Dr. Thomas burst into tears. Marco, thinking of his own son, sympathized with the Harvard intellectual,

"Great men also cry. The problem is that they don't know what to do with their tears."

"You're right and so is Peter. I don't know how to talk about myself or penetrate the world of those I love. I am isolated in my intellectuality. Only now I can see that I've always lived in a solitary bubble. I need to break it."

"Why don't you encourage him to look for a psychiatrist?" Sofia asked.

"I did, but he resisted."

"If you humanize yourself, it will grow inside him. Peter will certainly listen to you," Dr. Alberto, his friend, advised.

There was a sharp silence on the round table. Touched, some participants in the audience took notes. Others took the risk of telling their own story, which was unusual.

A thirty-year-old man spoke out.

"My father is a military man. He has never talked to me. He was an expert in demanding from me."

A twenty-five-year-old psychologist, in tune with the other young man, got up and said.

"My father is not a military man, but a psychology professor. Despite that, he has never sat with me. He has never asked me about the tears that I cried or the ones that I never had the courage to cry. That's not the upbringing I want for my future children."

Everyone wanted to get out of their social bubble. Members of the audience started to lose their fear of speaking not only about the world they lived in but also about the world within themselves. They found that they not only lived on the surface of the planet Earth, but also on the surface of the planet Emotion.

"Behind a person who hurts there is always a wounded person. Understanding the ones who hurt us doesn't change them, but it changes us. The worse the quality of emotional management is, the more important the role of psychiatry and clinical psychology will be."

With these words, Marco closed another round table. Several people came to greet him.

"I was on the verge of committing suicide before I heard these debates," an eighteen-year-old girl, who had just started her life and was already giving up, told him,

"You don't want to stop your life, but your pain. Find a good therapist."

Everyone went home thoughtful. Michael had to stop at the supermarket. He, who was always so closed, began to greet people on his way.

"Why are you so happy, Dr. Michael?" the supermarket cashier asked.

"I'm buying self-esteem," he teased.

Sofia sat down on the bed and thought about what they had debated. She had been in many round tables, but this one was causing a visceral reaction.

Marco, as he always did when he was restless and struggling with ideas, began to pace in his hotel room. After that, he opened his computer, went to his 'logbook' and began to write some his thoughts.

'A thesis starts to nestle in my mind and makes me anxious: psychology, sociology and pedagogy, the human sciences, made the mistake of not studying intensely and with discipline Jesus' biography. The most famous man in history has become a taboo. Amazing Tools of emotional management are no longer used. The universities failed! I failed!'

Marco remembered that Mary received the news that her soul would be pierced by the irreparable losses she would suffer. He remembered that he was pierced by Anna's loss.

Tears are universal poems. When our mouths shut, our eyes proclaim them. Those who don't know how to cry don't know how to make poems out of chaos. Marco, alone in his hotel room, began to cry.

CHAPTER 16

THE WORLD COLLAPSING AROUND MARCO POLO

A year before

Marco and Anna had gone to the Caribbean. They were celebrating another wedding anniversary. It was rare to see two people so in love.

"You are unforgettable, Marco, my eternal boyfriend."

"And you're irreplaceable, Anna."

It was a celebration trip, but it was also a moment to rest. Both Marco and Anna worked hard. Marco was a psychiatrist, researcher, and university professor; she was a clinical psychologist and expert in depression.

For Marco, his patients were not sick; they were pieces of art that he tried to understand. While he was watching Anna play in the waves, he thought about the complexity of life. He took a piece of paper and wrote another metaphor.

'Human personality is like a wave and time is like the beach. Each wave has a shape, just like each person has its characteristics, some of them are quiet, others are sparkling, but all of them play their role in the theater of time and,

sooner or later, they return shyly and mysteriously into the sea of existence, leaving few traces behind.'

Many people loved applause, awards, and social columns, but Marco loved to think about the mysteries that surrounded life.

"Come and enjoy the sea," Anna invited full of joy.

"I'm coming, my dear. But be careful, the waves are strong!"

Anna dived as if she was breaking the barrier of time and professional stress.

She insisted,

"Come on, Marco. Don't let this moment pass."

He dropped the paper immediately and let himself be embraced by the sea. Deep down, all he wanted was the best of all hugs, hers. Anna swam trying to overcome the resistance of the waves. Marco swam behind her. Both knew that simple, anonymous things nourish the emotions. Moments later, they were walking on the beach. Staring at him, she said, only,

"We don't need much to be happy. What is the point of caring about others if we forget to care about ourselves?"

"The thirst for relieving human pain consumes me. But I need to slow down,"

Marco confessed. "Professional success without emotional success isn't success; it is self-destruction."

"Do you care about yourself?" she asked the simple, vital question. Marco dove into his mind and was honest.

"Not enough. I'm 47 years old; my hair has started turning white. But you, being 37, are still a girl. In fact, I've done you good; you're prettier than when I met you."

"I did you good!" Anna said, agreeing with the joke. "I could bring a little balance to this crazy researcher who has always been off the curve."

"I still live off the curve, but there is no doubt that you brought me a little to the center. Thanks for existing."

Suddenly, two attractive women passed by them. She felt his eyes looking discreetly toward them.

"Are you looking at other women, Marco?"

"My eyes are yours," he said with a smile "Are you jealous, Anna?"

"Jealousy, that old ghost that haunts both men and women? It touches me, but it doesn't surprise me anymore. In fact, I read your essays about jealousy."

"Are you interested in my ideas?"

"I have always been. I remember well; Are people in love, jealous? They are if we consider it a way of getting closer to the beloved person. But jealousy nurtured by the fear of loss creates the need for control, which, in turn, becomes a sick deviance from the need of getting closer, producing the search of an excessive and insatiable attention." She added, "I liked that so much that I even memorized it. I think you may have a future as a researcher and writer."

"After writing ten books, maybe I've learned something," he said softly.

Although Marco had his books published in several countries, he never lost serenity. He knew that the virus of pride could kill creativity.

After that, he said,

"Soft jealousy is harmless; it becomes a counterpoint to indifference. Those who are indifferent don't love, sometimes not even themselves. Otherwise, those who are over-jealous destroy themselves, lose their self-confidence and hasten the loss. I will defend a new thesis in psychology: people who are jealous don't want other's attention, but their own, because they have abandoned themselves. Therefore, no matter how much attention you get from the other, your thirst is insatiable. You have missed the target."

She was astonished and proud of her husband once again. He also commented that jealousy is another cruel way of draining the natural resources of planet Emotion.

"Wait, I didn't read that," she said.

That was when he told her he was about to launch an Emotional Management program. They were a smart couple with pleasant and interesting dialogues.

"What about you, Marco? Are you jealous of me?"

"You are more beautiful than the prettiest girls."

"Demagogue," Anna said, pinching him gently.

"Honestly, as I look at you, I still get excited. How could I not be jealous? But I manage it."

"Do you know why my jealousy is also calm?" she asked.

"Tell me, my dear."

"Because I'm beautiful, wonderful and intelligent and you are privileged for living with me. If you leave me, you will miss out." Anna said, cheerful and with selfconfidence.

She was no longer that young woman, who had been a hostage of the past, whose mother had committed suicide and whose father was an authoritarian millionaire, insensitive, and extremely critical. She had become a free woman. After saying those words, she ran off down the beach.

"Wait there, young lady. Well, you will not die from low self-esteem." Marco said, smiling and running after her.

When he had almost reached her, something unexpected happened. Anna's heart began to beat faster, she gasped and felt dizzy. She lost her balance and fell face first into the sand.

"Anna! Anna! What happened? Are you okay?"

Marco was desperate. He thought she was having a heart attack or a convulsion. There were no muscle spasms or deviation gaze or oral rhyme. Soon she woke up, but she was dizzy.

"What happened? Where are we?"

"We're here on the beach in the Caribbean. I ran after you, but suddenly you fell and passed out."

"I think it is overwork."

He gently cleaned every grain of sand from her face and caressed her.

"Darling, you scared me."

He kissed her gently on the forehead and then on the lips, and hugged her.

"What a friendly hug. I will do it again," Anna teased.

"I remember when we were getting to know each other. Your father saw you in the arms of a stranger and shouted: 'Who is this guy, Anna?' 'It's Marco Polo,' you said.

'An adventurer? What does he do?'"

"It almost killed him when I said you were a psychiatrist," Anna remembered.

"It was not easy to beat the tiger."

"But you haven't defeated Dr. Amadeus yet."

Seeing her more relaxed, Marco asked:

"Don't you feel anything else?"

"I'm just breathless and with a slight pain in my chest."

He scrutinized her. Her lips were blue, reflecting the lack of oxygen. Marco was a psychiatrist, he wasn't an expert in that area, but he didn't like what he saw.

"Let's go dear. Maybe we will have to do some exams."

"I don't need exams. I just need to relax. Lunch didn't agree with me."

Curious bystanders surrounded them, one or two trying to help. Marco thanked the people and put her right arm around his neck as they walked back to the hotel. Anna took a painkiller and an antipyretic. Soon she got better.

"I was so happy when you told me that I was still a beautiful girl that I tried to run like one. I'm out of shape."

"Maybe you fell because you were jealous of me."

"You fool," then she added, with emotion "I miss our Luke, I will call him."

At 16 years old, Luke was their only child. He was a young man who did very well in school. He dreamed of studying medicine at Harvard. Luke wanted to follow in his father's footsteps, not by imposition, but because he admired him. While they were on vacation in the Caribbean, Luke was at his grandfather Dr. Amadeus's house and that worried Marco. His father-in-law would always say "If there's anyone who can teach Luke how to be an entrepreneur, it's me his grandfather you, are intellectuals…dreamers."

Luke used to live like a king in Dr. Amadeus' house, without control. There was no routine, no curfew, bedtime, and no limit to spending money. Dr. Amadeus had lied when he said that he kept the boy on a 'short leash.'

"Where is Luke? He doesn't answer the phone."

"We've always told him not to stay connected all day on the cell phone. It's five o'clock on a Saturday afternoon. The boy has common sense. He must be at the movies with some girl."

Anna lay down, relaxed, and slept for two hours. Marco, alert as he was, had already contacted a medical center. He expected a call. Unfortunately, Anna woke up breathless and with pain in her chest again. They quickly went to the hospital.

At the medical center, an experienced general practitioner, Dr. Franklin, examined her. After asking questions and examining her, he asked for an X-ray and a blood test. When the results arrived, the doctor was anxious.

"Anna, you have bronchopneumonia. Bilateral pneumonia. That is what's causing your short breath and diffuse chest pain."

"Is it serious, Doctor?" she asked anxiously.

"It's treatable. You are strong," Marco intervened.

"The ideal would be to know the type of causative agent, whether virus or bacteria. If it is bacteria, we need to know what would be the most effective antibiotic.

But I will prescribe you a good broad-spectrum antibiotic and observe its evolution."

Anna placed her right hand over Marco's left hand and lamented,

"I ruined our vacation, dear."

"Not at all ..."

* * *

At night, Luke called.

"My son, I miss you. Where were you?"

"I went to the movies with a girl I met a few days ago. What about you, mom; how are you?"

"I have pneumonia, but I'll be fine."

They talked for a while. After that, Anna's father, Dr. Amadeus, picked up the phone.

"Are you sick, Anna?

"Dad I have pneumonia. But I have taken medicines."

"Is Marco looking after you?"

"As always, dad ..."

"I don't know. Do you want me to send a plane to pick you up?"

"It is not necessary."

Three days later, Anna was still feverish and was finding it hard to breathe. The X-ray images were getting worse.

"It must be a resistant bacterium. I recommend that you look for a bigger medical center and do some more exams," Dr. Franklin said.

"We need to leave, my dear," he said, frowning and grabbing her hands softly.

"The pneumonia didn't subside. We should deal with it in the hospital where we work."

"I'm worried, honey, but it's going to be all right," she said gently.

"We will beat this bacterium!" he assured her.

They took the first flight to Los Angeles, the city where they lived. Marco was concerned about the super bacterium that was antibiotics resistant. He didn't say anything. Anna traveled with a mask. She was careful to ensure that passengers were not infected and that she wouldn't be infected with other diseases. Tired, she fell asleep.

She woke up when the plane landed. A wheelchair was waiting for her. There was an airport employee available to make their exit easier. It was a sad scene. They went straight to the hospital. Marco had set up a team led by his friend, Dr. Matheus, a pneumatology's. Showing kindness, Dr. Matheus carried Anna through the long corridors.

She worked in the hospital and also did social work at the children ward, so she was recognized by everyone as soon as she arrived at the lobby.

"Anna? What happened?" a nurse asked, worried.

"Pneumonia knocked me over. But it will be all right."

"Hello, Anna! I wish abandoned children's mother the best," a doctor said, waving her hands.

"Anna! Anna!" Three children of five, six and seven years old, from a childcare house, to which she gave free assistance, shouted as they ran and kissed her.

"Jorge, Rafael, Leo? It's good to see you," she said, recalling their names. She was so thrilled that she started to lose her breath.

"Anna, we need to go," the doctor said, worried. The boys looked sad. With tears in her eyes, she gasped and left them.

Dr. Matheus and his team completed the examinations and looked worriedly at each other.

"Look, Marco, the tests show that she has a diffuse and severe pneumonia in both lungs. Comparing the images made in the Caribbean with those of now, the pneumonia is in progression."

They gave her other antibiotics.

"The ideal would be to exam the lung secretions, but you, Anna, can't cough. If the images don't improve in three days, we will have a bronchoscopy to remove a small fragment for analysis."

"Ok doctor, let's do what is necessary," she said, worried, but not desperate.

"Take care of her, Dr. Matheus."

The pneumatology's smiled and said,

"In our circle of friends, we have always commented how much we envy you as a couple."

At that very moment, Anna again became short of breath. Dr. Matheus quickly put an oxygen mask on her to help her breath. After that, three friends with bouquets of flowers; Julia, Beatrice, and Hillary showed up. One of them held a card with the words,

"The dearest friend in the world!"

Anna took off her mask and smiled. She and Marco were very sociable. They led a project in more than twenty orphanages that taught children and teenagers to develop social and emotional skills.

"Dear friend, we love you. Children in the orphanages miss you."

"How are they?"

"Watching their progress brings tears to our eyes. The children are becoming resilient and learning to think before reacting."

"Many people work for a wage; others work for their dreams. Thank you," she commented gently.

"I'm sorry, but you must go now," Dr. Matheus intervened. Anna needs to rest.

Suddenly, she had another attack. This one was more intense. Dr. Matheus had to quickly help her. Her friends left the room crying at the sight of her distress. Minutes later, Anna was given another cocktail of antibiotics.

After three days, some improvement was expected. Unfortunately, that didn't happen.

"Don't give up, my love," Marco pleaded.

"I'm not afraid of dying, I'm scared of losing you and Luke," she said heartwarmingly.

Marco's voice broke.

"Forget about us, my dear. For now, focus on your health."

Ten minutes later, Dr. Matheus came into the room to make his daily visit. He said in a serious voice,

"I compared the previous days x-rays and tomography with those of this morning.

Your pneumonia is tough, Anna."

In the middle of the bad news, Anna got a call. It was her son.

"Can I answer this, Dr. Matheus? It's my son, Luke."

"Of course, but try not to get too excited."

"Hello Luke, it's good to hear your voice. How is your vacation?" She asked slowly and with a fragile voice.

"Grandpa's been letting me do lots of fun stuff. What about you? Why are you panting?"

"We haven't got it right yet with the antibiotics. But we will kick this pneumonia."

"You're not well. I'll try to get a flight today. I want to be by your side."

"It's not necessary ... Enjoy your vacation. It will end in a few days ..."

"But, mom, you can hardly speak."

Suddenly, Anna's father, Dr. Amadeus, realizing that his daughter wasn't getting better, took the phone from his grandson in an angry outburst and, without emotional preparation, told his daughter,

"Get out of there immediately, Anna! Go to a better hospital! Send me the bill!"

Her father paid bills. He was terribly afraid of diseases, never went to hospitals, and rarely went to funerals.

"They are taking good care of me, dad ..."

Marco noticed that Anna was more tense and breathless when she spoke with her father. He picked up the phone and tried to lighten the tension load. Even being an experienced psychiatrist, Dr. Amadeus was hard to manage.

"Good morning, Dr. Amadeus."

"Don't you 'Good morning' me! You're killing my daughter!" He said, throwing up the historical rejections against the 'psychotics' friend.'

Marco tried to control himself. Luke was next to his grandfather, and he confronted him,

"Don't talk to my father like that!"

Marco heard his son's words, but assured to his arrogant father-in-law,

"She's getting the best care. Doctors, friends of mine, who are university professors, are assisting her ..."

"University professors like you? You have no competence to act in private companies, so you imprison yourselves in universities! Take my daughter to the best private medical center now!" The man whose god was money ordered.

"She's in the center of excellence. I have to hang up. Thanks for your concern," Marco replied.

He tried to preserve Anna's reassurance. After saying goodbye to Luke, he hung up.

Luke criticized his grandfather,

"My father is an excellent doctor and makes mom very happy!"

"Naivety is a blessing, Luke."

"What do you mean? My father is a respected thinker."

"Thinkers die of hunger and sometimes kill others by starvation. Silence your tears! Men don't cry!"

"Who cries then? Computers?"

"Shut up! Respect you are elders; your insubordinate!"

After scolding Luke, he left the room. He didn't even try to comfort him about his mother's disease.

The boy went to the bedroom and began to quietly shed tears. Then he took a pillow and put it against his face. He wasn't sure, but he felt like he was losing the person he loved the most.

CHAPTER 17

A HAPPY BOY WHO LIVED TWO THOUSAND YEARS AGO

A five-year-old boy was fascinated watching as some butterflies flew over him. He ran around as if he wanted to dance in the air. With open arms, he reproduced the insect's movements. His parents and two religious leaders, Josefus and Benjamin, who were visiting, carefully watched him. Overjoyed, the boy kept shouting,

"Fly, beautiful butterfly. Fly!"

He laughed and followed one butterfly's path, then another's, and another's. He was full of energy. Josefus, one of the guests, was impressed and told his parents,

"I've rarely seen such a cheerful boy."

"Where does such happiness come from? You are not rich, your house is not that comfortable, you struggle every day to survive, but this boy smiles as if he were the richest one in the world," Benjamin, the other guest, said.

"My son is special," his mother said.

"All children are special," Benjamin replied.

"But this boy turns small things into music," his father agreed.

"Interesting," Benjamin said, suspicious. "And who teaches him to admire nature? Joseph or Mary, is it you?"

"It's his nature. We taught him a little, but it seems that he is thirsty for the living. He wants to explore everything, to know everything and to play with everything. Every night he asks me to tell him stories. Only then will he fall asleep."

"Is it safe?"

"He seems to have no fears. Look, he wants to ride a sheep!" his mother exclaimed. "Be careful, my son." Then she continued, "He plays with wild dogs, and they calm down."

Joseph looked at Mary warningly so that, so she wouldn't reveal everything. It was better to protect the child.

"How can he do that?" Josefus asked, scratching his long beard.

At that moment, a knight passed by quickly. The boy went towards him.

"Be careful," Benjamin said, afraid that he might be trampled.

"My son," his mother cried desperately.

The animal interrupted its march and slowly approached the boy, and then it turned its head down as if bowing. To everyone's astonishment, he reached up and touched the horse's head.

"Amazing!" Benjamin, an important Pharisee who observed the scene, declared.

"You should not be irresponsible letting him free," the other religious leader warned.

"But we cannot stop him," his mother said.

Suddenly, the boy shouted,

"Come, Dad, come on Mom, let's play with the horse!"

"Not now, Jesus," his father admonished. "Come, let's go home."

The boy stopped and obeyed. The knight, impressed by his skill, continued on his way but could not help looking back.

"Does he cry a lot?"

"Only in extreme situations," his father answered. "But he soon recovers and smiles again. I'm a carpenter, gentlemen, and my son is as strong as the hardest woods."

Running toward his parents, the boy didn't see a stone and tripped and fell, slamming his face into the pebbles. Mary ran and she was the first to help him. Soon after, Joseph and the two leaders arrived.

"My son, did you get hurt?"

His right cheek was bleeding and he cried for a moment, but soon he recovered and, as Joseph had said, he smiled.

"I'm all right."

"Who is this child? He should have been moaning in pain," Benjamin affirmed.

The religious leaders looked at each other and were intrigued by Jesus' recovery. His ability to deal with pain was unusual. He was active, yet obedient, sensitive, but strong.

"Let's take care of this bruise."

"It doesn't hurt. Let's play."

"Life seems to be an eternal game for him," his father said wonderingly, fascinated by so much energy.

Joseph took Jesus' right hand and the three of them said goodbye. However, something else mysteriously happened. The boy heard the bleating of a sheep with her cub, as she gave a painful groan, and he was the only one who heard it.

"The little lamb is sick."

"What? What little lamb?" his father asked.

The boy let go of his father, took a few steps and pointed,

"That one."

The animal was far away, so he ran after it.

"Jesus! Jesus! Come here."

"Mom, the lamb is in pain!" he said. "Let's go!"

They were all intrigued. Everyone followed Jesus. When the boy approached, the lamb's mother threatened to butt him.

"Be careful, son!" his mother cried.

The sheep immediately calmed down and they were surprised again. Mary reaffirmed, embarrassed though,

"I told you that animals love him."

Breaking the tension, his father intervened,

"My son, the lamb is fine. It is walking."

"But it is not sucking," the child said.

Suddenly Josefus, who was familiar with sheep breeding, looked at the mother's teats and saw that they were full and dripping.

"Wait, the boy is right. The lamb is not sucking; it was rejected by its mother. It was weak and staggering. If no one gives it milk, it will die."

They all looked at each other amazed. Then, to everyone's astonishment, the boy approached the mother sheep, stroked her head and then hugged the little lamb. With much effort, he held it in his arms and led it to the sheep's teats. Suddenly, the lamb that had been rejected began to suck the mother's nectar.

"It's incredible. I've never seen anything like that. A mother who rejects a cub rarely accepts it back," Josefus commented.

After that, they said goodbye and without asking permission, the boy gave the leaders a hug. As they parted ways, they looked back, as everyone always did, at Jesus and thought to themselves, "Who is that boy? What will happen to him when he grows up?"

* * *

Sofia woke up suddenly. She sat on the bed and smiled, realizing that once more she had traveled in her dreams. She thought of Marco. She needed to tell him about her dream. However, it was a painful experience to translate into words. She was sleepy and decided to let it go. She went back to bed and had a good night sleep.

CHAPTER 18

JESUS' STRANGE MARKETING MAN

A man, who looked mad, and dressed like a scarecrow, was shouting with a vibrant and eloquent voice about the great revolution that would start from the inside. He proclaimed that a leader was coming and would change the status quo of human relations. He would be the leader of a fair and generous government. He seemed delusional. He was putting a price on his head by speaking up and pointing out the bystander's aches and pains, and the corruption of the leaders of his time. Poking the bears, he said,

"Race of vipers. They incite you into running from the wrath that is coming."

In a time of political persecution, people had never seen such a brave person. It was advisable to be discreet, but he was unable to stay quiet. He very much wanted to penetrate people's minds, dissecting the tumors hidden under their skin, such as the arrogance and exclusions. His name was simply John, but his objectives were complex.

"I'm a voice that prepares the way for my leader, the Lord of the World. He is so powerful and magisterial that I'm not worthy of even bowing before him."

People drew an unimaginable supreme being in their minds, a leader like they have never seen, followed by a triumphal escort, carried in a golden carriage. His beauty would bring ecstasy to those ravaged by hunger, at a time when the Roman Empire spoiled Israel's barns.

The man did not show up, though. At night John tried to rest his voice, exhausted by the cries, but his disciples and aggregates nagged him. They questioned,

"Why is the Messiah taking so long?"

"Calm down, all of you; he will eventually come."

"But what characteristics does he have for us to recognize him?" a Pharisee, a leader who had joined the pack of reactionaries, asked.

John swallowed hard but did not lose his confidence.

"When you see him, he will be unmistakable. His gestures, reactions, and words proclaim his identity. His power is immeasurable, and his eloquence is ravishing."

"How do you know that if you don't know him?"

The fatal question was elaborated by a scribe, a Sacred Scriptures teacher, who had also taken an interest in John.

The most famous and strange personal marketing expert that had ever existed took a breath and smiled. His emotions were running high.

"I know it because I know it," he said, confident.

He inaugurated a thesis that would surpass Socrates' thesis which had been uttered three centuries before, "I know that I know nothing."

"But how can you announce a stranger with such confidence?" a local political leader asked.

"Enough! When he comes, he will surprise us!" John said, trying to end the sea of doubts.

"John, many people hate you for pointing out their crimes. Herod has been thinking about sending you to jail. Many Pharisees have insomnia because of your accusations. Your name makes them tremble. If the Messiah doesn't come to give you protection, sooner or later your head will roll," a disciple commented, worried about his strange master.

"Am I afraid of death? Don't wallow in the mud of conformism. This world needs to be turned upside down," he said, turning his head, not down, but to the side, trying to rest because of the dampness of the night.

Many who followed John's teachings didn't sleep, eat or dress like him. During the day, they stayed at Jordan River's shore and at night, they went to their homes or to hostels. Early in the morning, John repeated the same ritual. The tireless master of ceremonies announced the leader of his dreams, the author of a new era.

If Einstein came in through a time window to advise the prophet, he would certainly discourage him. He would say: 'It is easier to disintegrate the atom than to get rid of prejudices.' If Martin Luther King also could travel in time to guide John's mood, it wouldn't be different. Perhaps he would say, 'Abraham Lincoln freed the slaves in the Constitution, and, a hundred years later, I am struggling to undo social paradigms, rescuing the civil rights of black people, showing that white and black people are the same in essence. We are all one family.'

At that time, as in all eras, people didn't internalize or criticize themselves; they didn't survey their own failures. In many ways, John proclaimed that they, especially the leaders, had three unhealthy needs that infected their minds: the need to control others, the need to be the center of social attention, and the need for power. What an incredible mission it is to remove the debris from a human's mind.

"He will change the human heart," he said, confidently.

"But the human being is unchangeable," others with the same confidence said.

"How should we be prepared to wait for him?" others, who were more sensitive, asked.

The answer was bombastic, literally and metaphorically.

"Whoever has two robes, share with those who have none. And whoever has food will do the same."

The same feeling of Mary's *Magnificat* was in this unusual character's soul.

Weeks have passed, and the Messiah didn't appear. Impatience grew. Days felt like months; months felt like years.

When everything seemed like a mirage in the desert, a man, entirely different from the grandiloquent descriptions made by John, unexpectedly appears. There were no carriages, escorts nor social glamor. However, John sensed it and yelled, "Silence!"

They looked at each other. Their hearts pounded and their lungs quickened. The solemn moment was finally approaching. Everybody wanted to see what John saw, but no one could.

"Where is the awesome Messiah? Where is the Prince of time? Where is the rescuer?" his intimate friends wondered. Clear sky, blazing sun, and sweat on the face.

John didn't take long to point him out.

"Here is the man who fell in love with mankind, the man who will sacrifice himself for it, as a lamb sacrificed on an altar. Here is the lawyer who will defend us from our madness."

Everybody got excited and struggled to identify him, but he got lost in the crowd.

"Open your eyes and see the most solemn gift sent by God!"

He didn't have superlative beauty or exceptional physical endowments. Touching the shoulders of those in front of him, he gently opened his way. No one noticed him, except John, his announcer, the man who did his marketing, who smoothed down the ups and downs of the human mind. By identifying him, the distinguished master of ceremonies looked like a boy who sees his father late in the afternoon, after a day working in the field.

"Behold the leader of the leaders, the Prince of my dreams!"

"But where is the man?" miserable, politicians, Pharisees and learned scribes asked. Their disappointment could not have been bigger. "It can't be ... Would he be able to free Israel from Tiberius Caesar's grip and the massive taxes paid to Rome?"

They wanted a political rescuer, but Jesus was the rescuer from psychological jails. Like a movie that often frustrates the reader of a story that had already been shot in his mind, John's character didn't correspond to the expectations of their imagination. Hands injured by wielding hammers, the scars on a face that had been exposed to sunlight for hours were shocking. If he had disappointed on the outside, he overflowed with boldness and lucidity though.

He looked at John, but didn't identify himself. He didn't say his address, his origin, his life project, nothing. Transpiring silence through his pores, Jesus just started bowing before John to live the disturbing psychosocial baptism's metaphor. He would touch the waters and come out of them proclaimed a new man, capable of taming the ghosts that terrorize human minds, from phobias to jealousy, from egocentrism to feelings of revenge. Surprised, the master of ceremonies said,

"Do you bow before me? I am unworthy to untie the thongs of your sandals. I should bend before you."

Hearing this reverence; the scribe was in shock.

"How can such a daring man, who daily puts a price on his head, act so humbly before such a simple man?"

"Incomprehensible!" another man of letters confirmed.

From now on, this man would stand on the stage and shake the prejudices of the spectators. As it had been told to his mother when he was still a baby, that man would dissect hidden thoughts.

Discussion Room

Marco spoke at the round table about John's story, point by point; his modus operandi, his life project, his performance as master of ceremonies, according to Dr. Luke's descriptions. He described in detail the meeting between the announcer and the announced. He interpreted not only the written texts but also deduced phenomena and induced the ideas that were incomplete.

It was like watching a film directed by a skilled director, with an eye to details that were imperceptible at first glance. Films, based on books rarely do them justice. The round table spectators were amazed. After this approach, Marco would do his critical analysis.

"Incredibly, Jesus didn't say that John was exaggerating in his humility when he stated that he was unworthy to take off his sandals. His simple words reveal his dramatic superiority, 'Let us honor the scriptures."

Michael was intrigued by the disclosure. In an anxiety crisis, he slammed the table, outraged, almost out of his mind. He scared not only the members of the table but also the attentive audience who was listening to them,

"This round table is disturbing, Marco!"

"What is it?" Sofia asked, worried.

"Sofia this man's story drives any intellectual crazy."

"Why?" Dr. Thomas said.

"What do you mean, why? Do you, Christians, believe without critical awareness?" he said sharply. "As Marco has exposed, the nonsense that accompanies Jesus' story is at least mind-blowing. Be honest when you answer."

After a pause to take a breath, he began his series of questions.

"Was he announced as King?"

"Yes," Dr. Alberto said.

"Did this advertisement come out on front pages of the court as the Princes' son?" Michael asked again.

"No! He was secretly announced by a stranger that appeared in Mary's room," Sofia said.

"Was he conceived with the participation of a man?" Michael asked.

"Not according to Dr. Luke," Dr. Thomas said.

"Did he have a decent birth?"

"No," Dr. Alberto said. "He was born in a stable."

"Was he protected in childhood?"

"No! He ran to Egypt," Sofia said.

"Just those points are enough to make any thinker mad."

After another pause to think, he continued,

"Did the educator in charge of taking care of the Almighty's son have noble status?"

"No! She was a poor teenager from a troubled region," Dr. Alberto commented.

"Was her life and the boys at risk?"

"Probably," Sofia said.

"In the midst of this whirlpool of danger, did she have a fragmented self-image?"

"No. We saw that Mary had very high self-esteem," Dr. Thomas said.

"Did Mary live in the illiteracy era?"

"Yes, although Alexander the Great spread the Greek culture."

"Who did she learn to read with?"

"We don't know," Dr. Alberto said.

"Mysteries and more mysteries! Everything here is a sea of secrets," Michel affirmed.

Marco admired his friend's capacity for synthesis.

"And there's more," the neuroscientist said. "When Jesus, son of the supposed Author of Existence, decided to open his mouth to the world, he used a marketing 'team' made up by one man. Even worse, a man who ate, dressed, and spoke like an alien." Many people in the audience laughed, but they were thoughtful. He was right.

"This is not a laughing matter; you should be crying. Besides that, John was the first marketing professional that advertised a man without knowing him. To make it worse, instead of being polite or discreet, this marketing man fought the leaders of his time."

"There are countless paradoxes," Dr. Thomas said.

At that moment, Michael stood up, stared at his psychiatrist friend and science partner and concluded, anxiously,

"Jesus' story is disturbing my rationality, Marco."

"Sit down, Michael," Marco asked softly. "You are too tense."

"Tense? My mind is a boiling cauldron." Then, he warned, "Marco, you are a remarkable psychiatrist. Let's get out of this round table; otherwise, we will have a psychotic outbreak!"

Many people in the audience laughed again at the way Michael made his approach, including Dr. Thomas and Dr. Alberto. But he was serious.

"That's not funny, Dr. Thomas and Dr. Alberto! Maybe you have already gone mad and don't know it," Michael said.

People laughed even more, but, at the same time, they considered his words.

"These paradoxes are fantastic. A field day for whoever likes to think, but neither science nor religions are fascinated and will bend to them," Sofia concluded, seriously.

Suddenly, a gray-haired man, who was a physicist at Oxford University, commented,

"I'm not a religious person, but I'm as perplexed as Dr. Michael. Europe treats the most brilliant mind in history with superficiality. We've been losing the ability to question."

Marco took a deep breath and made a serious comment,

"Michael, my science friend, what disturbs me is that with all of the paradoxes, that we have been analyzing and that you have synthesized, say once more that Jesus couldn't be a made-up character."

"What do you mean, Marco?" Michael asked, confused.

"Let's think along. Would you use John as your marketing man to apply for the headmaster of the university department?"

"Of course, I would not, Marco. No one with a healthy mind would use a man like him. He would make me lose many votes. By the way, the election's result may be out tonight. I'm confident that I will be the winner."

Some people in the audience applauded. They liked his irreverent way. He held up his hands to thank them.

"Anyway, it seems like John really wanted to smooth down the ups and downs of people's minds, no matter who he'd hurt. Even if the result was anti-marketing." "You are right," Marco admitted.

"Which writer would have the ability to build a character with these social phenomena? In fact, Jesus' story disturbed not only us but also its writers, including Dr. Luke. His texts show an astonished man as the character he was describing. He had so many things to write, but he always tried to be brief. Besides that, his writing had some punctuation problems, as if he was so fascinated that he didn't take pauses to breathe."

"The boy we are studying is very different from the calm Christmas's child. Everything about him is unpredictable," Sofia added.

"When our students graduate from universities, although they are unprepared for life, their parents hold large parties, as if they were heroes. Jesus had zero social privileges from birth to death," Marco concluded.

"This is crazy! Wasn't that cruel?" Michael said.

Suddenly, Sofia came to a staggering conclusion.

"Perhaps the privileges were taken from him so that his light shone from inside out."

Marco put his hands on his head, annoyed.

"Are you defending the thesis that the supposed Author of Existence controlled time and space for his envoy to be born without social privileges? Are you saying that all these paradoxes' purposes were to reveal his psychological notoriety without any makeup?"

"Sofia's conclusion makes perfect sense!" Dr. Alberto said.

"This father threw his son into the lions' den," Michael said.

At that, Marco commented smartly,

"Would this Christian's God be willing to take such a risk?"

"What do you mean?" Sofia asked, intrigued.

"Take the name, power, status and material possessions from kings throughout history and see if they would be able to shine in anonymity, by themselves."

"Many of them were so unqualified that they would be nothing more than vassals," Michael said. "Not even sycophants would be left."

"Even some presidents elected by democracy, if we take their power, status, and populism and test them on the grounds of anonymity, they would be unable to run a salon, a pub, even a microenterprise," Marco said.

"Since everything was taken from the most famous character in history, we will also investigate him without shame," Michael concluded solemnly.

"Correct. From now on, we will analyze Jesus' intelligence without prejudice or dogmas, no matter what remains, no matter who gets hurt. We may be very disappointed," Marco said.

"Or admire him even more," the Vatican intellectual said.

"I very much doubt it," Michael said.

"Wait, Michael. You are going to have a psychotic outbreak," Dr. Thomas teased, just like he had done before.

"I am managing my emotions better," he said, sidestepping the questions.

At that moment, Michael's phone started to buzz. No one looked at their cell phones while they were debating, but there was an urgent message.

"Sorry, but it is urgent."

As he read, he looked more disturbed. The message was, "Beware of this debate! On any of these nights, your family could be taken away."

He handed the phone to Marco so he could read it. Marco was distraught. Michael showed the message to everyone, who also became disturbed. He recovered and commented,

"It can only be a sick joke. It is rare to have civilians kidnapped in Jerusalem."

"Is anyone trying to stop us from participating in these debates?" Sofia asked.

"Many people are watching over the internet. There are always some crazy people in the virtual world. Empty threats," the neuroscientist said.

"Feel free, Michael. If you want to give up the round table, we will understand."

"How? I advise masters and doctoral students, but there is so few interesting and innovative thesis these days. Even when I think about giving up these debates, I know they have become my biggest intellectual challenge."

Sofia remembered the risks that she and Marco had gone through, but she tried to get motivated.

"After all we have seen studying Jesus' mind has become a great mission even though we found obstacles along the way."

"I confess that I have never been so worried and, at the same time, so interested in dissecting the personality of the man I follow," Dr. Thomas said.

The venue was crowded; there were even some people sitting on the floor. They all stood up and applauded the debater's boldness and honesty. In more than eighty countries where the debate was being watched live, even during the night, countless people also applauded. Everyone wanted to go on that fascinating journey, full of unpredictable and surprising routes.

CHAPTER 19

JESUS AND THE MOST DRAMATIC STRESS TESTS

The next morning Marco was focused, thoughtful, and was reflecting on the ideas and thesis they had been debating in the last meetings. He picked up his computer and wrote his impressions on the mysteries of human existence once more.

"Life is a high-risk contract. And one of the most important clauses of such a contract is that we should live each day as a new chapter and each chapter as an adventure. People who get trapped in the prison of routine don't dream, don't recycle themselves and don't learn anymore. They have given up being the author of their own stories to become zombies, even if they are physically alive. I was like that!"

After writing these ideas, he studied Dr. Luke's book. On his desk, there were dozens of books. He referred to texts from all religions and several thinkers to formulate his critical analysis. Many intellectuals create their ideas in chaotic moments, and Marco acted the same way. There were books on the floor, texts and more texts on the table and note papers everywhere.

As he read and elaborated on the questions, his mind opened memory windows.

When he read the books that followed the meeting with John, the Messiah's announcer, Marco got stunned. He was taken aback by the discovery that before Jesus opened his mouth to the world; he had been through the most dramatic stress test. Intrigued, Marco wondered, 'Forty days in the desert without eating? Is that fiction or total pressure? How, at the peak of physical and mental exhaustion, could he think, Man, shall not live by bread alone? Which nutrient was he referring to; physical or metaphysical?

Kingdoms and political power that no man has ever had at Nazareth's carpenter's fingertip? Would that be a metaphor or did he have intellectual abilities to seduce nations? Temple pinnacle and religious star, could he take control of mankind, but had refused it? It is not possible. Did the carpenter have tools to sculpt a political and religious world throne?'

Marco was a rare researcher. He used much more than the Socratic method to foster his questions; he used the art of doubt as a scalpel penetrating the deeper layers of the texts he read to revive them, to dissect their implications and see their limits and outreaches. All that to see the facts with the least possible contamination. That's why he was hard on himself, questioning his propositions all the time. He wanted to see the world as it was, not as he wished it was.

Debate: 1st stress test - Taking the body to the limit.

Marco took a slow, deep breath. He looked at Sofia, at the Harvard theologian, and at the Vatican theologian. He stared at his friend Michael and looked around the packed audience in the classroom.

"I hoped to have questioned Jesus' mind in every way, but I didn't imagine that, before scientists asked their questions, he had already been evaluated by tests that were almost humanly unbearable. Did you know about that?"

"I don't know what you are talking about," Dr. Alberto exclaimed.

"Haven't you ever been mesmerized by Jesus' stress test in the desert? Haven't you ever been perplexed by his incredible rite of passage before he started to talk about his great life project?"

"Are you talking about the temptation of darkness?" Dr. Thomas asked.

Marco reacted immediately. He wanted to make the milestones between science and religion evident once more, although they overlapped in some areas. For example, science strives to control anxiety and religion strives to control existential anguish.

"Let's make the boundaries between science and spirituality clear. We are in a round table to discuss possible events that can be interpreted, analyzed and criticized. I repeat: when faith speaks, science is silent."

"Perfect, Marco," Michael pointed out.

"We reaffirm our agreement," the two theologians said.

"OK! However, we will not discuss evil forces, miracles, supernatural phenomena or any other elements for which scientific investigation is impossible. For example, if there is an almighty God, why doesn't he remove the debris from the universe, and why doesn't he eliminate the evil forces? Whoever builds a big house has to deal with its sewage!" Marco declared.

"Jesus was sent to treat this sewage. That is our belief," Dr. Thomas said.

"Beliefs. How to discuss them? On what basis?" Michael asked, exasperated.

"Calm down, Michael," Marco said.

Suddenly, Sofia had an insight.

"If occasionally, we discuss things that are beyond logic, we must do it philosophically, not scientifically," the moderator commented.

Michael clapped, and the audience followed him. At that point, Marco was ready to move forward.

"Jesus' tests were unusual and almost unbearable. We need to analyze them in the light of the human sciences."

"Do you mean the crucifixion?" Sofia asked.

"No!"

"We are all tested throughout our lives: students during school tests, professionals during interviews, startups by the market, and executives through achievements of goals. As a neuroscientist, I am expert in tests. How can you say that Jesus' tests are unusual?" Michael questioned.

"That's what the Greek doctor's text says!" Marco said.

"I need a better explanation," Michael asked.

"Would you bear going four days without eating?"

"Of course not. I was obese when I was a child. Today I can control myself, but I still have a love affair with the refrigerator," Michael said.

"Luke says that Jesus did not eat for forty days in the desert."

"But this is impossible."

"Well, without drinking, we would be dehydrated in two or three days. Without eating, it is almost impossible to survive. But that is what Luke said. Unless he is making it up."

"But he was a doctor, a logical man," Dr. Thomas reminded.

"This is only the first test. Luke says that he didn't submit to such a trial against his will. If this is real and not a fantasy, then he broke all the limits of physical stress. He had that kind of self-control that no man has ever shown. He must have lost weight until he almost died."

Marco, who studied and wrote long texts about the history of the Holocaust, mainly about the unbearable drama that the Jews in concentration camps went through, commented,

"In concentration camps, they ate only 300 or 400 calories daily. Most of them died within a few months."

"At this extreme point, no compassionate or tolerant mind is capable of developing complex thinking," Sofia said.

"Exactly Sofia. At this point, Homo bio (instinctive man) prevails over Homo sapiens (thinking man). At last, the memory circuit is closed, indicating that survival is more important than thinking and giving yourself to others. Therefore, my friends, many Jews, due to starvation, had selfish reactions; they hid food and dissimulated. Some of them betrayed their friends for a piece of bread, although they were good people before living such a dramatic stress," Marco commented.

"Dr. Polo, I read one of your articles pointing out that in countries where there is food scarcity, for example, where it rains less than 700 liters per square meter per year, there is more disagreement as well as more wars and fights," Dr. Thomas commented.

"Exactly, but this can be corrected by education, especially the one that stimulates cooperation, teaches people to think before reacting, putting themselves in other people's shoes," Marco stated. "On the other hand, in countries where there is abundance, for example, of sunshine and fertile lands, such as Brazil, they promote joy, parties and social gatherings, but don't encourage reading, researching or overcoming barriers."

"Wow, I've never thought about that. Since both extreme scarcity and abundance bring traps that only social and emotional education could solve, countries with a temperate climate are more developed," Sofia commented.

"Of course, there are many variables, but climate and education helped them. However, let's go back to Jesus' paradigms. He passed through Mary's womb tests, the escape to Egypt and the silent and humble work as a carpenter. However, now his body is starving," Dr. Thomas commented.

"How can anyone choose to pass such a test? That is insane, Marco," Michael said, outraged.

"Do not fight me, Michael. Your fight is with Dr. Luke, the biographer. He stated that his narrative would be judicious. He dealt with many people who were starving to death. Now, the person he loves is starving. He should have aborted the thought right after this stress test."

"He was told that he could turn stones into bread. Of course, I know we will not go into that field," Dr. Alberto said. "But, in order to agree with your reasoning, my point is that he did not abort the thought," he said, "Man shall not live by bread alone, but on every word, that comes from the mouth of God!" "That's the thesis," Marco said.

"Wait. They told him that he could stop the physical laws of physics and change matter? That he could turn stones into bread? How is that even possible?" Michael asked disturbed once again.

"Michael, this is not the thesis. We agreed that we would not discuss the supernatural powers of this man. So why are you arguing?"

"I'm sorry. But...,"

"The thesis is that he had a clear thought when his body was dying. But before I talk about that, let me speculate about it. The text says that he got hungry after forty days. What about the previous days, didn't he get hungry then? Of course, he did."

Marco kept saying that the Greek doctor pointed out in a magnificent way that Jesus was in the process of internalization and that this is what suppressed his instincts. And then completed his reasoning,

"Could any human being have this kind of self-control? What we know is that when an earthquake happens, some people who get trapped under the wreckage can unleash a mental power that preserves their body health. Something shocking for the medical science."

"Amazing. I had never thought of that mental power," Sofia said.

Marco continued,

"Now, concerning the thought; 'Man shall not live by bread alone, but on every word, that comes from the mouth of God!' First, this is logical thinking. Second, Jesus had a comparative critical awareness, physical bread versus metaphysical bread. Third, it's an impossible field for science to investigate, human temporal survival, which provides and is symbolized by wheat bread versus timeless survival, which provides the direct supply produced by the mysterious Author of Existence."

"But ... where did you get all this from?" Dr. Alberto commented, admired.

"That is absurd," Michael said. "Science cannot actually investigate this."

"But, Michael, the interesting thing is that while Jesus' body was on the verge of collapsing, of dying, he shocked medicine, fighting against death every day. He spoke about the mortals' greatest dream: eternity."

"Interesting, interesting…," Dr. Alberto said. "Even before death, he didn't lose the romanticism for life. He irrigated his life with hope, because without hope we die, even if we are still alive."

"We cannot say these facts are not at least curious," Sofia said. "Jesus talked about the 'antimatter,' not in the classical sense of physics, but regarding timelessness. I know it is not the subject of this debate, but it is a sophisticated philosophical discussion. He seemed to have no kind of fear."

Animal instinct and individual rational thought inhabit the same human being. Depending on the stress levels, the animal instinct prevails over the logical, leading people to commit unthinkable acts, demonstrating anger, hatred, impulsivity, and feelings of revenge. Jesus' body was pushed to the limit, and it would not be the first time. However, instead of succumbing to instincts, he was able to preserve his critical awareness. He wrote poetry out of chaos.

CHAPTER 20

THE POLITICAL AND RELIGOUS POWER TEST

The intellectuals who were studying Jesus' mind continued to discuss the most dramatic stress tests that a human being can bear. Most humans couldn't tolerate this kind of pressure throughout life, especially people from the middle and wealthy social classes. After studying the tests that took Jesus' body to the extreme, they would evaluate the tests that would take ambition to the extreme, emotion to the limit, and even the intellect to its furthermost boundaries.

Marco said,

"The second stress test Jesus went through is no less astonishing and challenging than the physical test; the obsessive need for power. His self-control was thoroughly tested."

"Are you talking about when he was taken to the top of a hill and saw all the kingdoms and his glory on earth?" Dr. Thomas suggested.

"Yes. Though this shouldn't be a physical place but a metaphorical one."

"Testing the eagerness for power isn't so difficult; I am not an ambitious man," Michael pointed out.

"I agree," Dr. Alberto said.

They were both sitting in front of Marco. Suddenly, Marco took a sip of water and squirted it into Michael and Dr. Alberto's faces. He immediately shouted,

"You are weak!"

Both of them got very angry. Everyone who saw the scene was shocked.

"Are you crazy, Marco?" Michael shouted.

"Did this round table upset you?" the calm Vatican theologian said out loud.

"You are hypocrites! You wanted to sabotage me from the beginning," Marco continued attacking.

Everyone was shocked. The two men who had been attacked snorted with anxiety. Their hearts were in their throats. Then, Marco sat down and apologized to his two friends.

"I am sorry. But, please, tell me honestly; what did you feel with this test?"

"What? Was that a test?" the American theologian asked, astonished.

"Are you kidding me? Did you test my self-control?" Michael asked, shaking.

"Yes, I did. Did you feel angry and willing to attack me?"

Both said yes.

"The obsessive need for power doesn't happen only when we want the power that we don't have, but also when we exercise power we already have without management. You wanted to attack me, your friend, in this controlled environment, let alone in an open environment and in front of the disaffected." "But what is your point?" Sofia asked, puzzled.

"Dr. Luke pointed out that after Jesus had gone through extreme physical stress, he was tested to pursue the power ambitiously and to use it excessively during his journey."

"What an incredible test," Dr. Alberto confirmed.

"Men sell their souls for power; they corrupt themselves, destroy their values, crush their ethics, kill themselves, control their peers and encourage wars. Maybe that is not your problem, Dr. Alberto. If you had too much power and someone touched a nerve, you wouldn't think twice before using it."

"I am shocked at my reaction. The man I follow was completely detached from power."

"The Crusades, the Inquisition, and many other aggressive behaviors indicate that, at given times in history, a 'Christ' was built in the image and likeness of its leader's egocentrism," Sofia commented.

"Last month I fired my assistant just because she confronted me in front of two other scientists. I was egocentric," Michael confessed, honestly.

After that episode, Marco made a surprising comment.

"Jesus' biographer points out that Jesus had the ability to seduce people and kingdoms and dominate them. He says that, in other words, Jesus 'would have all the kingdoms on earth if he had bowed down and worshiped his power.' He would have reached places that not even Caesar had ever reached."

"He was tested in the hell of hunger and in the glory of nations," Michael said.

"It is an overstatement to say that he had the ability to dominate kingdoms," Sofia said.

"Yes. However, I have analyzed Jesus' behavior in his final moments. He reacted like a nobleman, not as someone imprisoned. Pilate looked like a child before him.

Herod Antipas felt like a child, amazed by his reactions."

"That is remarkable," Dr. Thomas said. "Was Luke, right? If he had used all his physical and mental powers, Jesus would have conquered a supreme power on earth?"

"If I came to change destinies of mankind, I would never give away power, even if I had it," Michael said.

"No one with a healthy mind would do it, Michael. But the most intriguing and complex man that had ever walked the earth did," Marco said, adding, "To finish the debate tonight, his third test was the religious one. The third test was conducted when he was raised to the temple's pinnacle. But I will not waste time on this."

"What do you mean? Are you saying that Jesus could have had the ability to control all religions?" Dr. Alberto asked.

The American theologian took the lead.

"The text to which Dr. Polo refers says that he could throw himself from the temple's pinnacle, which would symbolize the many kinds of religions, and he would be miraculously supported. That means that, if he had used his intelligence and his miracles in order to promote himself, he could have seduced all religions, thus leading them. Marco refused to enter this field because it talks about supernatural acts."

"That's it!" Marco commented, straightforward.

Incredible as it may seem, Michael, who had always been so skeptical, decided to make thoughtful comments on this thesis.

"It would be fascinating if the characters we are studying weren't fictional, but real; a man who had both political and religious power those leaders never had, but refused to use the power, wishing only to be human."

And, as a human being only wanted to change humanity. Many people who follow many religions want to be Gods, but Jesus was eager to be human," the American theologian said.

"Perhaps 90% of the people who have any power isn't worthy of it. Power infects them, closes the memory circuit, imprisons the Self in traumatic windows and suffocates their humanity," Marco concluded.

"Only the one who bows before society to serve it is worthy of power. Not the ones who make society serve them," Sofia commented with wisdom.

"Even people who were seemingly humble became unrecognizable with power in their hands," the Vatican theologian said.

"Many thinkers stop thinking critically," Michael said.

At that, Marco said,

"Many employees want to be entrepreneurs, many entrepreneurs want to be politicians, many politicians want to be kings, and many kings want to be Gods, but, to the astonishment of human sciences, the only man who was called the Son of God wanted to be human."

"Jesus proposed a revolution of mankind's essence," Sofia concluded.

After all this debate, Marco, who was one of the rare researchers of the thinkers' formation process, assured everyone that Jesus' personality seemed to be very different from all the characters he had researched; Abraham Lincoln, Nietzsche, Sartre, Kant, Robespierre, Freud, and Einstein.

"You expected to be disappointed as soon as you began to analyze his intelligence," Sofia accused.

Marco just shook his head.

"I expected him to be knocked down in the first round, but I am confused," the atheist neuroscientist Michael said.

"I conclude this thesis with a lump in my throat: there has never been such a generous person who wanted to be small enough to make the little people bigger," Marco, one of the most prominent atheists that science has ever known, argued.

The intellectuals finished another round table session feeling both staggered and silent. Millions of people that had been watching the debates understood that the damage to mankind throughout history had not been produced by humans, but by those who postulated themselves as Gods. Those who made wars, even though they were mortal, humiliated and excluded without being aware that one day they would go to the solitude of a tomb.

There were many political and religious leaders watching the debates. Some of them were applicants for Gods, but now they felt the need to be what they had always been, human beings, fragile and imperfect, who would eventually need a shoulder to cry on and another one to lean on. In fact, a human revolution was about to happen.

CHAPTER 21

THE FOURTH STRESS TEST: PUBLIC HUMILIATION

The debates created at the round table that studied Jesus' mind had shaken the debaters and spectators' paradigms, concepts, dogmas and vision for life.

Marco ordered breakfast to be delivered in bed for the next morning. He was immersed in books. He had never been so deeply focused.

Sofia had breakfast with the other guests. There was a buzz in the huge dining room, but she didn't seem to hear it. All the knowledge she was receiving was messing with her way of being and thinking. The newly acquired knowledge made her review the chapters of her life story; rewriting her conflicts and feeding her boldness.

Michael had started to have sleeping problems. He woke up frightened. His wife did not understand what was happening to him. He used to be strict, Cartesian, and extremely critical; however, his behavior was changing. The morning after the stress tests analysis of Jesus, his class at the post-graduate course in medical science was different.

"There is no use in blabbering; in talking about things you don't understand. My classes' goals are, first of all, to change you into autonomous human beings, minimal managers of your minds. You will not be able to be a good professional if you are not kind to yourself."

"Managers of our minds? You've never said that to us. What's gotten into you, Dr. Michael?" a young doctor asked, surprised.

"Intelligence has gotten into me. Life is a high-risk contract. You can only succeed if you are resilient, give up foolish ambitions and are minimally prepared for the unpredictable curves of existence."

The students looked at each other in amazement. As they were intrigued, Michael joked,

"Thank you for the applause."

The group applauded him, smiling. Michael had a scathing wit, however, thanks to the round table; he was learning the art of being nice.

Dr. Thomas and Dr. Alberto, in turn, were also flooded by a wave of thoughts. They had never imagined that the man they loved and considered the 'Son of God' had experienced the most incredible stress tests of all time.

"Dr. Alberto, if Jesus had preserved his memory, he would never think that Mary's womb could be an unimaginable jail."

"It is true, my friend. What about his childhood? If the Son of God had preserved his timeless memory in his early childhood and hadn't had amnesia until the meeting with John the Baptist, it means that he had gone through unbelievable tests. If he hadn't waded into the deep waters of patience and tolerance, he wouldn't have tolerated those tests. Nowadays, who can be patient enough to live in a society where everything is urgent?" Dr. Thomas said.

After that, Dr. Alberto commented about the last analysis of the debate.

"What surprises me is that the biggest tests to which Jesus Christ was submitted occurred before he opened his mouth to the world and started his work. I never thought that the cross was just the 'icing on the cake' in his huge sacrifice for mankind."

"He went through the sordid valleys of physical, mental, and social exhaustion." Dr. Thomas commented. "Who would have loved being backstage at the theater if they could be applauded onstage as the leading actor?"

After that, the debaters immersed in a cauldron of thoughts and dialogues about each one of the round table sessions.

At the next debate, Marco commented,

"Jesus had nothing, and he was all alone. He was physically in chaos, mentally in distress and socially fragmented, but, as we have seen, he refused to use his intelligence to conquer kingdoms and religious power. Who would give up on maximum power if they had it? Would you, Michael?"

"I ... I am not an ambitious person," Michael said.

"No? How did you feel when you lost the election for the leadership of the University department?"

"I was betrayed, Marco. Betrayed!" he said, punching the table, but he soon realized what he had just done.

"We are so humble that we are proud to be humble," Marco emphasized.

"Are you calling me a hypocrite?" Michael asked, anxiously.

"Being hypocritical means disguising, dissembling, and acting. We are all hypocrites, at least by hiding our feelings from people we love. I am. Sometimes you are, aren't you?" Marco asked his friend.

"I am," Michael confessed.

"Jesus came to change mankind, but he refused to use the traditional means of excessive criticism, intimidation, yelling, sermons, and punishment," Dr. Thomas said, wisely.

"The risk of this innovative method was huge. It was a new language, a new process, a new project," Marco pondered again.

Michael took the opportunity to question the table members.

"Assuming that Jesus' father was the Author of Existence, the Big Bang mentor, and the physical events monitor, wouldn't the son be hurt because of all the stress tests that he had been submitted to by his father?"

"Jesus must have been the most perfect of humanity, so he went through the most dramatic tests. He was the prototype of a new man," Dr. Thomas affirmed.

"Interesting. You seem to have all the answers," Michael said. Then he aimed all his questions at them, "Hasn't the God you believe in hurt you?" he asked the theologians. Or are Christians' lives a bed of roses?"

They swallowed hard. Dr. Alberto decided to open his heart.

"I confess, I have already been sad with God." As Dr. Alberto spoke, he traveled back in time. "My mother died when I was nine years old. Before she closed her eyes, she said, 'God will take care of you, Alberto. Be sure of that.' But he did not, at least, not from my point of view. My father abandoned me when I was 11 years old. 'Dad, where are you going?' I asked him with tears in my eyes, realizing that something was wrong. He said, 'I am going on a trip, but I will be back soon.' Afterwards he married another woman and never came back. I had to wash stinking restaurant toilets to survive. Two years later, the brother I loved the most was hit by a car and died. I blamed God for my misfortunes. The more I rejected him, the more I felt attracted to him. I wanted to help mankind. Finally, I decided to join the Franciscan Order, and that decision made me very happy," he said, wiping his eyes.

Michael was surprised by that answer. He had never seen so much transparency. Michael believed that religious people were superficial, that they didn't think or meditate about life; neither had they complex existential thinking. Because of his atheistic prejudice, he believed that they followed their religions because they were fragile. At that moment, he saw powerful men. He was even more astonished when Dr. Thomas decided to talk.

"I have also been sad with God. I helped the poor people in the Sub-Saharan of Africa for five years, and I gave my best every day. I often had to bury boys and girls killed by starvation, diarrhea or dehydration. I died a little inside every time I had to do that. I as well contracted meningitis but what was killing me was not the disease, but knowing that I could not help the little ones anymore. I was weak, and questions hammered my head; 'God, what is the point of being in this hospital if I am not able to save a sick child? Where are you?'" he said, sadly.

Marco was intrigued by those accounts. Tense, he asked,

"Haven't you ever thought of giving up on everything and shouting, 'God, don't you exist?'"

"If I stopped believing in God, my hope that one day those children killed by starvation would smile in eternity would die. If I considered God a utopia, my dream that all the pain in the world would be relieved and all human injustice would be repaired would die. The dictators would win, violent people would be heroes and Mary's *Magnificat* would not be accomplished," the American theologian said.

"But ... but ..." Michael stammered, feeling embarrassed and paralyzed. "But, if God is real, then at this present time God is neglectful."

"You disbelieve in God because of his silence in this stage while I believe in God because of his action in eternity," the Vatican's theologian said.

Marco and Michael, both atheists, were on the opposite side of the theologians, but, for the first time, and in a profound way, they admired the intelligence of their arguments.

"In my opinion, God is not neglectful in the present. He gives the ink and the paper, but we write our own stories," Sofia said, wisely. Then, thinking of an earlier debate, she concluded: "It seems that Jesus' great goal was to humanize the human being."

Marco also commented that all religions, Buddhism, Islam, and Brahmanism, always had the apostles of peace, who accomplished the arduous task of taming their instincts and getting vaccinated against authoritarianism.

"The more successful a human being is, the more difficult it will be for him to deal with frustrations. Some of them are kind at the beginning of their careers but become relentless when they get on the podium. No one can go against their ideas or actions. The fourth and sharpest stress test Jesus went through was in this field," Marco said.

"I don't remember another test," Dr. Thomas said, curious.

Everyone was impressed when Marco told them about the test that would evaluate the other trials of Jesus. So, that would be his hardest test, which could lead Jesus to regret giving up all the power that he supposedly had.

"What test was that?" Michael asked, trying to disguise his curiosity.

"A social humiliation test."

Marco said that after Jesus had successfully passed the physical and mental exhaustion test, as well as the ambition for political and religious power, it was necessary to rest, to be socially applauded and spiritually acclaimed. None of that happened. He left the shadows of an anonymous life and went to the place where he grew up to spread his message.

"Now I understand. By assuming himself as the people's liberator, he was hated by his friends, shunned by society and excommunicated by religious leaders," Dr. Thomas commented.

"After winning the Oscar for best actor and director for the forty days he spent in the desert, the carpenter of Nazareth was booed in his own home. When he was about to collect the prizes, they took away his glamour and remarkably he was rejected. Carving wood was not enough anymore; he had to cut an emotional masterpiece not to get traumatized."

Everyone was amazed by Marco's presentation. He asked something to his friends at the round table and then to the audience in the room.

"Who betrays us: our friends or our enemies?"

The audience was divided.

"Friends betray us!" Marco pointed out. "Enemies can upset us. But only friends, those we rely on the most, can stab us in the back."

After some discussion, he asked again,

"Why did Jesus say; 'Physician, heal thyself.' to his friends and colleagues from Nazareth?"

"He was referring to a proverb that would portray his imprisonment and crucifixion," Dr. Alberto said.

"It is more than that, Dr. Alberto. He was managing his emotion, so he would not be disappointed with his friends and social leaders."

"What do you mean?" Michael asked, interested.

"Jesus used two modern techniques of emotional protection. The first one: giving himself to people without asking too much, reducing the return on expectations. The second one: don't ask people for things that they cannot give. They would tell him, 'You have helped many people, but you are incapable of helping yourself. Heretic! Liar! Impostor! Heal yourself!' By predicting those highly stressful stimuli, he managed his emotion and, consequently, didn't turn it into debris. What about you, can you protect your emotion?"

"I am stunned by this man's mind. I ask too much from my children, my wife, and my colleagues. I sell my peace at a base price. At the beginning of my medical career, I was tolerant and patient. Now, however, at the peak of my professional status, I am too demanding with everything and everyone. I cannot handle myself. I have no emotional protection at all. My brain cortex is a garbage can," a doctor, who was watching the debate, confessed.

The round table was no longer made up of five people; it involved the whole audience. This multifocal debate was uncontrollable. Michael knew that doctor and of his fame. Motivated by him, he was brave to declare,

"My emotion has always been a bag of rubbish. I am an expert in expecting too much from others. Some people even avoid me in the halls and the teachers' lounge."

"People who demand too much from others work in a financial institution, but they do not necessarily have beautiful love stories," Marco commented, making the audience laugh. But, deep down, that was a sad case.

After that, the scientist talked about some important secrets of mental functioning. Marco said that compared to computers we are like gods, saving and deleting everything we want. Nevertheless, in terms of the human mind, that was impossible. Everything we hate is registered in a privileged way.

"If you hate someone, I'm sorry to tell you, this person will sleep with you and disturb your dreams." He made the participants laugh again. The techniques they used were making them sleep with their enemies. Marco completed this concept, "Jesus, in the most intelligent way, prevented the formation of traumatic windows and preserved his emotional health in his social stress tests by reducing the return on expectations and not acting as a collector."

Marco also explained that it was impossible to delete the infected files, except with brain damage, such as head trauma or cortex degeneration, as it happens with Alzheimer's disease. After that, he said that emotion could never lead itself.

"Emotion cannot have an unlimited credit card. It brings sense to life, but it cannot lead the mind; cannot buy what does not belong. Otherwise, a cockroach will become a monster, criticism will trigger enemies, and public humiliation will create feelings of revenge or an inferiority complex. I repeat, without emotional management, the psychological heaven and hell are very close."

Everyone was very pleased with Marco's explanation. A lady from the audience, a sociology professor, was so moved by everything she heard that she stood up and said,

"Dr. Polo, I've been a sociologist and professor for 25 years, and I've never thought that one of the biggest causes of social conflicts, such as wars, homicides, violence in schools and psychological harassment in companies would be a lack of emotional management. This is as new as it is revolutionary. The attacker metaphorically has an unlimited credit card; he cannot bear being contradicted and, as long as I allow it, so too does the one who suffers the attack, because, irresponsibly, he buys what doesn't belong to him."

Marco stood up and applauded her. The other people followed him. The mysteries that surrounded the most famous character in history inspired minds. Sofia, excited, added,

"The tools Jesus used are so powerful that they can prevent stress that accompanies some types of depression. However, it is a shame that universities have failed to study and research Jesus on a scientific basis. He didn't suffer in advance, not even deliberate losses or frustrations. He had strategic thoughts about the future and prepared himself to bear the unbearable."

"His NEEE index was very low. He didn't spend negative emotional energy," the Vatican theologian said.

"Dr. Luke's writings point out that Jesus was very sociable. He was a scholar who often read published texts. However, there was a significant difference between being loved by people and being accepted as their leader," Marco commented.

"They couldn't imagine that a simple carpenter, who grew up among them, would change the world," Sofia said.

"Exactly, Sofia," Marco confirmed. Then, he concluded shockingly, "Maybe Jesus was the most tested character in terms of self-control. He was free, he could have decided to be quiet, go away or use his supposed power to both control and fascinate his opponents, but he behaved as a simple human being. He didn't need to prove anything to anyone. Which of you would give up your power when humiliated?" Marco asked.

"Honestly, I wouldn't give up my power," Michael replied. "Many intellectuals love to debate ideas, but they have a neurotic necessity to control others."

"Many religious leaders don't accept their authority being questioned. They love the applause, but they exclude the ones who criticize them," Dr. Alberto affirmed.

"However, to sociological astonishment, Jesus gave his opponents flowers. It didn't matter to him if they were critics or prostitutes; he treated everyone the same," Marco concluded.

"It seems that the most famous man of all time, the only one whose birthday is globally remembered, wasn't noticed for his remarkable specialty, being an emotional manager, writing poetry out of chaos," Sofia concluded.

The debate produced sparkling material, full of emotion, adventures and subtle touches of intelligence. However, when the round table session was coming to an end, Marco made everyone think about his final words,

"I study the formation process of thinkers, but Jesus' intelligence is so complex that I feel disturbed. A man who had gone through such caustic kinds of tests and went through all trials with honors must have been a unique genius. However, it is possible to infer that the biggest test

Jesus went through was not visible like physical exhaustion, political ambition, the neurotic necessity to control others or even public humiliation, his greatest test was invisible."

"I don't understand, Marco," Sofia said, startled.

"Neither do I ... One more test?" Dr. Thomas asked, suspiciously.

Marco just replied,

"Thirty years mapping human's minds ... Thirty years evaluating the emotional ghosts that haunt us ... Thirty years scanning social conflicts. Jesus submitted himself to the most rigorous test of all, patience. On the other hand, we, who live in this urgent society, fail this test. Our cell phone stops for one minute, and we stress out, don't we?" "Incredible," Dr. Alberto agreed.

"Didn't he go to India? Greece? Didn't he visit Egypt's savants?" Michael asked.

"No one knows," Marco said. "But maybe he hadn't gone anywhere. Maybe he was managing his emotion around Nazareth. Thirty years preparing him to sculpt humanity's mind ... Thirty years to open his mouth to the world ... Thirty years of patience ... Who would have such self-control?"

Thus, all the people who had heard Marco's words were feeling introspective as they left the debate. They had many doubts, but at the same time, they seemed convinced that the most famous man in history was also the least known man by mankind.

CHAPTER 22

THE DEBATERS' UNCONSCIOUS

Two thousand years before; my friends, my disaffections.

Many people in the Jordan River were impressed by John's reverence to Jesus, John who used to be ruthless with politicians and Pharisees. John, who would talk openly now bowed at a simple man's feet; a man in rustic robes, and of humble origin. That was the theme of the conversation between the spectators on their way back home.

"How could John exalt that Nazarene?" a disciple said, intrigued.

"It's not possible. John is as sharp as a double-edged sword. He said he has been waiting for him for years. I know Jesus, the carpenter."

"Do you know him? Did you live or play together? A man having such a profession and origin can't be the Messiah."

"No, but I assure you; many times, when he spoke, something burned in our minds. During any disturbance, he would remain calm. He was the first to help the community, the most capable of peacefully solving conflicts."

"He does not look like that type of person."

"He is a master in appearance, helping out and then disappearing. I have been applauded because of solutions he gave me."

"Interesting."

"But I have a fear. When the heads of the city find out about his new identity, they will be scandalized." Soon after, Jesus' friend found him at the entrance to Nazareth.

"Spring has come. It's time to talk about my father's kingdom."

His friend shuddered.

"I'm your friend, Jesus and I have learned a lot from you, but you should leave this place because when you speak, you make the leaders panic.

"I can't leave now," Jesus said.

"Then please be quiet," his friend said.

"I cannot stay silent any longer."

"For the sake of your life, please be discreet."

"Didn't you realize that I have been discreet all these years? It is time to talk about who I am and why I am here."

"But the leaders will say; 'we know your parents; how do you claim to be the Messiah? Impossible! Heresy!'"

"Using a favorite expression Jesus said, "I am the Son of Mankind." The next day when they went to the synagogue, as he always did, Jesus read a text. However, this time, after his dramatic stress tests, he took the prophet Isaiah's rolls and didn't read them in the sequence of the book. He took a part of the text in which he believed was a part of his biography, although it had been written many centuries before his birth.

"The Spirit of the Lord is with me because he has anointed me to proclaim good news to the poor. He has sent me to proclaim freedom for the prisoners and recovery of sight to the blind, to set the oppressed free."

Everybody was fascinated by his words. Joseph and Mary were listening to his speech and felt very satisfied. He should have stopped there, but he shocked everyone gathered when de declared, "Today, in your presence, this Scripture has been fulfilled." The reaction was immediate.

"Isn't this Joseph's son?" they said, astonished.

Others looked at his mother and said,

"That's heresy! Your son claims the power of being the Messiah, the rescuer of the nation. Tell your child to be quiet!"

Mary and Joseph were speechless and began to understand what was to come. Mary remembered the warning that 'a blade would cross her soul.' At that moment, the 'blade' began to hurt her. Jesus, watching the perplexity of his friends, relatives, and members of the city, used a well-known phrase that portrayed the virus of discrimination,

"Truly I tell you, no prophet is accepted in his hometown."

As Jesus pointed out human mistakes, including the Nazarene's lack of generosity, they became furious. His parents began to cry.

Days before, he had told his mother; "The time has come, my mother. I love you very much, but, from now on, I will give myself to mankind. Remember that you were chosen to receive me. Don't place yourself as my mother, but as a woman, the chosen one, the blessed woman. If you announce yourself as my mother, you will also suffer." It was impossible for Mary to separate things.

"I unquestionably love you, but I will follow your guidance, my son," she said, worried. "Woman, this will be the password that you should always remember," he replied.

The most tested man in history now tested people's hearts. He talked with conviction about his project. While his friends still loved him, they had gone from the heaven of admiration into the hell of rejection. Many of them turned their backs on Jesus.

In a riot of fury, people dragged him hundreds of feet to the top of a hill. There they shouted,

"Deny what you said!"

"I can't deny who I am," Jesus calmly responded.

"You are a simple carpenter."

"I am also a carpenter of the spirit and the human mind!"

His mother shouted out crying,

"Son, my dear son. Let him go!"

"Be quiet," a religious man said. "A young man who grew up and worked beside and now proclaims to be the Messiah is unacceptable!"

That is why Jesus would always give people a second chance. He never asked for what they could not give. He didn't ask for anything, even from his friends. If his friends had thrown him off the cliff that day as they had planned, Jesus would have died early, and that would have been the end. Jesus would have died from broken bones and severe trauma, but that did not happen, it was not the end, it was only the beginning.

* * *

At that very moment, Dr. Thomas woke up, startled. He had dreamed about those events. Jesus' last stress test disturbed him so much that his unconscious mind led him to retreat into the past. He was panting. Suddenly, he opened Luke's book and went to the passage where Jesus was about to be thrown off the cliff and read it. At the exact moment, when Jesus was about to die, something strange happened. He looked into his executioners' eyes, penetrating their minds, and they opened the way. Jesus passed between them like the air flowing between fingers.

A very powerful leader

It was the first century of the new era; the year was 32. The Roman emperor, Tiberius Caesar, the senators and the great generals of Rome were gathered in the Throne room. All were near a character that magnetized them with his wisdom, confidence, and strategies.

"What did you do to me?" Tiberius asked, stunned.

"Nothing that wasn't already inside Caesar," the man who made him embarrassed and dumbfounded said.

"I have never imagined that a Jew would be able to enter our nest, in Roman's elite, and leave us astonished," the emperor said.

Tiberius was born in 42 BC. His mother had divorced his father and married Octavian, the future Augustus, who would lead the empire with spiritual aspirations. He was officially adopted in the year 4 A.D. In September of the year 14, he became the second of the Julius-Claudian dynasty, succeeding Augustus, his stepfather. After reporting his astonishment of the character that had impacted him, he asked,

"Who are you?"

"I am who I am," the intruder answered with determination and mystery.

In different situations, such a vague response would be a desecration punished with death. Nevertheless, the intruder had them dazzled, his gestures shocked, his words penetrating. Tiberius, the senators, and generals looked like boys before a genius.

"I am an old man; I am tired of wars, although my campaigns in Pannonia, Germany, and Raetia have been successful."

"Wars dominate the body, but only knowledge dominates the mind. The strong ones use intelligence to lead; the weak ones don't have anything but weapons. This empire will break up into a thousand pieces," the mysterious character said.

"I am an anguished man. I was called 'tristissimus hominum,' the saddest man, by old Plinius. However, you penetrate my head like the air in my lungs. Your words transpire warning and encouragement. The Empire needs a new modus operandi."

"Where does all this knowledge come from?" Senator Livius asked the protagonist. "From the Greeks?"

"I told you. I come from the viscera of what I am."

"I have never seen such strategic skills coming from such a young man," Germanicus, the great Roman general, said.

"Time isn't the only ingredient of experience, General. I am the Master of all Masters," the intruder said.

"My throne is destined for my dynasty," Tiberius Caesar said. "But I can review my political project for the good of the empire."

"But, what about Caligula and Tiberius Gemellus?" Senator Marcus Tullius asked.

"It is time to change, senators. If this man called Jesus wants it he will be Caesar of the Caesars," he said, quoting his name. And completed: "A new order, a new relationship, a new policy would be installed in the Roman Empire's womb."

The senators and generals were confused by Tiberius' attitude, but he was so resolute that one by one they began to applaud his decision.

"Caesar! Caesar! Caesar!" the Roman elite cried.

The enigmatic character just smiled and courageously turned his back on, the ultimate power of the world. Opening his mouth, he left them even more shocked,

"I am a traveler of time, Emperor, and lords. If you knew about the power that I once had, you would be surprised. I came from far away looking for the human heart, not the political throne."

Shocked by his refusal to the throne, the emperor showed his indignation,

"Why do you refuse to take over the empire? Because of power, people betray, corrupt and kill."

"My scepter is called freedom! I don't wish to have servants, but friends."

At that moment, a counselor who was accompanying him tried desperately to dissuade him.

"Jesus, my Master, I know your message, your life's project," he said.

"Are you sure?"

"Yes! Why do you make things so difficult? If you take over the empire and dominate other kingdoms, you will be the Lord of the Earth; your teachings and wisdom would travel throughout the world."

"Didn't you hear that I want a change from the inside out?" the Master of the all Masters said.

"I understand it. But by sending some Galileans to spread your message and revise humanity's agenda will be an arduous and risky path."
"It is the right thing to do," the Master said quietly.

"It will happen very slowly. If you listen to Tiberius, your words will be spread like flames on the field's straw."

"The most important and beautiful things can't be rushed. We cannot stretch a child's personality; it is necessary to form it. Besides, love and power don't walk hand in hand." After these words, the Master concluded: "Power buys sycophants, but not friends. Power buys beds, not peace. Power buys the world, but never buys love."

After a brief pause, Jesus looked at the emperor and finished saying,

"I have unimaginable power. However, I am a time walker. I am looking for something power cannot buy."

Disturbed, and with tears in his eyes, his friend foresaw the future.

"Master, you will be rejected by your friends, detested by rich people, considered heretical by the religious ones and, at last, will be treated like... like..."

"Rome's greatest criminal. Love requires sacrifices."

"Your disciples will be thrown to the beasts, they will die by the sword of Gladiators, and will be considered the scum of the world."

"I will cry their tears with them. To those who will follow me, I will not promise heaven without storms, but strength in the storm. There will not be applause in the journey, but courage to endure the booing and ability to write great chapters on exciting days."

Emperor Tiberius envied his wisdom. Nevertheless, at the same time, listening to the refusal, even in the face of his pleading, he changed his mood,

"Throw this ungrateful man to the beasts and any of his disciples, who didn't dissuade him from rejecting the power of Rome!" Then the soldiers took him to the arena where all expected him to be attacked and killed by three lions.

* * *

Dr. Alberto gave a deafening scream. Now, it was his turn to wake up scared. He got up from bed shaking. In his dream, he was Jesus' counselor; it was him who had begged Jesus to become the Caesar of the Caesars, allowing the solemn dissemination of his project, of his message.

CHAPTER 23

MARCO POLO LOSING WHOM HE LOVES THE MOST

Marco, the first psychiatrist and researcher who analyzed Jesus' intelligence from the view of human science, was fascinated by the initial results. In researching how men and women throughout history have broken the prison of routine and have become thinkers and producers of new ideas, he felt that there was nothing more that would surprise him.

He had already examined Freud, Piaget, Sartre, Marx, Kant, Descartes and many other thinkers' intelligence. He had analyzed how they responded to the art of criticism and doubt, their healthy behaviors and their weaknesses, their cups of boldness as well as their setbacks. Now, studying the mind of the most famous man in history, whom he had always despised, disturbed his prejudices, recycled his arrogance, and expanded the possibilities of thought.

He began the round table by speaking openly and spontaneously,

"As we recall the main paragraphs of Jesus' written biography by Dr. Luke, some of us have revealed, without fear, it's difficult chapters. I have always been sociable, but in the depths of my being, I am both lonely as a man and as a professional. However, it is my turn to tell you about the saddest day of my life, my biggest stress test."

Everybody was amazed by those words. Michael looked at Sofia, Thomas stared at Alberto. Millions of people who were watching the debate on the internet were staring at the screen. Marco was so smart that he seemed unbeatable, far from mortals' emotional wounds. However, it was time for that intellectual to reveal the tears that he cried and those that he had never had the courage to share or show.

He told about the final moments of the woman he loved. Sofia didn't quite blink as she listened.

A year before

Anna, my eternal girlfriend, the sweetest woman I have ever met, was getting increasingly weak. Her crises because of a lack of breath increased and were horrible. Neither of us rested. I was so worried that I wouldn't let any nurse sleep near her. I was by her side every minute of her last days. At every crisis, she needed to put quickly on an oxygen mask.

Seeing the undisguised concern of my pneumatologist friend, Dr. Matheus, I asked him in a low voice so that Anna wouldn't hear,

"What's the next step?"

"The bilateral pneumonia is not getting better with any antibiotics. I am devastated. The next step will be to do a lung biopsy via video." Anna had read his lips.

"When will we do the biopsy?" she asked.

"Now," Dr. Matheus said.

She removed the mask and gave her assent,

"Let's not waste time. I don't know if I will survive...but I will fight until the last minute for life ..." Anna said, panting, trying to swallow the air that was around her, but it seemed so scarce.

Today, deaths from pneumonia are very rare, but I felt that something was wrong, that her lungs would suffer dramatic stress and her heart would stop. After the biopsy, the analysis was sent to the pathologist with a request for urgency. The result would come out the next morning. As much as I didn't want to, I left Anna's side and went looking for him in his office. Anxiously, I knocked on the door and entered.

"Matheus, did the result come in?"

"I think so, Marco. Let me open my computer and check my e-mails." After checking his inbox, he said, "Great. It came in."

His calm manner immediately turned into anguish. Each second, he spent reading the diagnosis of Anna's lung x-rays seemed like a lifetime to me.

"What is it? Is it serious?"

The pneumatologist contracted the muscles of his face and lowered his voice,

"Anna does not have a bacterial or viral infection."

"What do you mean?" I asked, puzzled.

"She has a severe autoimmune disease called 'bronchiolitis obliterans.'"

"I have never heard of this lung disease."

"Her own body is attacking her lungs, causing severe inflammation, blocking all bronchus which is obstructing her breathing."

"What are the reasons for this disease?" I asked.

"Genetic, emotional, environmental. We don't know the definitive causes."

"What is the solution? Is it serious?"

The pneumatologist shook his head.

I put my hands on my face and couldn't hold the tears.

"Am I going to lose my Anna?"

Matheus and his wife were our friends. He had to be completely honest,

"You are strong, but, unfortunately, yes."

"Life is a seesaw. We were in the Caribbean on vacation, very happy, but suddenly, she fainted, and we went from the emotional heaven to the psychic hell! What is the treatment?" I asked, anxious.

"We must administer high doses of corticoid as soon as possible to avoid lung failure. Her breathing is so shallow that it is better for her to go to the ICU, in case of emergency."

Dr. Matheus didn't have to complete the picture; I knew what could happen. I went to the room of the woman I loved trying to keep a good mood, but it was impossible. While Anna was physically suffocating, I was emotionally drowning. Anna knew me so well she could read my face when I walked through the door.

"I know ... I'm dying..."

"No, Anna ... No. We will try a corticoid therapy."

Gathering strength, she said,

"Death is an unwelcome visitor. It knocks on the door of children and adults.

Sometimes, at that moment ... we have no time to attend it..."

Again, she had a shortness of breath, and this was an intense episode.

"Choose life, Anna, don't give up. Please don't give up."

She took off the mask and, with great difficulty and said,

"No one dies ... when ... they are loved by someone..."

Soon, Dr. Matheus arrived and explained her illness better, the therapy with corticoid and procedures.

Just as Dr. Matheus had finished speaking, Anna suffered a cardiac arrest. The world collapsed at my feet. The doctor rang the alarm bell and, while they were urgently bringing a stretcher, he was doing chest compressions, in synchrony, I did mouth-tomouth resuscitation. We worked together, and after much effort, Anna's heart finally started beating again. She sighed heavily and breathed again.

As she was taken down the corridor to the ICU almost immediately there was a new drama: another heart attack. Desperate, I got the nearest defibrillator and gave it to Dr. Matheus. It was horrible to see a person you love close their eyes forever.

The shocks discharged by the defibrillator made Anna's heart beat again, but not strongly. She was taken quickly to the ICU.

I followed her holding her hand and saying,

"Fight! Fight for life! Fight for me! Fight for Luke!"

At that moment, I wasn't a psychiatrist; I wasn't an intellectual, but a man who was completely unhappy, although not out of control. Amazingly, Anna looked at me and showed a calm, detached smile. Then she moved her purplish lips and sent me a soft kiss. It reminded me of one of my thoughts: 'Sooner or later the calm or agitated water will empty into the ocean.'

When we got to the ICU, they stopped me from entering.

"Don't go in, Marco. As rational as you are, you are a human being. Let us take care of her," the intensive care doctor said.

Reluctantly, I stayed outside. The first procedure was to monitor Anna's heart; at the same time, they inserted the I.V. Looking at his colleagues, Dr. Matheus asked,

"What are you going to do?"

The ICU chief doctor answered,

"We need to medicate her and reduce her physical and mental stress."

"Are you going to ... sedate me?" Anna asked.

They said yes.

"And if it is necessary, we are going to intubate you, too."

"Induced coma?"

"Only if it is necessary," Dr. Matheus said.

"Not before ... saying goodbye ... to Marco."

"But Anna," the doctor said.

Resolute as she was, she stared into the two doctors' and nurses' eyes and said categorically,

"Not before!"

If Anna died, Dr. Matheus didn't want to have this weight on his consciousness. He looked to the ICU chief doctor and asked for his permission. He understood the seriousness of the case and nodded. Finally, I was able to be by her side once again, and the doctors and nurses witnessed one of the most beautiful moments that had ever happened in an ICU.

"Honey, I am here."

"Film me ... with your cell phone..." she said.

"What for?"

"Plan B ... Do this and put pure oxygen ... in me," she said with difficulty.

Dr. Matheus himself did it. With that, her vital energy improved. Gaining strength, she said in the footage,

"Luke, for me, you are the best son in the world.... Even though I close my eyes, I will never forget you ... Don't be afraid of life. Be very happy, be your father's best friend ... Drink from his wisdom..."

I shed tears while filming. Then Anna took a deep breath and sent a message to her inhuman and cold father,

"Dad, I forgive you. Thank you for giving me life and taking care of me."

At that moment, she gasped again. Her heart was fragile. Dr. Matheus pumped oxygen into her nostrils again. The ICU doctors and nurses, often distant as a primary coping mechanism were touched to hear Anna's words. Some of them also cried.

"Don't say anything else," I begged her.

But she continued,

"Plan A."

Raising her arms and putting the cell phone down, she showed that what she would say now didn't need to be recorded; it was to be kept in my memory.

"If I don't survive ... take care of Luke wisely, always reinvent yourself as a father. And I want to encourage you ... to love another woman."

I sobbed. She completed,

"Look for her like a pearl hunter."

"It is impossible to replace you," I said to her.

"According to reason it is, but not according to emotion."

Then, after another dose of oxygen, she took my right hand and gathered her strength to say these last few words,

"You are as generous as rain and as unselfish as the Sun, Marco Polo ... You turned my story into a show ... I know you don't believe in God..."

"Anna," I said, trying to silence her.

She added,

"But I believe that life is a great script and death is only one act of the show ... I will continue to play my role in eternity ... My beloved, allow yourself to think of other possibilities ... study Christ's mind."

My wife spoke of hope while she died. As she spoke, the device that monitored her heart showed it pumping the blood with more strength and rhythm. The human mind revealed its power and everyone who watched the screen was impressed. I squeezed her hands and, in a choked voice, said,

"Dear Anna, my love for you is indecipherable. Of all the things that I have conquered in life, you were the best one. You are unforgettable. Thank you very, very much for existing."

As I said those words, the 'beep' was even stronger. It seemed like Anna didn't have a serious illness. Then the doctors put their hands on my shoulders and asked me to leave.

As I was leaving the ICU, Anna's cardiac function began to lose strength and pace again. Panting, she could barely breathe. The doctors and nurses helped her quickly. I have never cried so much in my life than on that day. After I had gathered myself, I got into the elevator and could barely see the numbers. I didn't even notice that one of my rare distractors, Dr. Felpes, was in there. Dr. Felpes thought it was a heresy for a thinker of the present to produce a new theory about the mind functioning capabilities of the classical theories of Skinner, Freud, Jung, Piaget. The university was a bonfire of egos and vanity.

Dr. Felpes was astonished to see me dejected; he didn't know what was happening. He had become a predatory expert in attacking people who were hurting and acting similar to insensitive intellectuals.

"Is the unbeatable intellectual impaired?" he asked with a smile on his face.

I didn't answer. But he teased me even more,

"Unbelievable! Marco has feelings! I didn't know that you cried, too."

"Dr. Felpes, you don't even know the foreword of my writings, let alone the most important chapters. Yes, I'm crying. And if you want to know, I feel like the most fragile of men," I confessed.

Confused and realizing something had happened, Dr. Felpes asked,

"What is going on?"

"I am losing the one person that I love the most."

"I am so sorry."

Without saying anything else, I left the elevator and walked through the long corridors downstairs. Teachers, students, and professionals who passed by looked at me puzzled. Some of them asked,

"What's going on with the professor?"

Seeing me so emotional, a neurosurgeon spoke to his friends, quoting a phrase from the last class he'd had with me,

"'Human personality is a sophisticated construction, but, sooner or later, there is no stone left unturned. Collecting our fragments and reinventing ourselves is what distinguishes us.' Wasn't he the one who said that?"

What this neurosurgeon didn't know is that it was my turn to collect my pieces and rebuild myself. I knew that many people fail at that job. That is why I screamed to myself, 'It is worth living even though life is as brief as dew that briefly appears and soon dissipates in the first rays of day.'

* * *

As they heard Marco's speech, thousands of people from several countries were encouraged to collect their pieces and not give up on life, even in the face of death. Friends were deeply sorry for Anna's loss. They couldn't imagine that such a courageous and intelligent person as Marco could kiss the arid ground of weakness. Sofia took his right hand and caressed it softly.

CHAPTER 24

AN UNCONTROLLABLE AND AMAZING FAME

Marco said that after Jesus' unimaginable stress tests, his fame began to spread uncontrollably. His words and attitudes were so innovative that they occupied the imagination of the people and were on the first pages of the most reliable means of communication of human civilization; word of mouth.

"At a time when transport was rudimentary, there were no newspapers, TV, cell phones, social networks; Jesus caused a wave of news across the land. All people talked about was the man who wanted to change the world."

"But didn't this social brilliance come from the supernatural acts that Christians say he promoted?" commented Dr. Alberto.

"In the middle of the twenty-first century, this is a Disney story," Michael said.

"Sorry, Michael. After analyzing the facts that involved Jesus, from his birth to his stress tests, there is no need for mockery. You may doubt whether there were miracles, but you have to respect the facts. Unless you think Dr. Luke was having a psychotic outbreak when he wrote his story?"

"No, I don't think so. Dr. Luke proved to be a coherent and lucid writer,' Michael said, swallowing hard. "Marco concluded, all the paradoxes of Jesus' story reveal that he existed as a historical person. I don't believe in supernatural acts. I confess; I used to mock this belief. Today, I have evolved. I only respect them." Some people in the audience applauded him.

"We must always remember that our purpose at this round table is to study Jesus' mind, not to evaluate his supposed divinity," Marco declared.

"But do you think Dr. Luke was delusional in reporting extraordinary facts that went beyond the limits of quantum physics and the theory of relativity?" the Harvard theologian asked.

"I know it is intriguing that an intelligent physician like Dr. Luke wrote that Jesus suspended the laws of physics and used metaphysical methods to cure sick people. The classical sciences have not gotten into this field, at least so far."

"I never thought studying Jesus would be so disturbing. Everything in his story reaches unimaginable limits," Michael said.

"In my opinion, it is easier to say that Dr. Luke was a bad writer, that his narrative was weak, and that his ideas were childish and naive, much like the hundreds of books I read, but this man is a remarkable biographer. We will study at our next round table something that dramatically shook me. Jesus wanted to spread his message to the world, but not only did he refuse political and religious power in this endeavor but also, he refused fame. He preferred anonymity."

"Are you kidding me, Marco?" Michael asked. "One more paradox. I cannot take it."

Once again, the audience laughed about the deprived manner of the intellectual. At this point the debates recessed as they deserved a long rest. Especially Marco, who was tired of telling Anna's story. Despite that, he and Sofia decided to walk to the new hotel where they were staying. This hotel was closer to the Western Wall than the one that had caught fire. When they arrived at the Wall, he asked her permission and approached the old stones. There were few people there.

As he approached, he saw an old woman crying. In a low voice, she pleaded,

"Take my husband away from his coma. We had so many happy years. I cannot stand his silence."

A man in an Armani suit, president of a large Silicon Valley company, who did not dare to visit the Western Wall during the day, also shed tears. He was visiting Israel on business, but his real treasure was failing; his seven-year-old son was dying of cancer. With his right hand, he touched one of the old stones, and with the other, he wiped his face as he said, almost voiceless,

"David is still a child. Please do not let my son die. Extirpate his cancer."

Touched, Marco also decided to run his hands slowly over the rocks. He felt their cold temperature, but also their smooth relief. Millions of people had touched them. He thought. *What nightmares did they have? What dreams did they build?* It was a surreal place. At that moment, Marco broke his atheistic pride and understood that religion would be an ever-present flame in hearts of mankind. Hope is the secret. He recalled the words of his assistant: 'Socialism did not exterminate it, the theory of evolution did not stifle it, and the digital age did not silence it.' He concluded: we are mortals, there is not a religious person who has nothing to beg for or atheist who one day, will not have anything to complain about.

He thought of Anna and also cried. He did not know how to pray; he did not believe in God, he had no faith, he had no hope that she was pushing her existence beyond the parenthesis of time. If she were, he would be filled with hope. He was too scientific; he just could not. He remembered Luke, his beloved son, drug dependent. He feared he would die as he had already overdosed twice. Sofia approached him. She had never imagined seeing the famous head of the department of psychiatry, famous writer and respected researcher collapsing like that. She touched his shoulder. He was embarrassed, tried to wipe his face fast. Trying to revive him, she remembered one of his intellectual pearls.

"Remember: 'Great men also cry.'"

"The problem is they don't know what to do with their tears," he confessed.

At that moment, they both turned from the Wall and continued on foot to the new hotel. She offered Marco her arm, and they went the hotel like this. Suddenly, he stopped, looked into her eyes and said,

"I want to kiss you!"

Surprised, she encouraged him,

"Then, why don't you?"

"You're sixteen years younger me."

"But I am a woman."

"It is not fair. I'm a professional, and you're ..."

"You are not my boss here. Psychiatrists are complicated when it comes to love," she complained.

"You are also a psychiatrist."

"No, I have already told you; here, I am a woman."

He kissed her forehead and, to her astonishment, he commented,

"I dated many women before Anna. I need to relearn now. I discuss sexuality with my patients, but for me, a sustainable love has to be intelligent, and profound love has to be ..."

"Stop stalling, Marco, and kiss me," she said, giving him an affectionate scold.

Amazed and intimidated by Sofia's confidence, he risked a kiss. It was a long kiss. He felt her warm lips touching his; they were two worlds crossing horizons, two wounded humans sailing in the sea of emotion.

Two Thousand years ago

It was a reddish dusk; the sun seemed to bleed on the horizon. The heat was unbearable. A crowd flocked to see a man without masterful beauty, but with delicate gestures and powerful words. Husbands carried their wives; parents, their children; children carried their parents; friends, one another. Everyone wanted to see, to hear, to be touched by Jesus. Seeing all of that social movement in the land of hunger, it was possible to see that the carpenter of Nazareth was becoming famous, but it still was not possible to know that he would become the greatest celebrity of all time.

"My father is on the verge of death, sir," a person said.

"My friend is faint. He lost the ability to walk," another person said.

"My son has a fever, he coughs a lot and cannot even lift his head," a weeping mother said.

Everyone was looking for a doctor. If life is a winding road, at that time in history, the road was straight up a hill. Simple tonsillitis led to death. A virus caused an epidemic. Malnutrition, lack of vaccines and antibiotics made it an era of pain and uncertainty.

"Rich people at the gates of death would give up their treasures in exchange for health. Elders on the verge of the last existential sigh would give their knowledge in return for youth. That is why I declare that of all the goods you can acquire on this earth; nothing compares to what you already have; life," exclaimed the Master of all Masters to an eager crowd.

The ones who were thirsty for wisdom and the wretches who were thirsty for relief kept coming. The walker had no home; his classroom was outdoors, the canvas he painted was the world, his bed was any piece of ground. He loved mankind so much that he forgot about himself. If they did not offer him food, he would forget to eat.

Nevertheless, in those hard times, his fame spread quickly. Just before the sun set for the day, people sought out Jesus, and he started to teach. Moments later he would disappear. He looked for loneliness as a thirsty person would look for water, and it was there he had mysterious internal dialogues and learned more about himself. The crowd kept searching for him. When they met him, they surrounded him, and pressured him, and begged. That was their last hope. In seconds, the sick ones would smile. Jesus insisted,

"Do not tell anyone."

He was against celebrity worship. However, it was impossible not to share the most joyful day of their lives. It was impossible to keep the walker anonymous. Tiberius Caesar collected heavy taxes from those suffering people, and a significant part of grains and olives was destined to supply the noble caste and the powerful armies of Rome. For the people, having Jesus was like having refreshment, having him was having security, having him was having a charm for life.

The crowd took possession of him as if he was their property. The walker insisted,

"It is necessary for me to announce a new era, a new relationship, a new way of seeing and reacting to life."

People seemed not to hear him.

"Stay with us! Do not abandon us!" they insisted.

"In this Kingdom, the great ones control the little ones, but I must speak about the Kingdom of God, where all the people are brothers and sisters, where everyone is only of one family."

He was poetic, but people were not interested in poetry. They wanted him to solve their problems. He knew this, but he did not ask for anything. As he was gifted with awareness, he knew that when they suffer, the whole universe suffers, when they have insomnia, the whole universe does not sleep. The only pain they truly feel is their pain. The awareness that made us unique also made us egocentric. Empathy was a rare ability.

"Hey, you! Let him talk to us, too."

The pressure was intense. Jesus had no stage, but everyone wanted him to play the part; he had no pulpit, but everyone wanted him to speak. His eloquence was contagious. However, it was almost impossible to speak.

He was by the lake of Gennesaret. The crowd gathered to listen to him. He suddenly planned a strategy never imagined before. When he saw two boats by the lakeshore, he said,

"I need your boats."

"Master, everyone is looking for you, and you want to fish?"

"Yes. Fish for men."

His voice was so strong, but so delicate at the same time that it was impossible to deny his requests. The improbable then happened. Entering one of the boats, he asked the sailor to take him away from land. So, for the first time, someone spoke from a boat to a crowd on the shore. There was a long sermon, most of which was not recorded by his biographers.

"Learn to respect the differences. A happy person invests all he has to make others happy," he continued to teach,

"Selfishness and individualism are personality flaws. Share your robes and your food. The tired heads that you lift today will be the ones that will remember to lift you one day."

Suddenly, James and John, two promising young men, sons to a businessman, Zebedee, who had some boats, heard him.

"Who is that man?" James wanted to know.

John, the youngest one, replied,

"I don't know, James. But when he speaks, he makes my heart pound.

Zebedee also listened to that enthusiastic man. Soon after giving his lecture in the open air, Jesus approached the shore. When he found Simon, who would later be called Peter, he made a strange invitation,

"From now on you will be a fisher of men. Come and follow me."

Only a madman would leave a safe job to follow a stranger who did not even promise him a plate of food. But the Master used to attract hearts, freeing the imagination, and inspiring the capacity to dream.

Simon, seeing the remarkable status and fame of the stranger and, at the same time, being seduced by his message, had no doubt. He spoke to Andrew, his brother,

"I don't know what fishing men means. But it must be something much better than smelling like fish. Great decisions are made in solitude."

Simon made a decision that would change his story forever, and Andrew did the same.

"A fisherman of men? Are you crazy?" Zebedee thought out loud.

Suddenly, Zebedee saw Jesus coming toward him. He needed to hide his two children from that mysterious character. He tried to distract them by encouraging them to repair the nets.

"Come on, sew the nets. We are late."

The invitation could not be avoided. Jesus approached, looked at the two young men, much younger than Simon and Andrew, and made the incredible calling,

"Come and follow me."

Follow where? Follow in the dark. Being a walker with no social security, no escort, no food, no goods, with only the dream to help mankind.

The daring, the ability to venture, to break the prison of routine, have always made scientists more productive in youth than at maturity. Accommodated by applause and academic successes, later on, many become barren of new ideas. Jesus chose young people, although he knew they were always more irresponsible.

"My sons, no..." pleaded Zebedee, calling them to his side.

"Father, this is our opportunity," James said.

"What opportunity, my son?"

"We want to help change the world."

"But you cannot even change this place, and you want to change the world?"

The father had his reasons.

"And you, John? You are still a boy. You've barely turned 15 years old."

"Father, I know how to survive. I will follow him. He will free Israel," John said.

"Are you crazy, my son? Look at him. He has no armies; he walks like a beggar."

"He says what no one has ever said," Andrew commented.

"Even Simon left everything behind," John commented.

"Simon runs over everyone. He is as hectic as the waves of the sea," Zebedee replied.

Suddenly, Jesus approached the family gathering and said calmly and surely,

"Do not worry, Zebedee. I will take care of them."

"They have a promising future here. We have boats, a business."

"But I will give them the treasures of heaven. They will know mysteries that wise men did not see, and that Kings would give everything to have."

The master of all masters was alluring. His words had incomparable magnetism, they touched the depths of emotion, and they played with the imagination. Zebedee was full of doubts. Suddenly, a riveting episode deeply touched him. A fetid leper, deformed, intimidated by the sickness, threw his face on the ground when he saw Jesus and begged,

"Lord, if you want, you can heal me."

The reaction of the bystanders was immediate. The lepers were social pariah.

"Run from this man!" a heartless person said.

"The Leper is contaminating the Earth," another insensible man said.

"He will never make it to heaven," a religious person said.

Jesus looked at the man, who in the last years had eaten and drank from the menu of scorn, and felt sorry for him. Tears welled in his eyes. Feeling no fear, he did what no one had the courage to do. He touched the deformed face and felt the flabby, skin on his hands. Not only did Jesus respect the different ones, but he also loved and treated them like royalty. He started sympathetic love, unconditional love, the greatest law of human rights.

"Who are you?"

"I am Rubem, sir."

"What tears did you cry?"

"All that a man treated like filth can possibly cry."

"And what tears didn't ever flow from your face, my son? I want to know the ones you did not have the courage to cry."

Rubem was taken aback. He paused and, in a broken voice, talked about the moments when loneliness and rejection penetrated the depths of his emotion.

"My father abandoned me. My brothers ...turned their faces ... My wife excluded me, and my two sons are ashamed to say that I exist. My mother, ah, she was so kind, but she was the last to treat me with kindness."

Full of emotion, he tried to wipe away his tears, but with his wrinkled hands and face injured by leprosy, it proved to be a difficult task. Many were impressed by Jesus' clever dialogue with the miserable man. To the Master's eyes, they were not sick; they were only complex and complete human beings who needed more than having a healthy body; they needed a healthy mind.

"Protect yourself, Rubem. Do not buy what does not belong to you. Forgiveness does not solve the errors of those who hurt, but relieves the pain of the wounded ones."

"How do I do that, Master?"

"I'm a walker who teaches people to walk within themselves. Come and listen."

"But I am leprous. They all run away from me."

"Everyone can run away from you, but never run away from yourself."

While he was listening to the unusual man who invaded his mind and spirit, his skin was suddenly restored. He put his hands on his face and felt the smooth skin. Looking down at his limbs they were no longer deformed. "My God, what happened?! My skin is smooth. It does not detach from my body. Thank you! Thank you!" Rubem said jumping with joy.

His disciples were extremely happy and excited. Simon commented enthusiastically,

"We are right, friends! We have worked all our lives on boats. Now, let us board this most incredible voyage."

"Amazing! Who is he?" the young speaker John inquired.

"I don't know, but this man will dominate the world," Simon said.

"I want to be by his side when that happens," James said ambitiously.

To their astonishment, when he saw Rubem jumping with joy, Jesus called him and said,

"Rubem, I have a request to make."

Simon whispered to his brother Andrew and the brothers James and John,

"This man is intelligent. He will say: 'Tell the world about all my power.'"

But the message was exactly the opposite,

"Do not tell anyone what I did to you."

"Sir, why can't I tell?" the leper asked.

"What? Did he ask for silence? How? I do not understand!" Simon, the future Peter, commented.

"I repeat: do not tell anyone what I did to you. Do not promote me, promote love, promote the pleasure of giving yourself away."

The leper didn't understand. In fact, everyone was confused. Hiding Jesus was impossible. His fame was uncontrollably spreading. Crowds would anxiously seek him. Jesus talked to countless people, but would periodically disappear into the desert. There, he would meditate, relax, rest and would have, unfathomable encounters with the One who sent him. Loneliness has always been a unique moment to have poetic encounters with oneself. Those who hate loneliness have never been friends with themselves. The master of emotional management was aware of that.

Later, another incident occurred. When Jesus was teaching inside a house, a large crowd began to surround the home. Desperate, a group of friends wanted to bring one of their own, who was paraplegic to Jesus. However, it was impossible to get entry. In an odd moment of creativity, they climbed to the roof and, through the tiles, lowered the patient to the center of the room where Jesus was standing. They believed that the simple Galilean had superhuman powers. Seeing their courage, Jesus dared to say to the miserable man,

"Your mistakes and failures are forgiven."

That was not what the dying man expected to hear. He wanted to move, to walk, to stop being a burden to his parents. The walker wanted to get him to move first in his mind because he knew that millions of people could walk but do not have the belief that they can, they move their muscles, but they are incarcerated. The words of Jesus fell like a bomb on the heads of the religious people who heard him.

Amazed, one of them said, "Only God can do it."

"Your attitude is unbearable," another one answered back.

Then, they stood up. The man who knew human anxieties, the backstage analyst of the human mind, diagnosed the traps that imprisoned them. He looked at them and said in advance,

"What is easier to do; say that your mistakes are forgiven or move your bones and muscles, which has been paralyzed for years?"

"Of course, words are easy to say," a smart spectator said.

To the astonishment of the observers, the Galilean once again made them all amazed,

"Get up, regain your movement!"

The paraplegic man immediately became the freest and happiest man in the world. He had a long journey to learn to be free in the one place where it is unacceptable for a human being to be a prisoner; within himself. Unfortunately, he would have to learn that the worst prisons of mankind inhabit the human brain.

CHAPTER 25

THE "WRONG" CHOICE OF THE DISCIPLES

Marco started to comment that Dr. Luke's texts are about the important process a master uses to attract and start a sophisticated process of forming his disciples. Once again, nothing was ordinary. He talked about the calls, the unusual and audacious way in which they were approached, the risks, the first conflicts and the disappointments. After that, he brought to the round table an entire issue that may not have been discussed.

"If there was a human resources team assisting Jesus in his closest students' selection, would they accept? Was Peter's, John's, Thomas' and Judas' personalities and abilities to have self-control, and to undertake and reinvent them, remarkable? Jesus went through all possible and unimaginable tests, but could his disciples go through the simplest evaluation test?" They were all speechless.

"I never thought about that," Dr. Thomas said. "We, Christians, believe that he had made the right choices."

"Well, he didn't, in my critical analysis."

"I knew it. Jesus must have failed at something," Michael commented. "Any good professor must select the best students if they don't want the project to sink. In American universities, such as Harvard, Stanford, Yale, and MIT, only the excellent students are admitted."

"It's not possible that Jesus had made the wrong choices," Dr. Alberto answered back. "On what basis do you say that?"

"The subject is broad. I will make just a synthesis of the disciples' personalities and the risky choices Jesus made. Before that, I would like to ask the illustrious representative of Catholicism and, maybe, the future Pope, Dr. Alberto, and the renowned theologian of Harvard, Dr. Thomas: Which one of Jesus' students had the best psychological profile? Who is the best disciple?"

Marco also asked the audience to vote. John won, followed by Peter.

Dr. Alberto had no doubts,

"Of course, they were Simon and Peter. The most honest and available of the disciples."

On the other hand, Dr. Thomas made his choice clear,

"John, the kindest of them all."

Marco's answer was pretentious,

"A selective analysis reveals that Judas Iscariot was the best."

The packed audience was amazed. The two theologians immediately stood up and showered Marco with arguments.

"You are wrong in your judgment," Dr. Thomas said.

"You don't have a psychological basis for saying that," Dr. Alberto commented.

"Marco, even I think you have gone too far," Sofia said.

"A traitor considered the best of the disciples. It is inconceivable," Michael commented.

Without defending his idea, Marco presented the characteristics of Jesus' bestknown disciples' personality.

"Peter was energetic, anxious, acted without thinking and didn't know how to put himself in other people's shoes. He judged quickly and thought slowly. His impulsiveness put his Master in very delicate situations. He almost caused countless deaths when he cut a soldier's ear in the act of betrayal. If he were a student today, the teachers would want to see him miles away from their classroom. Do you agree, Doctors?" he asked the two theologians.

"Yes," they both said, embarrassed.

As Marco exposed his readings, the theologians remembered the texts they had read. They interpreted the Gospels only in the light of theology and, because of that, they had asphyxiated their analysis of the disciples' minds.

"John, the kindest of the disciples, was bipolar."

That statement immediately caused astonishment in everyone.

"Where did you see that he had bipolar disorder?" Sofia, as a psychiatrist, questioned.

"No, John did not have bipolar disorder, his emotion did not swing between depression and ecstasy Sofia, he had a bipolar personality. He was generous when people came up to his expectations, but when they didn't, he had extremely aggressive reactions. He wanted to set fire to those who didn't follow Jesus. Do you agree,

Doctors?"

"Yes," the theologians said, embarrassed again.

"Wow, Marco. These students wouldn't even have passed at a second-rate university," Michael said.

"Matthew had a questionable character. He was working for Rome, treated as a traitor by his people and, furthermore, had a debased reputation. Thomas was paranoid and insecure; he didn't trust his own shadow," Marco said and asked again, "So, who was the best of the disciples?"

Nobody dared to answer, but they knew the answer.

"Judas Iscariot!" Marco concluded. "He was the most self-centered and serene one, he had a social vocation, worried about the poor people, was not impulsive and didn't put his Master in delicate situations."

"But why did he betray Jesus?" Sofia asked.

"I will not go into details on Jesus' betrayal right now. I will study this subject in due time. But, although he had a calm and serene personality, Judas had a severe fault: he wasn't transparent."

"Now I understand. A person who is not transparent takes his conflict to the grave," Sophie said.

"Exactly, a person who is not transparent has no self-criticism, pretends to be another character and disguises their conflicts. Besides that, they save killer windows or traumatic windows in every frustration. The other disciples, in spite of their serious personality problems, were eager to change themselves, overcome their limits and rewrite their stories. They edited their traumatic windows in their cerebral cortex, while Judas accumulated them."

"Jesus failed as a master by selecting such problematic students," Michael said.

The silence took over the audience and the round table. Millions of people from the most diverse countries were haunted by the question; 'Did Jesus fail?'

Suddenly, Marco said,

"Either Jesus made a mistake, or he had such high confidence as an educator that he was able to turn any rough stone into a masterpiece," Marco commented, making Michael silent.

Dr. Alberto reacted immediately. As if he had had one of those rare insights, he reported,

"It is admirable! Any student who wanted to could have had the opportunity to enter Jesus' academy and become a brilliant mind."

"If Judas hadn't killed himself, he would have been a great thinker, such as the apostle Peter, who wrote two elaborate letters at the end of his life. The Master of all Masters was so intelligent that he could change anyone who was at his feet," Dr. Thomas said, stunned.

"What we can learn from this previous analysis is that Jesus, as emotional manager, gave everything he had to those who had little. What kind of teacher is that, which in the act of betrayal, called his traitor a friend, and gave him a question so he could build the answer himself: 'Friend, why are you here?'" Marco said. "Which of the biographers pointed out this question: Matthew, Mark, Luke or John?" "Luke?" Sofia asked.

"No, Matthew. Did he have a sociological purpose in registering that question? Yes!" Marco said. "Matthew was corrupt, but he was embraced by his master at the beginning of the journey. Judas was coherent, but betrayed Jesus and was embraced by him at the end of his life. They did not deserve it, but they were generously welcomed even then. Maybe Jesus is a very rare teacher, who does not give up on any student, even if they spit in his face. It was the students who gave up on him."

"I am very strict as a graduate and post-graduate professor. For Jesus, the subjects do not matter. He performed social inclusion. He was able to turn clay into stones, stones into building material. I am disturbed," Michael said.

Dr. Alberto masterfully completed,

"The best universities in the world choose the best heads, but Jesus transformed the last ones in class, the intellectual scum, into the best minds."

"There should have been a complete change of mentality from the inside out to fulfill his enormous task as an educator, so he said: 'No one puts new wine into old wineskins because they will break,'" Marco commented.

"I'm stunned," Sofia said. "A new education with new knowledge, represented by wine, would require new wineskins, a new mind with new skills."

Suddenly, a history teacher who was tired of seeing the same things in education commented,

"Our education is linear. We bombard students' brains with data and get a mass of repeaters of information as a result. Any computer, no matter how sloppy it may be, can save and recite more data than the human memory. Only the exceptions become thinkers. What were the new paradigms of education that Jesus proposed?" Marco listed a few:

"For now, I will mention only seven, which are the results of my analysis of Dr. Luke's entire book:

1. Each student has an incredible potential, even if it is inconspicuous;
2. No one is unrecoverable;
3. No one can change anyone; only the person can recycle himself;
4. The social and emotional skills, such as thinking before reacting, empathy, resilience and emotional management, are vital for saving the healthy windows in the cerebral cortex;
5. Using metaphors and stories is important to free the imagination and creativity;
6. Dynamics and life experiences in the educational process break the jail of theory;
7. Mistakes are opportunities to grow, not opportunities to new punishments."

"Astonishing. I'm curious to see the result of this educational process. If uneducated fishermen, corrupt tax collectors and paranoid and unstable young people were transformed into brilliant students, then I'm going to become a priest," Michael joked though he was shocked.

That was how participants and spectators become thoughtful. There had never been a master who was so confident in his methodology to turn restless and insane minds into calm and intelligent minds

* * *

Michael was the most feared post-graduate professor of his famous university. He controlled his students with an iron fist. Everyone had to make the highest grade with honors in their defense of their master's thesis or Ph.D. He was authoritarian, austere, a person of few words. At the round table, he was unrecognizable, relaxed, good-humored, and prone to admit his faults.

The day after the last debate, he caught some undergraduate medical students cheating on one of his most difficult tests. When he found out about the cheating, he called the group, made up of two men and two women, to his room,

"You will be expelled or at least will fail my classes."

The students were in shock. They had thrown their future away.

"Professor, forgive us," a student asked, in tears.

"We were wrong," another student said, almost voiceless.

"Every action has reactions. Every attitude has consequences. You played with fire and burned yourselves."

"Your tests are almost impossible," a student said, annoyed.

"Don't raise your voice. For me, a student who cheats on tests is out of my class. However..."

"Aren't you going to fail us?"

"I will discipline you. A master should invest his best in those who have little."

One of the students, who was following the debates, told his colleague, softly,

"It is the round table ..."

"You have disappointed me. I will exchange the zero, the end of the year failure or expulsion from the university, for a challenge: you will give a class about the subjects you have cheated on. And you will have to say things that I didn't teach in class."

"How can we do that Professor?"

"Sparing you doesn't mean overlooking your bad behavior. You are capable of going much further than you realize."

"Are you praising us?" the student who was crying asked.

"Reinvent yourselves. I'm betting on you."

After looking at each other amazed, they accepted.

"Challenge accepted."

The students left with the mission of being much better than they were. And they used chaos as a creative opportunity. The master used their mistake to discipline them and not to destroy them. It was fascinating. The four of them took a huge leap in their intelligence. They were below average students, but, from that episode on, they soon became the best in the class.

CHAPTER 26

THE PASSAGE THAT LUKE DID NOT TELL

The most penetrating round table to study the intelligence of the man whose story has changed the humanity calendar continued to map the vampires that were in the basement of the debaters and spectators' minds. Not only Christians but people of all religions, including atheists.

"I have received many messages from people who are watching our debate around the world," Dr. Thomas told them, enthusiastically. "I've never imagined that, at my age, I could feel this indecipherable joy. A Buddhist from Japan said that he used to criticize his son every day for not living up to his expectations, just like I did. Later, his son confessed that, by praising him more than criticizing, he prevented him from killing himself. Suicide among young people is high in Japan."

He continued,

"An Arabian gentleman, practitioner of Islam, who hadn't talked to his brother for thirty years because of an argument over an inheritance, said that, after he had viewed the round table, he looked for him and said; 'Brother, money buys sycophants, but not friends. You are my best friend. Take what you think is yours.' They reconciled and cried together. He also said that Jesus is mentioned in prose and verse in the Koran. Now, he discovered some universal tools capable of uniting Muslims and Christians."

Michael also shared the experience he had with the students from the medical school who had cheated on the test. Everyone was touched. Marco thought of his son Luke when he listened to all those narrations. He also needed to be a light windows engineer, sound files capable of containing altruism, betting, support, and encouragement.

"This debate has been a success, but poorly worked success makes more damage in the human minds than failure does: it stifles creativity, blunts feelings and promotes egocentricity," Marco assured. "We must never forget the great example of young Mary."

"Remarkable self-esteem and solemn humbleness in the same mind," Sofia recalled.

Speaking of Jesus's teacher, Marco stared at the two theology intellectuals, one, representing Catholicism, and the other one representing Protestantism, and said,

"It is important to remember that, at this round table, we will not study the supposed supernatural acts of Jesus. If they were real or not, whether Jesus had superhuman power and ability to shrug off physical laws or not, this all goes into the field of faith.

"When faith comes in, science departs," the psychiatrist, Sofia, reaffirmed, adding, "But if we discuss these issues, it will be in the philosophy field."

"Exactly! And, from the philosophical point of view, I ask the theologians, what was the first supernatural act of Jesus that was described by his biographers?"

"It was at the wedding of Cana from Galilee," Dr. Thomas said.

"He turned water into wine," Dr. Alberto said.

"Very well, this episode is known all over the world, but it's hard to know the social and emotional facts behind the scenes. How did that happen?"

"Mary came to Jesus and said, 'They have no more wine,'" Dr. Alberto said.

"And was his answer delicate?" Marco asked.

Dr. Alberto swallowed hard because he knew that Jesus' answer to his mother didn't sound generous. For centuries that response had been questioned by theologians. Many of them even avoided commenting on it.

"Apparently not," Dr. Thomas said. "Jesus said, 'Woman, my time has not come yet. You must not tell me what to do.'"

"What a strange answer! Where is the compelling relationship between mother and son?" Michael asked.

Dr. Alberto tried to explain that in many ways, he mentioned the start of Jesus' project, the interference of Mary, the public environment, but nothing could justify the fatal doubt. The answer was unkind, considering that the mother-son relationship, so valued by billions of Christians over the ages, had been put into question.

At that very moment, Marco began to make his critical analysis,

"In the first place, why did Mary say that the wine was gone?"

There were many explanations, but none convinced Marco. Then, Marco said,

"Follow my line of thought. She just pointed out that the wine was gone. Why? Without intending to discuss faith matters, Mary's brief words, 'They have no more wine.' were more than a synthetic thought. It was a password saying, 'I have seen you doing incredible things. If you want to, you can change that,'" Marco commented analytically.

Sofia was enlightened.

"Of course! She must have known that he had done superhuman acts during his younger years. It must be that."

"If that was true, Mary's son was not only an extraordinary person in his mind only, but also in his attitude, just like Sofia dreamed about," Dr. Alberto said.

"Mary must have undertaken a considerable effort to protect her son Jesus. She knew that people would threaten his life," Dr. Thomas said.

"You understood."

"You are driving me crazy," Michael said, completely lost.

"I have never analyzed those facts from the psychological point of view. It makes sense, because Mary says to the servants, 'Do whatever Jesus tells you to do.' Son and mother knew each other so well that they used to speak through codes and looks," Dr. Thomas affirmed.

After Mary's password, Jesus said his password, 'Woman,' and he said 'My time has not yet come. You must not tell me what to do.' It is likely he had prepared his mother many times so that she could separate things. Let's imagine this scene together. Jesus took a slow and profound breath. He wanted to tell something that would shock her. She never thought she would lose him, especially not in an inhuman way. He had been born thirty years ago. Her memory no longer revived the first events. She knew who he was, but she didn't know the facts that would happen later. The sky was beautiful, without clouds, without storms on the horizon.

'Mother, I need to tell you something. It is my turn to leave. I am deeply grateful for all the affection, care, and attention you have given me. From now on, I will stop being your son, first, instead, I will be humanity's son. The risks are enormous.'

His mother must have told him, 'I will not be able to stay away from you, my son.' To which he replied, 'If you cannot stay away from me, if you want to follow me, you will have great joys, but huge frustrations.' 'I am ready,' she said, always bold.

He commented sensitively, 'To reduce your suffering; you will have to return to your roots. You will have to be the Blessed Woman, not my mother. Always remember the mission to which you have been called.' 'I will not forget, my son.' 'There is no worse pain than a mother losing a child.' 'My son, are you going to die?' she asked, shaken. 'Mother, remember: I am the lamb of God.'

She felt an intense pain. She had tears in her eyes. She wiped her face with her thick clothes. Her soul would be pierced.

'I unimaginably love you, my son ... Help me if I forget,' she said in a choked voice.

Taking both of her hands, he kissed her cheek and tried to spare her, "If you forget, I will give you a password, 'woman.'"

After Marco had told this possible story, Dr. Alberto was deeply touched.

"So, when Jesus said that phrase, apparently cold, to Mary; 'Woman, my time has not come yet.' In fact, he was reminding her of the password," Dr. Alberto said amazed. "It is justified ...it is justified... This analysis solved an equation that had been without a solution for 2,000 years."

Marco also concluded,

"Even though he had told her the password, Jesus heard Mary. He may have shaken his head to indicate that he would do what she wanted. Maybe, it was the only significant action Jesus did that didn't relieve someone's pain."

After that comment, Marco asked the astonished audience,

"When did Dr. Luke report this episode of water being turned into wine?"

People who knew the biography he wrote were intrigued. They didn't remember. The two theologians, who were debating at the round table, were looking for the passage, but they did not find it.

"Nowhere," Dr. Alberto said. "But it is strange; If Mary had an intimate friendship with Dr. Luke, why didn't she tell him about such an important fact?"

"The thing is because she thought it wasn't necessary. It was not important."

"Even if Jesus hadn't wanted to do the act, he finally did what his mother wanted. But, I don't understand why she didn't tell Dr. Luke about that," Sofia pondered, confused.

"Because of her discretion," Marco said. "She got what she wanted, but nobody's suffering was in question. That may have made her keep quiet."

"Where did you get all that from, Marco?" Dr. Thomas asked again, intrigued.

"A gold miner does not produce the nuggets; he just removes the sand. I will not take the credit."

After that, Marco concluded that it had been a huge loss to humanity the fact that religions and science had not studied Jesus' intelligence with the depth that he had always deserved and he made a *mea culpa*, confessing the stupidity of his prejudice.

CHAPTER 27

GROWING IN WISDOM

The beginning of the Christian era

Joseph was carving a thick, decaying olive tree trunk. It was difficult, painful work. Rehoboam, a friend, was next to him. Suddenly, Mary approached him, worried. She was with Judith, Rehoboam's wife. The boy Jesus' behavior once again worried her.

"Jesus is gone again."

"Where did he go this time?"

The boy was eight years old. He was determined, smart, astute, an explorer. His ability to ask questions was fantastic, and his generosity dazzled everybody.

"Doesn't he listen to you?" Rehoboam asked.

"No one is as obedient as he is, but as a thirsty person seeks water, he is eager to discover the world," Mary said.

"Then, this child of yours will bring you many joys," Judith assured, trying to comfort her.

"The problem is that he is only a child, he risks being hurt, stolen, and sold as a slave," Joseph said.

"But isn't he afraid to go out alone in these difficult times?" Rehoboam asked.

"My son seems to be afraid of nothing," Joseph said, wiping the sweat off his face. "I will look for him."

Mary, Judith, and Rehoboam accompanied him. They searched for hours.

"Have you seen my son?" his father asked people on the way.

"My son, Jesus, we are looking for him," his mother said.

"Did he run away again?" some people would say.

"No. Jesus didn't run away. He is talking to strangers," his father assured.

"With strangers? He needs more boundaries," some people would criticize.

They went through the village trying to find where he was. Here and there people gave them hints, but, whenever they arrived, he was already gone.

"Has your son ever done this before?" Judith asked, with a perspiring face.

"Sometimes, but he always came back. I fear that one day he will not come back," his father said, very worried.

Meanwhile, a few miles from there, the boy approached an elderly man. Talkative as always, he started a conversation,

"Good afternoon, sir."

"Good afternoon, my son."

"Do you live alone?"

"I do."

"Is it difficult to be alone?"

"A little," the old man said, amazed at the question.

"Don't your children visit you?"

"They have their own lives, my son."

"Shouldn't parents be vital to their children?"

"Yes, but time goes by and many children forget they have parents."

"They shouldn't forget," the boy commented.

"How old are you?" the old man asked in amazement.

"I am going to be nine." He changed the topic of the conversation. "Have you suffered a lot?"

"Many times, my son."

"Why?"

"I feel abandoned. Sometimes I have a pain in my chest. Other times I don't have enough to eat."

The old man noticed the boy shed a tear. Suddenly, the boy offered up some of the bread.

"Are you hungry?" the boy asked.

"Thank you, but I am alright my son, the old man said, not wanting to reveal his massive hunger.

Then, the boy broke his bread in half and gave one piece to the old man, who was overcome with joy.

"Who are you, my son?"

"I am just a boy who doesn't like to see the older ones suffer."

The old man ate without taking his eyes off the boy. Suddenly, the boy surprised him even more,

"Look at the clouds painting the sky. See that bird? What a beautiful flight." A gust of wind blew on him. He opened his arms, closed his eyes and said; "Feel, grandpa, how good it is to be hugged by the wind."

The old man ate the bread and intently listened to the boy's words. Between one bite and the other, he asked,

"Tell me your name. Who are your parents? Where do you live?"

"My name is Jesus."

Instead of answering the other questions, the boy asked, "Where are the lepers?"

The old man scratched his head, tense.

"Why? The leper's nest is a perilous place."

"Please, tell me how I get there."

"It's on that mountain," he pointed to the horizon. "But don't get too close, boy."

"Why?"

"Lepers live like beasts. They attack people, steal, hurt and even kill."

"They are not evil. Lepers only hurt because they too are injured."

The old man thought about this and again asked the boy who he was. Jesus answered,

"I am just a boy who loves mankind."

Then he left without saying goodbye. The elder tried to follow him, but he ran away. He seemed to run like a calf freed from the farmyard, full of joy. Two hours later, his parents showed up with a couple of friends. They were exhausted.

"Have you seen a boy alone around here?"

"Is he slim, with straight hair, talkative, smart, with a wit that leaves you speechless?"

Mary looked at Joseph, and Judith looked at Rehoboam.

"Yes, it is him," Mary relieved said.

"Where is he, sir?" his father asked, anxious.

"He left two hours ago, but he doesn't leave my mind."

They thought the old man was crazy, but he said,

"I am not crazy, my children. The boy who was here gave me food, twice."

"I don't understand, sir," Joseph said.

"He fed me with half of his bread and with the joy in his way of being."

Mary was thoughtful. Once again, her son had shaken those who had listened to him. She always asked him to be careful, not to talk to people he didn't know. However, that was almost impossible. He was extremely sociable.

"Are you his parents?"

"Yes," Mary said.

"Who taught him the things he told me?"

Jesus' parents looked at each other.

"We teach him; he teaches us."

Not wanting to reveal anything else, but, at the same time, concerned, Mary went straight to the point, "Tell me, sir, where is he?"

"He is in the leper's nest."

"He is in the leper's nest?" Rehoboam, Joseph's friend, said, startled. "It is a perilous place."

"I warned him, but he ran away. I tried to run after him. I am sorry, but I couldn't catch him."

"No one can, sir. We must go," Joseph said.

The four of them hurried out and took several turns until they reached the place where the lepers isolated themselves from society. The lepers hid in that location because they were afraid of being stoned, burned, mocked, and excluded by the 'healthy' people. Some relatives and friends, showing sparks of compassion, used to throw pieces of bread from above the cliff so they wouldn't starve.

Inside the huge cave was a well of water. There, from time to time, the Lepers took baths, relieved themselves, drank the contaminated water and became infected all over again. The Leper's nest was a dump of human beings. Fearful, Mary, Joseph, and their friends approached slowly. As they entered the cave, they saw a torch burning and several lepers around the boy. His parents and their friends were stunned. The boy was talking to the miserable ones, trying to cheer them up.

"Which was your happiest day, Isaac?"

"That is when my son was born; his name is also Isaac. I held him tightly to my chest, and I felt like the happiest man in the world."

"What was your saddest day?"

"That is when Isaac, 15 years old, told his friends he didn't have a father. He was ashamed to say that I had leprosy. I heard those words when I was behind an olive tree. I cried for three straight days."

"What about you, Moses? When did you jump with excitement?" the boy asked with the willingness of a master.

So terribly deformed by leprosy many of Moses's friends and relatives believed that he was no longer a human being. His face was horrible. He looked like a cross between a leopard and a wolf. "That was when I married Rinna. She was a beautiful, happy, and funny woman. A week of partying, wine, roasted lambs, grapes."

"When did you have your greatest sorrow?" Joseph and Mary's son asked.

His parents listened in amazement to his son asking those questions to the lepers. As they were so distracted, they didn't notice the presence of strangers.

"I was despondent when, at the first signs of leprosy, Rinna began to avoid me and question my sins. If I was a leper, I deserved it, because I was a sinner. After her, my friends abandoned me, then my brothers. But nothing was sadder than when my parents stopped visiting. They left me to die. Today, I look like a monster."

"Whoever has leprosy doesn't deserve to live, boy," Salus, another leper, said.

"You are giants. You manage to live even when you are treated like the dregs of society."

"Where did you learn that, boy?"

"My father taught me. Let me touch your wounds."

The Lepers immediately rejected his request, but the boy insisted and started to rub their wounded, stinking, deformed faces. Miraculously the burning on their skin got better.

Suddenly, a cry echoed in the dark, dismal, humid cave. It was Rehoboam,

"Don't touch those wounds, boy!"

More than twenty lepers were immediately filled with rage. The 'normal people' only invaded that cave to hurt or kill them.

"Attack them," Moses commanded.

The Lepers went to the invaders with their sticks in their hands.

"Don't do it," Jesus cried.

Suddenly, Jesus heard Mary's voice,

"Jesus, my son."

"Mom! Mom!" he shouted.

Then, something surreal happened. Some lepers ordered,

"Don't touch them! They are his parents!"

The boy ran and hugged his parents.

"Son, it is dangerous to be here."

Suddenly, Jesus looked around and saw the suffering lepers with their severely deformed appearance. It seemed like a horror scene. He then said,

"But, Mom, they are my friends."

With those simple few words, Jesus was able to calm everyone; it was then time to say goodbye. The boy gave each one a hug. It was a beautiful scene. Touched, the wretched people cried and asked to each other, "Who is this boy?"

As they left, something incredible happened. Moses, the most deformed leper, whose face the boy had touched, suddenly recovered his health and his face was restored. He jumped with joy.

After that episode, the lepers anxiously started looking for the boy, but they could not find him because Joseph was now working in another city.

Wherever the Lepers would go they would ask about the child that had cured Moses; however, because the 'normal people' were still so frightened; the Lepers would be stoned or beaten. It was at that very moment, Sofia woke up in despair. She had another intriguing dream about Jesus' childhood but didn't know why. Sofia felt that she had penetrated the essence and personality of the most famous boy in history. She was happy for him, but she also cried for the excluded ones.

CHAPTER 28

MARCO POLO: THE EMOTIONAL EARTHQUAKE

During breakfast, Sofia told Marco about the "movie" that had passed through her mind. She told the story with such emotion and detail that he was genuinely touched. He was aware that the intelligence of the man who had changed history was playing with their subconscious minds once again. Staring into his eyes, she said,

"Of course, it was just another shocking dream. At least, in my unconscious mind, the missing bond between the charming adult Jesus and the inspiring boy has been solved.

Marco commented,

"Our mind has a fascinating creativity, especially when induced as it is at the round table."

"I confess that since I was a little kid, I have always thought about the baby we celebrated at Christmas. I kept seeing him in his crib and tried to imagine how he would grow, who he would play with, how he would deal with pain and with his parents. In my dream, he was an indescribable boy."

"I have the impression that the billions of human beings who have followed Jesus Christ throughout history and still follow him are not entirely aware of the exact causes for believing in him. They valued his superhuman acts, his death on the cross, and his promise of eternity; but it was his small and most intelligent gestures, his intriguing attitudes, and revolutionary ideas that seduced them. The ten parameters I am using to study his mind reveal it."

Sofia remembered that Marco would use those analytical tools, which led her to ask out of curiosity,

"Could you summarize those parameters and the points in which Jesus had been extraordinary?"

"It is too early to have a full analysis. Remember, we are still at the beginning of our debate. Jesus's skills to filter stressful stimuli, to reinvent himself in chaos, his empathy, his resilience to endure frustrations, his self-control in focus of tension, his pedagogical skills to form and focus brilliant minds and to be the author of his own story are keeping me awake at night."

"Remember the conference you gave here to the UN. You said that you had never studied an intellectual who had managed his emotion to this point." "I think of it every day. By the way, I failed," he honestly declared.

At the same time, he made those comparisons; he got immersed in his own story. In ordinary situations, Marco was very healthy emotionally. However, the emotional earthquakes that he had gone through were devastating. They showed him that he didn't have the mastery to filter anxious stimuli, to empathize with his child, he didn't have the ability to rescue him and stimulate him to turn chaos into a creative opportunity.

"I am a loan shark of my own emotion. I ask too much of myself, I try to be great for others, but I am aware that I am my own executioner."

Sofia took his right hand and gently said,

"You need to hug yourself, give yourself and the ones you love new chances."

"I know. It's not enough to be a psychiatrist or a researcher. I need to become a human being under construction. I need to break the routine jail and reinvent myself in my relationship with Luke; otherwise, I will lose him.

In fact, Marco's international fame and intellectual prestige did nothing to attract his son; quite the contrary, it only increased his challenge. He thought of the thesis: 'Power buys sycophants, but not friends.' There was no doubt that he had to rewrite his story.

A year before

After losing Anna, Marco tried to get even closer to his son. Luke was more important to him than all the gold in the world. Nevertheless, the problem had never been the love of parents for their children. The real issue was how to translate that love. Demands are a remedy that produces many side effects. It suffocates dialogue. Without dialogue, relationships lose spontaneity; without spontaneity, you suffocate reliability; without assurance, the relationships become sterile.

Even in the case of intelligent and generous parents. If they don't develop some emotional abilities with their children, the relationship dies. Marco experienced that himself. No one had ever imagined that the resourceful psychiatrist would live such a dramatic script. Before Luke sank into drugs, he had many conversations with him. Some of them were quite stressful.

"How is your life, son?"

"I am fine."

"Do you want to talk about your mother; about your loss?"

Luke got tears in his eyes. He wanted to avoid the subject. He couldn't deal with tense themes.

"No! I want to go to my room."

"You are always running away. Let's talk."

"I don't want to talk! I have already said that!" he said rudely.

"Why don't you?? What do you do at night? Where do you go? Who are your friends?" Marco enquired.

"They are the same ones," Luke said, trying to end the conversation.

"Are you doing well with your psychologist?"

"She is very superficial," the boy replied.

"Is she superficial or are you tough?" his father asked.

Marco didn't want to break into Luke's mind vault. While he knew his boundaries and respected his son, he hated the fact that Luke would not open up. Marco noticed that Luke continued to use drugs. He suffered in advance, which was understandable in such cases, even for an experienced psychiatrist.

"Are we going to talk about the reasons that led you to use drugs?"

"I don't want to talk," Luke said and walked away.

Marco raised his voice slightly,

"Why not? You despise me and treat me like crap."

"I don't despise you. I have no reason to use drugs. You and mom have always been kind to me. We always talked about things, including drugs." "So, why did you get into that trap?" his father asked.

"You are a psychiatrist, and you don't understand."

"I am a psychiatrist, but I am not a magician or a fortune teller. I can only analyze what people tell me."

Luke sighed. He didn't want to talk about that, but he quickly sputtered,

"I was in this cool group, where a pretty girl was flirting with me. They offered me cocaine once; I rejected it; they offered twice, I rejected it again. The third time the girl told me 'Stop being uptight.' That is when I gave in. That's it."

"Would you rather be uptight or a drugs prisoner?"

"It is over. I promise. Trust me."

"Son, be yourself. I am your father and your friend. You can tell me whatever it is that you didn't have the courage to say to me until now."

"I have nothing to say. I want to go to my room."

So, he left the room. Luke had always been an open, transparent boy, but the sudden loss of his mother, the traumatic experience in the police station, his grandfather's outrageous and cruel accusation plus his father's overwork made him close himself in his own world.

Before those episodes, there were no significant conflicts in his personality. Marco knew, unlike Freud's beliefs, that no loss or deprivation is required in early childhood to make a sick adult. Even having a happy childhood, if the Self, as the manager of the human mind, doesn't learn how to protect emotion, stressful experiences can build psychic prisons.

Drugs were one of these experiences, although a significant portion of people who have tried them can get out of the process without being dependent. That was not the case for Luke. The difficulty of dealing with loneliness affected him and slowed down his brakes. He started having a relationship with a group of drug users in school. Soon, they were also seduced by some drug dealers who pretended to be social leaders. Fifteen days later, Marco had another tense conversation with Luke.

"Son, you look strange. Have you been using drugs? Be honest."

"I didn't. You don't trust me," he said with conviction, but he was lying.

"Be careful to whom you associate," Marco said.

"Relax, I know how to take care of myself," he said sharply, which was odd.

"I am going to send you to another psychotherapist. You need to find someone you identify with. Lately, you seem to be suffering from a severe tension overload."

"I don't want it."

"But you have missed the sessions with your current therapist."

"Alright…alright I'll think about it," he cried and left without saying anything else.

Days later, Luke went to a friend's birthday party. As he had classes the next morning, he needed to come home early. An older friend said that he would bring him home. However, he arrived at midnight.

As he came through the door, Marco could tell that something was wrong. Luke was unusually excited one moment and then paranoid the next. Luke looked like he wanted to run away; it was a typical behavior of those who use cocaine.

. Marco was waiting for him, very worried. When he passed through the living room, he didn't see his father.

"Luke, my son, wait," he said, interrupting his steps.

"I'm going to bed," Luke said, very disturbed.

"Wait, I beg you."

"I have to wake up early."

"I have already told you. Wait!" Marco said in a louder voice.

"Damn it!"

"What? You've never seen me offending anyone, how dare you talk to your father like this?"

"You control me too much," Luke said after a brief silence.

"Do I control you? You have no self-control. Why are you so restless?"

"Don't try to be my psychiatrist."

"I am your father. Why such restless behavior?"

Marco approached him and saw he was tense, watching everything around him.

"I didn't use drugs."

"Don't let this particular vampire drain you."

Luke was quiet. His father understood.

"My son, we have lost mom I don't want to lose you. Drugs can be a path of no return."

Luke then began to cry.

"I am weak, Dad."

"Let me help. I love you."

"I don't even know if I love myself anymore."

They hugged. Marco realized that his son's case wasn't only a serious and temporary experience. He started putting up boundaries, controlling his money and his schedules. He kept trying to get closer to him. Luke, however, began to get even more depressed and stopped talking altogether. Marco sent him to more and more psychiatrists, but he didn't adapt to any of them. He found a clinical psychologist, Dr. Susan, but the relationship between father and son got worse after that. Trying to gain Luke's confidence, and without understanding the nuances of his conflict, she pitted Luke against his father.

"Your father is very controlling."

"He doesn't let me breathe."

"You must impose what you think. Otherwise, you will always be in his shadow."

If there was something Marco didn't do, it was to try and control people. He always said, 'People who win without risks win without merit.' He always gave people the right to express their ideas, including criticizing him. He encouraged his students and collaborators to have their own ideas, even to disagree with him.

Marco talked to the psychotherapist.

"Dr. Susan, the relationship with my son is worse. What is going on?"

"You dominate Luke."

"How can you say that I dominate him? I always encouraged him to fight for his dreams."

"You must give him freedom."

"But freedom without responsibility is self-destruction," he said, questioning her.

"You may be a respected thinker, but you have to respect your child's rights."

"Of course, I have to respect his rights, but I can't agree with him using drugs."

"Drugs? What do you mean? He didn't tell me he was using drugs."

"Luke has been coming to the sessions for two months, and you didn't know he was using cocaine?" Marco said, annoyed.

"Do you think I am a goddess who knows everything?" she replied with arrogance.

"You don't have to be a goddess, but at least you must be human because only humans can treat humans. Goodbye Dr. Susan."

Marco found another psychologist for Luke, but there was another problem he didn't know. Without his permission, Luke's grandfather had given him an unlimited credit card. The stinking rich grandfather didn't know that money badly used impoverishes as much or even more than the lack of it. Luke was getting the money and still using drugs. He had become an expert in disguising, dissembling, and lying. Marco struggled to win his son, an increasingly difficult task, and suddenly he received news that made his world collapse. His cell phone rang.

"Doctor Marco Polo?"

"Yes, Marco speaking."

"This is Dr. James from Saint-Louis hospital emergency room. Your son had a heart attack."

Marco's heart felt like it would collapse too.

"What? How is he?" he asked desperately.

"He is doing well now," the doctor said.

"What happened?"

"He overdosed."

That was Luke's first overdose. The second one was just before his trip to Jerusalem.

"How? But... But..." he said, sweating.

Marco got into his car and immediately went to the ER. When Luke saw his father, he burst into tears. He was lying on a stretcher attached to an I.V. Desperate, Luke asked for help.

"Dad, I almost died!"

"Luke, my son, what are you doing with your life?"

"I don't know. I don't know," Luke said in tears.

"Where did I do wrong?" the psychiatrist asked with tears in his eyes, feeling guilty.

"It is not your fault. It has been two months since mom died. I can't live without her," he sobbed. "I miss her."

"Me too, son," he commented, wiping his eyes. "Your pain is unimaginable. But, honor your mother by being happier, not self-destructing."

"I can't control myself. Please, put me in rehab!"

Never before had Marco seen Luke so fragile. He hugged him for a long time. He was a good young man, but he was losing himself. He asked worried,

"Where do you get the money to buy drugs?"

"With the credit card, grandpa gave me," Luke confessed, taking the card from the bag and giving it to his father.

"What is the limit of this card?"

"There is no limit. I can spend as much as I want to."

"How could your grandfather do this to you?"

"I don't know. Maybe it is because he had never been a good father to mom. But he loves me."

"Overprotecting is a way of sabotage, my son. Without limits, our animal instinct overcomes the rational," Marco said, completely outraged.

His father-in-law had tried to sabotage him all his life; now it seemed that he wanted to destroy his son. After that sad episode, he went home very upset. The future, it seemed, was a horizon without direction, a sky without stars. They would have to feel their way along together to survive.

As he studied the last science barrier, the formation of the Self and the construction of awareness, Marco once said something to an audience of educators that would describe his future emotional state,

"We all must be critical of anthropocentrism, of putting ourselves in the center of the universe, but it is an inevitable fact that, for having an existential awareness, we become unique, different from each other. When we suffer, it seems that the whole universe suffers, when we experience loneliness, the whole world feels lonely, at least for our emotional awareness."

Those words scanned Marco's mind while he took his son from the ER. He cried, and it seemed that the whole universe was in tears. He had tragically lost his wife, and now he was terrified of losing his only son. It appeared that the whole world was a victim of the same terror. The world was collapsing around Marco, leading him once again to understand that there are no giants in life, our fragility eventually emanates from our pores.

* * *

After quickly remembering of those episodes, Marco called Luke. The round table led Marco to think a lot about the bridges he had built. He was a mental health professional. He didn't want to win arguments or defend his point of view; he wanted to win his son. He remembered the debate he was conducting and had the courage to apologize.

"I am sorry, my son. I am an expert at judging, but I need to listen more to what you have to say."

"No, dad, I am wrong."

"No, my son. I have been trained to listen to what people have to say. I confess that I tried to hear only to what I wanted to hear; not what you had to say." Luke was touched.

"I never thought you would say that. You are more transparent than I imagine. But I can't open myself up to you."

"Maybe it is because I didn't give you my experiences."

"What do you mean?"

Marco swallowed hard and got tears in his eyes.

"I give you guidance, advice; I am an ethics manual. But I forgot to tell you about my tears so you could learn to cry yours."

"I have never imagined that you could cry, except now that we have lost mom and I am in trouble."

"You are wrong. I also want to tell you about my failures, so you can understand that no one is worthy of a podium if one doesn't use one's setbacks to conquer it."

"You look invincible. Do you have failures?"

"Son, I have many."

"But I always thought your life was perfect."

Marco smiled.

"Do you know I had the most fantastic grades at your age?"

"I know, you have a genius title from a European Institute."

Marco paused because his son did not know him.

"That was twenty years after school. At school, I was one of the worst in my class."

"I don't believe it."

"Well, trust me. I was unfocused, irresponsible: I had no life project. I only rewrote my story after I joined my dreams with discipline."

"Who would have imagined that the great Marco, an intellectual, internationally renowned, was a disaster in high school," Luke, said, opening a smile.

"You know the applause I received, but you don't know the booing I got. You know my intelligence, but you don't know about my failures from youth."

"But... but... why didn't you tell me this before?"

"That is one of my faults. I told you that I have failed to give you the essence of my experiences. That is why I declare: you are the greatest treasure in the world to me." "What do you mean? Drug addicts are considered to be human trash."

At that moment, Marco was very much touched and didn't answer his question. He started to sing happy birthday to his son,

"Happy birthday to you, happy birthday to you, happy birthday dear Luke..."

"Dad, are you crazy? Today is not my birthday!"

"I know, Luke, but I am singing "happy birthday" because every day I am privileged to have you as a son. Thank you for existing."

"Daddy, I... I always ... disappointed you. And you say ... it is a privilege to be my... father... I love you... I love you... Forgive me."

Luke burst into tears. He couldn't say anything else. Neither did Marco. They both lived the language of silence. A new and compelling chapter was about to begin between them.

CHAPTER 29

MICHAEL AND HIS DAUGHTER: THE ROUND TABLE IMPACT

Although he was recycling himself, Michael was not only strict as a researcher and tough as a teacher, but also a lonely lover. He didn't know how to charm and involve Sarah, his wife. His most typical performance was as a father. He had an only daughter, Isabela, who had Down syndrome.

When she was born, her face gave signs of the syndrome, the neuroscientist was disappointed, silent, and ended up being isolated. He dreamed that his daughter would shine in science, just as he did. Children are either their parents' happiness or their frustration, especially if the parents are myopic.

"Michael, play with Isabella," Sarah said a thousand times.

He always had excuses. His lack of time was, in fact, lack of love. He rarely got involved with his little girl, and when he did, he did not enjoy the moment.

Five years had passed, and it was still difficult for Michael to take her in his lap, go out with her, walk hand in hand in parks and play peekaboo behind the trees. He was an intelligent, responsible, and ethical man, but the bullying that he had suffered in childhood for being obese, his parents' stiffness, and his shyness during adolescence made him hide his feelings.

"Do you have a daughter? How is she?" his colleagues from the University asked.

"She is docile, intelligent ..." and, embarrassed, he soon ended the conversation. He never said she had Down syndrome.

Michael couldn't make Isabela the individual flower she deserved to be. When he got home, he went to his office to read, write articles or watch television. Sarah, in turn, was an oncologist. She worked hard; often dealing with death. She was a sensitive woman; she needed warmth, fellowship, dialogue. Michael was an expert on asking too much from people and not giving enough of himself. He lived the thesis of his friend Marco, 'Without emotional management, couples begin their relationship in romantic heaven and end up with conflicts in hell.'

However, Michael was in the process of change. The round table was stirring his emotions and changing his parameters. Sometimes he shared some moments of the debate with Sarah. He didn't tell much, though. One evening he greeted her differently, "Sarah, how was your day?"

"What happened to you?" she asked, curious.

"What do you mean?" Michael asked.

"You never ask me how my day was."

"Oh? I thought I was a kinder husband."

Sarah looked him straight in the eye and said clearly,

"Don't you realize that I'm a widow with a living spouse? No, rather, I am a wife consistently betrayed by her husband."

"Me? Betraying? You're getting crazy, Sarah!"

"There is more than just sexual betrayal. There are betrayals by indifference, social networks, the internet, and television."

"But I don't think I am indifferent."

"You have lost your sensibility, Michael. Do you know how long it's been since you gave me a real kiss?"

"Well ... Has it been a long time?"

"One year!"

"One year? So, I am asexual!" he said, playfully.

"Do you know how long it has been since we made love?"

"Don't ask difficult questions."

"Thirty-seven days."

"I really am asexual," and after that, he gave a weak excuse. "It is the science. Scientists exhaust their brain thinking; they rarely have much sexual vigor."

"When confronted, you joke; when you get upset, you become a lion. Who are you? We look like a couple at the end of our lives. It's not working anymore," she said, taking a deep breath. She was tired of their cold relationship.

"Sarah, I love you," he said, worried. For the first time, he was afraid of losing her.

"True love is not perfect, and I know that. However, without affection, it becomes sterile. It doesn't charm or inspire," Sarah said with maturity.

Michael swallowed hard. He tried to pay off his huge emotional debt,

"I am going to change. Really!"

"Do you know how many times in the last year you promised you would change?"

"Demanding again?"

"I won't demand, but I insisted on taking notes. There were 22 times. Twenty-two broken promises. Twenty-two times you betrayed me, Michael. In fact, you betrayed yourself."

"But ..."

When he was going to argue, she continued to pour out her resentment and reasons,

"I used to admire your intellect, your wittiness, the dreamer scientist. Today this kind of science disgusts me. I am tired of Cartesian, logical, critical, but empty, men.

People like you only love their ego and no one else.

"Sarah, what are you saying? You sound like Marco speaking."

"Marco loved Anna. He praised her every time we went out together. It was inspiring. He cared about her feelings. He was a gentleman."

"So, am I an obnoxious person? You always accuse me, always ..."

When Michael was going to continue to argue, causing another interpersonal war, he interrupted his arguments and suddenly said,

"Paul!" He remembered Luke's mentor.

He remembered that Paul was brave enough to share his madness with Luke and allowed him to tell his story to the world. While he, Michael, was a black box. He never recognized his mistakes, never apologized, and was an expert in defending his positions. The only important thing was winning the arguments, never thinking about the person with whom he argued. "What did you say?" Sarah asked, curious.

"Nothing. I thought of a character we studied at the round table."

"Even as I speak, you are thinking of something else. It's always like that! I am merely a footnote to your story."

He noticed that a tear came out from her right eye. Touched, he said,

"My sincere apologies ... You are right."

Amazed, she let out,

"Are you saying that I am right? Stop being a liar. You never apologize ..."

He was genuinely humble and mapped his mental jails with no fear for the first time.

"In fact, I am Cartesian; I have only logical thoughts in my brain. I don't know how to surrender; I don't know how to help others, I am impatient, and my level of tolerance for frustrations has always been small." He continued with a broken voice. "I don't know how to give myself away ... except when I met you ..."

Sarah was surprised by his words. He was not the same. However, she was so hurt that she took the opportunity to spew her past sorrows,

"You really don't know. You've never known how to love Isabela. I'm sorry, but it seems like you are ashamed to have a daughter with special needs." Michael could not bear that. Sarah had touched the forbidden wound.

"Don't say that! You insult me!" he shouted.

She lowered her voice and reminded him,

"So, why don't you play with your daughter?"

He knew he was beaten and his eyes began to well up with tears.

"I am an oncologist; I am going to keep dissecting your emotional tumor unless you don't let me," Sarah continued to use the words' scalpel. "Why don't you hide behind the couch to play to get Isabela's attention? Why are you so shy about making her smile? Any self-respecting father is an expert at making his children happy."

Michael put his hands on his face and got desperate. He couldn't wear a mask anymore. He cried unrestrained tears and confessed his frustration about having a daughter with special needs.

"I dreamed of having a child who would grow up and be a thinker like me. I imagined that she would write books; leave a legacy for mankind ... but Isabela ..."

"Your daughter may not leave a cultural legacy, but she may leave a legacy for you. Don't you understand?" Sarah said with tears in her eyes.

Sarah, watching him collapse, was generous with him. She didn't point out his faults; anymore, she just hugged him. Every man, no matter how strict he may be, hides a child who needs a woman's lap. Michael, who had always been self-sufficient, removed his armor and allowed himself to be protected by his wife.

"Don't punish yourself. I know this diagnosis is hard for you, but it is the first time in years that you speak about the human being within you. If you hide behind the intellectual, the scientist, you can never recycle the debris from your mind," she said, kindly. Then, she added: "You can, and you must be a real father."

Those words inspired him. After all the impact that the last discussions with Marco had, he concluded something he kept for himself, but now he would share with Sarah,

"Emotional hell is paved with well-meaning parents. I need to educate my emotions and manage my mind. This is so new to me that I am at times lost. I need to reinvent and recycle myself. It is hard to admit it. It seems that I am ashamed of our daughter, but deep down I am truly ashamed of myself." At that moment he started to cry. "That is why I never took her to the University, to the school; to the shopping mall ...

I am a monster."

"No, honey, you are just an imperfect human being," and she hugged him again.

In her arms, he thanked her.

"Thank you ... I will remain a human being under construction."

Suddenly, in spite of the late hours (it was 11 pm) Isabela woke up. She went to her parents' room. When she saw the tears flowing from Michael's face, the girl was touched. She grabbed his leg and said, urgently,

"Dad, Dad ... I love you. Don't cry ... Isabela is here."

He bent down, placed her in his lap and said,

"You have more emotional intelligence than your dad."

Naive, she shouted,

"And you are ... the best ... father in the world!"

At that moment, something unexpected happened. The apartment door was kicked open. Scared, they heard footsteps and realized that their house had been invaded. They were in the master bedroom and desperate; they hid in the bathroom. Three hooded people began to turn over drawers, closets, desks. They entered the bedroom and took Michael's notebook. Then, they tried to open the bathroom's door. As it was locked, one of the burglars at kicked it.

The family was shocked. Michael grabbed his daughter tight, but with the greatest affection in the world. He wanted to protect her with his own life. He realized that the burglars could break in the fragile door, so he cried,

"Take whatever you want, but leave my family alone!"

They kicked the door again. Isabela, frightened, began to sob.

Michael hugged her and tried to comfort her, speaking quietly,

"Daddy is here! Daddy is here."

"Thank you, Dad. I love you," she said, generously.

"Open the door, or we'll shoot!" another burglar said.

Anguished, Michael said again,

"I am with my little daughter. She's terrified. Please, take it all. Just spare us!"

Michael thought of the threat he had received when he was at the round table and was terrified. When the burglars shot at the lock, they all heard police sirens. Several police cars arrived at the scene, and the invaders quickly left the apartment.

After the shock, Michael didn't leave Isabela. He kept her in his arms all the time while telling the police what happened. Sarah, in spite of her depression, looked at them with joy. She wanted to take Isabela away from him to rest, but she was no longer a weight on her father, she was an unspeakable source of happiness. He insisted on keeping her close.

From that moment on, Michael's relationship with Sarah and Isabela took an unprecedented emotional leap. The next afternoon, he changed his routine, insisted on taking his daughter to the University. Everybody fell in love with the girl. Affectionate and talkative, she hugged and kissed everyone she met. Michael realized that his daughter was more sociable and admirable than him. Sensitivity had won over reason.

The neuroscientist also made a great discovery. He understood that children with special needs are so fascinating that they can calm the anxiety of their educators because they are more patient, docile and tolerant than the average. That was how a mentally wooden father started to dance the emotional waltz with free legs.

CHAPTER 30

THE TERRORIST ATTACK

It was an ordinary day; however, the events that would happen next would turn it into an extraordinary time lapse. Dr. Alberto was in his chambers, reading, thinking, and writing. He was very excited about all the discussions on the biography written by Dr. Luke. Suddenly, someone knocked on the door and handed him a letter with the papal seal. The stamp was identical to the ones he was familiar with, but he had never received an individual letter before. He opened it right away. The content was overwhelming. There was only one sentence.

Dr. Alberto, return to Vatican City immediately. The debate in which you are in involved in Jerusalem is scandalous!

Dr. Alberto was deeply disturbed. He could not understand what was happening. *Had I somehow offended the Roman Curia?* He thought distressed. The urgency of the request was so huge that he would not even be able to say goodbye to his friends. He was weakened and saddened; 'What *mistake did I make? Our debates had a different depth. Is it forbidden to think nowadays? Just when I came back to my first love; The Author of Life; as I did when I first started my career!'*

He felt tired and distracted while packing. When he was done, he picked up his cell phone and was about to call Dr. Thomas but before dialing his number and giving him the bad news, he received a call. It was the secretary-general of St. Peter's Cathedral. He trembled.

"Dr. Alberto?"

"Yes!"

"This is Antônio Carminati."

"It's a pleasure, Dom Antônio. Is there anything wrong?" he said, breathing uneasily.

"No, quite the opposite. I would like to congratulate you for the most intelligent debates with the round table."

"I beg your pardon? Have you been following it?" Dr. Alberto asked nervously.

"How could I miss it? Millions of people watch you every night; it's like a TV series. For many of the people I know; that is all they talk about. These discussions are getting to our minds, making us think and talk."

"I did not know about that."

"We got to know Mary from a perspective we had never studied before. How intelligent she was. How daring she must have been. She was so able to protect her emotions. What an amazing self-esteem she had. The impact is so significant that the role of women in the Church is being questioned more and more. They must be more active, more influential, and participate more often. More than a thousand cloisters in several countries have been discussing the subjects you talk about."

"Well, I'm thrilled to know that," Dr. Alberto said as happy as he could be.

Dom Antônio Carminati was so enthusiastic that he continued to show the impacts of the round table,

"Jesus' intelligence is simply incredible. The stress tests he went through made us sleepless. His emotional skills and self-confidence to make thinkers out of hard stones are astounding. We only knew the Son of God, but not the Son of Mankind."

"I'm puzzled too. I'm reviewing my paradigms."

"We have failed to study the mind of Jesus from the angle of science. Two thousand years of gross error." Then the papal secretary said; "The Pope would like to meet Dr. Polo and the other members of the round table one day."

"I'll tell them that."

"Continue, do not stop it."

"But, secretary ... I'm worried. I received a papal letter telling me to return to the Vatican immediately."

"That is very strange. It can only be a forgery."

"The seal looks like the Pope's. Why are you so sure it's fake?"

"Because I'm the one who distributes the letters sent personally by the Holy Priest," Dom Antônio Carminati said. He added; "Either someone is playing a sick joke on you or someone is attempting to sabotage the round table."

At that moment Dr. Alberto became extremely worried.

The round table started at seven every evening. As soon as Dr. Alberto arrived for another session, he reported the facts to his friends in the hallway of the University. Then, Michael came in and intently listened. Dr. Alberto spoke of the joy Dom Antônio Carminati had given him and, at the same time, of the strange letter he had received.

Michael twitched, and he kept clenching and unclenching his hands. After the Vatican theologian's comments, Michael recounted the dramatic experience of being locked in the bathroom with his daughter and wife. At that point, everyone was feeling very tense and anxious.

"What's behind all these dangerous acts? Is there a connection between the risks that Marco and Sofia had with the gunmen and the fire? The mysterious letter Dr. Alberto received; and Michael's drama?" Dr. Thomas asked, tense.

"Are these isolated events the fruit of lone wolves or a conspiracy by a radical group?" Michael cautiously asked.

"They cannot possibly sabotage our debate. We did no harm to anyone," Sofia said.

"Except to the strict minds who hate to think of other possibilities," Marco speculated.

"We may have to interrupt the debate's broadcast on the Internet," Michael pointed out.

"However, the gains are enormous not only for us but the viewers as well," Dr. Alberto said.

By the time they had discussed these matters, they were running 15 minutes late. Many people were outside the debate room waiting for them to come in, as the doors would only open after the debaters' entrance.

"We'll talk about it later," Marco said.

They all headed into the debate room but had to go through the crowd who was eager to listen to them. Some asked to take selfies, delaying them even more. When the room was open, and the five intellectuals began to walk toward the table, there was a deafening roar. There was a bomb hidden under the table, ready to explode as soon as the debate had started.

The commotion was tremendous; people fell on top of each other trying to get out of the room. There was panic, crying and screaming everywhere. Marco had to protect Sofia so that people would not step on her. Luckily, no one was hurt. If there had been no delay, the consequences would have been horrendous. Not only the debaters would be dead, but also many members of the audience.

The Counter-terrorism Bureau had to search every corner of the University. It was the first time a bomb had exploded inside the institution. The Bureau officials questioned the debaters for a long time. Sofia was crying, leaning on Marco's shoulder. After the detailed interrogation and a recount of the many comings and goings, Dr. Thomas suggested,

"There is a deafening cry inside me telling me not to stop the debates. But we must consider the risks."

"It is an irreparable loss, but perhaps ... we had better take time out," Dr. Alberto said in distress.

"My life is turning upside down with this round table, but I cannot hide my fear of continuing," Michael said.

Sofia, who seemed the most fragile in the group, proved to be the strongest.

"Why are you all so apprehensive? You back off at the first obstacle. Aren't there millions of people watching us?" "Yes," the others said.

"Aren't there many people using the emotional tools we've discussed to expand their quality of life in this crazy, consumerist society?" "Yes," they said again.

"So, don't be cowards!" she said brightly.

Marco looked into Sofia's eyes and solemnly admired her. In tune with her, he said,

"I have resisted studying the intelligence of this historical character for two decades. I thought it was a waste of time."

Then, he rubbed his face and completed his reasoning,

"But I reaffirm: while analyzing the psyche of Jesus, I expected to find someone who was fragile, predictable, and ordinary, without individual attitudes. A person with poor emotion and a rough intellect, but I never felt so overwhelmed in the face of such sophisticated intelligence and, at the same time, I have never been so challenged to self-knowledge and to build new ideas. I will not stop studying him even with all these risks!"

Sofia smiled and said,

"Remember, the man Jesus was alone throughout the most rigorous stress tests, and he hadn't backed off his project an inch, and I will not back off either."

"But the University Dean closed the doors. He's afraid of new attacks," Michael considered.

"Then let us go to the streets of Jerusalem," Marco insisted, having an irreverent idea; "Let's follow the footsteps of this mysterious man! Let's go to the places where Jesus spoke and acted in Israel and Palestine! It may be safer to be outdoors in Jerusalem than indoors."

The other debaters kept thinking about the proposal. In a burst of joy, and in unison, they said,

"We are in!"

"The next round table will be about the Sermon on the Mount, which was the subject I had prepared for the debate we canceled," Marco said enthusiastically.

"Will we have the discussion in the very place where Jesus proclaimed his famous speech to a dazzled crowd?" Sofia asked, ecstatic.

"That's the idea!" Marco confirmed.

Two people who were watching them overheard Marco's proposal. They had participated in the debate as spectators and had formed a group called "The Most Intelligent Man in History." Soon they released the informal meeting to all social networks.

Even at unpredictable risks, Marco, Sofia, Michael, Dr. Alberto, and Dr. Thomas began to discuss Jesus' ideas and behaviors on the streets of the magical city of Jericho, Dead Sea, and other sites. Unlike the millions of tourists from more than a hundred nations who visited those famous sites, the debaters were interested in entering areas never walked before, in discovering the backdrop of the intelligence of the man who had revolutionized most of mankind.

Jerusalem had rarely been so electrifying and enigmatic.

CHAPTER 31

THE SERMON ON THE MOUNT THE MOST FASCINATING TREATISE ON HAPPINESS

Marco was wearing a light green shirt with some yellow flowers. He took off the dark blazer that had always characterized him. The intellectual couldn't understand how to make clothes match. As he was color blind, sometimes he used two different shoes and different color socks. The discussions weren't going to take place at night anymore, but in daylight, in the afternoon. He seemed happy to be free to debate the master lecture. The psychiatrist slowly went up the mount where tradition says Jesus delivered a speech.

At the top, he wondered whether the crowd at the foot of the mountain was hearing the echoes of the words of the intriguing man of Nazareth. More than a hundred people followed the debaters. When they arrived at the summit, the breeze cooled their faces. They sat on the rocks and at the improvised benches. The people made a circle around them. Some were filming them on their cell phones.

It was surprising how the debate looked like an orchestra. Marco was the conductor who caused everyone to play the instrument of critical thought. They did it brilliantly, even when they disagreed or questioned each other. Soon Michael, who was relaxed, commented,

"Marco, your analysis on Jesus' mind is stimulating. I haven't become a religious person, but I began to question my strictness and my prejudices."

His daughter, Isabela, was on his lap, touching his hair. It was a surreal compelling image on that mysterious mountain, a reflection of the fact that Michael would never be the same after the debate. At the same time Sarah, his wife, was present, mingling with the audience.

"What other surprises are yet to come?" Sofia asked right away.

"I know the Sermon on the Mount," Dr. Thomas confirmed. "I defended a doctoral thesis based on it."

"Then, please, Dr. Thomas, the word is all yours," Marco humbly said.

"You are the one who should do it, Dr. Polo. I wrote it in the religious field. I am eager to learn Jesus' speech from the psychological and sociological perspective," he said, as a pupil in love with learning.

Without further delay, Marco began to present his analysis for further reflection and discussion. In his original thesis, he had already surprised the audience,

"First, the Sermon on the Mount is the greatest treatise on happiness and the prevention of emotional disorders in history!"

"What do you mean? Are you saying that Jesus was 2,000 years ahead when he talked about psychological prevention? Science is still crawling on the subject to this day! How is it possible? I am anxious to check the foundation that sustains such a thesis," Sofia commented, puzzled.

"'A treatise on happiness and prevention of mental illnesses?'" "I've never heard the Sermon on the Mount from this perspective," Dr. Thomas said, surprised.

Then, Marco continued,

"As the subject is vast, let's talk about happiness now. My question is the following: Is happiness a vital psychological phenomenon to human beings? What does, 'to be happy,' mean?"

"Although this question is difficult to conceptualize and has a thousand variants, such as joy, pleasure, well-being; there is no doubt that the search for happiness is the paramount goal of scientists, lovers, the poets, children, parents, in short; human beings," Michael said.

"I love you, Dad," Isabela said after her father had spoken. Then she kissed him on the cheek as if she had understood his ideas. Michael was elated, Sarah, her mother, got tears in her eyes.

Marco, in a poetic way, talked about the theme,

"Happiness has always run through the arteries of human motivation. Kings sought it out with their power, but it told them, 'Power cannot control me.' Celebrities have tried to get it with their adulation, but it cried, 'I don't mind the spotlight.'"

Everyone clapped at the scientist's words. Inspired by him, Sofia continued the poetry,

"Generals tried to conquer happiness with their weapons, but it assured them, 'I do not submit to the prison of fear.' Millionaires sought to possess it with their money, but it shouted, 'I'm not for sale.' Young people tried to take it by risking their lives, but it cried out, 'Calm down, or I'll hide inside you.'"

Everyone clapped at Sofia's sensibility as well.

Marco began to say that one of the earliest reports on the search for happiness was by one of the wisest Kings from the past.

"Solomon was perhaps the first great leader to seek happiness as the goal of life. He was an ethical and literate man. For him, to be happy was to have healthy social relationships. That's why he wrote his enjoyable book of Proverbs. However, he got infected with power and believed that being happy was nourishing his emotion with everything his eyes desired.

He exhausted his brain, got depressed and took his NEEE index to its maximum."

The audience was upset because, for many of them, wise King Solomon was an untouchable historical figure.

"But ... But ... where is the compulsive error of Solomon?" Dr. Alberto asked.

"Solomon, in fact, had gold, beautiful clothes, palaces, servants; and he was also married to a thousand wives: seven hundred wives and three hundred concubines," Marco pointed out.

"That man was obsessed with sex!" Michael exclaimed.

Many laughed.

"I will not judge Solomon's pathology, but he was tormented by one thousand mothers-in-law!" Marco said. More laughs. "Jokes aside, the wisdom of that King was magnificent. Even a brilliant man may get lost in power if, throughout life, he doesn't return to his origins, if he isn't self-critical or contemplative, and doesn't manage his emotion. Therefore, Jesus once observed, 'Consider how the lilies of the field grow: they do not labor or spin. Yet I tell you that not even Solomon in all his glory was adorned like one of these.'"

"From the bias of emotional management, this passage criticizes Solomon's emotional health," commented Dr. Thomas. "Perhaps this King was the first world celebrity! Even the Queen of Sheba, a distant kingdom, came to honor him. But he was ... he was ..."

Noticing Dr. Alberto's difficulty to conclude his reasoning, Marco completed boldly,

"Emotionally naked. Solomon was covered with gold robes but was uncovered, unprotected, and unable to conquer what power cannot dominate or buy. In short, he wasn't wearing 'the lilies of the field.'"

"Fascinating! The pursuit of happiness leads to self-destruction if we take the wrong path. The result was that Solomon was such a pessimistic and unhappy man that he ended up writing, in a poetical way, that everything was about vanity. He had lost the pleasure of living, while Jesus was overjoyed by observing a lily," Sofia, who also knew those texts, considered.

"This is the contrast between a great emotional manager and a lousy manager. Consumerism led Solomon to be an emotional beggar living in a palace. Today, in modern societies, anxiety feeds consumerism and consumerism feeds fear, becoming one of the great causes of the emotional beggars' era. This theme should not be forgotten!" Marco declared.

Two beautiful young women looked at each other; they felt emotionally miserable. Every week they bought a brand-new item of clothing.

"How can this uncontrolled need for pleasure lead to unhappiness? What is the mental mechanism?" one of the girls named Marina asked.

Marco looked into her eyes and answered,

"Emotion is the most widespread phenomenon, even more than political democracies. People who have ten houses are not ten times happier than the ones who have only one house. Having is not being. An unconscious phenomenon called psychological adaptation causes such feeling. The frequent exposure to the same object or act of purchase triggers this event by lowering levels of pleasure. For instance, at the beginning of a career, a celebrity writes autographs with pleasure, but at the top of the career, if the emotion is not managed, signing the autographs may cause misery."

"Let me see if I got this. Over time, rich people lose the pleasure of driving their Ferraris, because they psychologically adapted to the stimulus, whereas a poor person can be thrilled when driving a rusty car for the first time," Michael commented.

"Absolutely!" Marco said.

"I think I deserve some applause," the neuroscientist joked.

Isabela, his daughter, was the first to clap. Then, the others followed her.

Both atheists and religious people attending the debate were able to identify their emotional ghosts, including Marco. His reasoning was revealing historical human conflicts.

"Besides Solomon, another unstoppable quest for happiness lies in the Epic of Gilgamesh, King of the Sumerians, reported many centuries before Christ," Marco said.

Dr. Alberto had studied this epic poem in his theses, so he said,

"Gilgamesh pursued immortality as the ultimate goal of a human being. For him, there wouldn't be full happiness without immortality."

"It is undeniable that death is an incredibly serious challenge in every mortal's story. Trillions of cells react against a risky situation because they are genetically programmed to live. Cancer is the result of cells that want to be forever young. Cancer cells are selfish; they live only for themselves, disrespecting the organism as a unit," Michael, the neuroscientist, said.

"If your cells loathe dying, why are you an atheist, Michael?" Dr. Alberto asked, smiling at him.

"These religious people like to make atheist's lives hell," Michael said, accepting the joke, and adding, "I think some atheists are as armed as the most steadfast religious people. I confess I was like that. I am skeptical, but my mind is no longer a closed vault, Dr. Alberto. I admit that I have never felt so good about discussing religion with such different people."

Sarah, in the middle of the audience, sighed and grinned. That was the Michael she had married. Intellectual power had stiffened him, but now he had returned to his roots.

"The anguish generated by the fragility of life and death itself makes up a significant part of world GDP," Marco recalled.

"It makes sense." Jacob Moscovitt considered an Israeli colonel who in was the audience. "The health system, the safety devices in products, the insurance industry, the judiciary, the military forces only exist because human beings can feel pain and can silence life."

"Interesting," Sofia said. "Does it mean that the pursuit of Gilgamesh in overcoming death is the essential search, even for atheists?"

"What do you mean?" Marco asked curiously.

Sofia concluded,

"When atheists defend their ideas, they are in search of freedom of expression, but sooner or later they are run over by death, which mangles this freedom." "It is an intelligent reasoning," Marco humbly said.

"As I said earlier, when Socrates was condemned to drink hemlock so that his ideas would be silenced, he told his enemies that he would keep philosophizing in eternity."

The boldness of the ancient Greek thinker was indeed admirable.

"We, atheists, make every effort to face death with ease. Our tears expose us," Michael said.

Sofia completed,

"We use psychotherapeutic techniques and anti-anxiety medication to control anxiety, but we cannot be arrogant and deny that the search for God, regardless the culture or the religion, is a legitimate pursuit of relieving anguish before the inevitability of the finiteness of life." "It also makes sense," Michael said without further ado.

"But religion, whatever it is, without altruism, empathy, emotional protection or threshold increase for frustrations, suffocates the emotional health and turns happiness into utopia," Marco said once more.

"I agree," said Dr. Thomas and Dr. Alberto at the same time.

Thus, the round table orchestrated by Marco debated the most diverse themes freely without fear. They found out that religious people and atheists who didn't agree to sit and discuss respectfully and intelligently were immature.

"Europe is on fire because of Islamists, Christians, and intellectuals. It's like they are on their own islands. I think that there should be thousands of round tables like this, but they are rare as brilliant diamonds," Marco commented.

Then, he continued his explanation,

"In the seventh century A.D., Solon had the concept that happiness was gloriously dying for the homeland or a loved one. His thesis shocked a certain king, called Croesus, who believed that happiness was to accumulate material wealth and power."

"Well, King Croesus' thesis is very modern, as this is the belief of capitalism," the evolutionist Charles Deloid, who was also in the audience, said. "I became an atheist because I saw some extreme religious leaders who were unable to be generous and others who were more concerned with lining their pockets than with helping others." "Maybe you are not an atheist, but an antireligious," Sofia said.

"In Goethe's famous work, Faust, an anguished, depressed man, whose brain was exhausted by self-punishment, sold his soul to the devil too, in another life, to find the secrets of a happy life: traveling among the stars, eating until you are full, dressing in the best clothing. According to this thesis, being happy was a primary need of the human being," Marcus Gebbe, a literature professor who also followed the debate live, commented.

Marco instigated everyone to give their opinions if they wished. After the big cauldron of ideas, he prepared the group to talk about the ostentatious theses of the Sermon on the Mount.

"In 1972, the King of Bhutan, a small country jammed in the mountains of the Himalayas and whose natural resources and land was scarce and inhospitable, introduced a new parameter to determine the wealth of his nation. Instead of using GDP, the Gross Domestic Product, which measures services, grain production, and industry, he proposed the

GDH, Gross Domestic Happiness. The GDH took into consideration peace, harmony, and compassion, the quality of housing, the environment, and schools. Wealthy countries can have people with low levels of happiness and vice versa. What do you think of the GDH thesis?"

"Fascinating," Sofia said.

"Lovely," Dr. Thomas said

"Spectacular," Dr. Alberto confirmed.

"Brave," Michael said.

But Marco made a correction in the concept,

"The GDH is intelligent but insufficient. Introducing GDEM, namely, Gross Domestic Emotional Management is necessary. Otherwise, dramatic mistakes may occur."

"I didn't get it," Michael said.

"Follow me: there can be peace from the outside, but storms on the inside, a restless and tense mind. Therefore, high GDH and low GDEM. You can be compassionate towards others, but generous people can be executioners of themselves, whether they are suffering in advance, ruminating losses or overcharging themselves."

People started to further think after hearing those arguments. They understood that exterior happiness was of no use if the internal Self was not master of its domain. Enlightened by such knowledge, an avalanche of people began to state their mental terror publicly. It was a breathtaking scene.

"I have a comfortable bed, but I can't rest. I wake up in the middle of the night, and I can't go back to sleep. Anguished, I get my cell phone. I'm always tired! It seems that I just carry my body along," a fifteen-year-old boy commented. Anxious as millions of young people, he was destroying the engine of life; sleep. Everyone was worried while listening to him.

"I am completely insured; home, company, life. I am wealthy. However, I don't have any emotional insurance. My mind has no protection. Offenses, criticisms, and setbacks overwhelm me," Antony, a wealthy American businessman, said.

Sofia, inspired by the entrepreneur, completed Marco ideas,

"Gross Domestic Happiness is only sustainable if the collective emotion is managed. From the GDP angle, the 100 richest people on the planet control 70% of the world's wealth. They are wealthier than seven billion other people. However, there are many names listed on Forbes who live on crumbs of pleasure. And when the emotional management is mediocre, the NEEE index is very high. They become executioners of their own brains."

After the whole explanation, Marco asked,

"And what about Jesus? Why did I tell you that the Sermon on the Mount is a remarkable treatise on happiness?"

The people there didn't know how to answer it. At that moment, he shocked everybody by saying,

"The theses of such an intriguing man did not talk about 'self-help' happiness, neither about spiritual, romantic or poetic happiness. They are about intelligent happiness."

"Are there two kinds of happiness, an intelligent and an unintelligent one?" Dr. Alberto asked.

"Clearly there is," Marco said. "A careful analysis of this famous speech, given 2,000 years ago, probably in the very same place where we are gathered today, shows that there are two types of happiness.

1. Intelligent happiness is sustainable, it renews itself, whereas the unintelligent one is unsustainable, it ages fast, it dies when pleasure ends;
2. Intelligent happiness is cultivated; the unintelligent one is sloppy;

3. Intelligent happiness is resilient, nourished by crises; the unintelligent one succumbs to frustrations;
4. Intelligent happiness manages anxiety; therefore, it is patient, whereas the unintelligent one is impulsive and intolerant;
5. Intelligent happiness gives itself away a lot and charges a little; the unintelligent one gives itself away a little and charges a lot;
6. Intelligent happiness does much from little; it is contemplative; whereas the unintelligent one does little from much, it is consumerist;
7. Intelligent happiness respects the differences, whereas the unintelligent one has the compulsive need to change others, it raises the voice, criticizes, compares, pressures."

Marco gave many other explanations of Jesus' thought on intelligent happiness. For him, being happy was not having a perfect life, without failing, making slips or mistakes, but using our craziness to nourish sanity, to nourish the crises to support tolerance, to feed the tears to enrich wisdom. Everyone was amazed.

"Hold on a minute, Marco. We know that psychological disorders, such as depression and suicides, are expanding in modern societies. There are discordant statistics out there, but they are all explosive. Probably one billion people, or 20% of the world's population, is likely to develop a life-long depressive disorder. If schools taught students to manage emotion to have the intelligent happiness, would these statistics be more generous?" the dean of the University of Jerusalem asked.

"I have no doubts, sir. The Sermon on the Mount reveals essential tools for a sustainable and healthy emotion."

"But ... but ... I've always thought of the Sermon on the Mount as a set of rules and principles of conduct," Dr. Alberto commented, intrigued.

Marco said that Edward Jenner created the smallpox vaccine more than two centuries ago. From that episode on, natural medicine invested a significant part of its resources in prevention, while psychological medicine has become overly curative. He added,

"I don't know if I will be disappointed with Jesus's intelligence in the chapters that follow the biography written by Dr. Luke. There are daunting challenges, complex texts that are difficult to be analyzed, but so far it has been possible to say that he was the Master of all Masters regarding emotional management. The millions who follow him do not prevent their conflicts because they never understood and incorporated the tools proposed by him."

Marco then stood up and proclaimed,

"He criticized the neurotic need to be the center of attention, that's why he used to say that what his right hand did, the left hand should never know. He was enchanted by a prostitute the same way he was by a queen and paid attention to a dying man as if he were a prince."

"Amazing!" Sofia commented.

"Spectacular," Sarah, Michael's wife, said.

"From now on, we shall study the depths of the Sermon on the Mount. The speech portrays the concern of this mysterious man with the future of mankind, who was very famous and, at the same time, remarkably unknown. He wanted to make it viable!"

"Are you saying that the Sermon on the Mount is an emotional vaccine to make human life viable?" Michael asked in shock.

Marco looked at Michael and then at the crowd, and completed his reasoning,

"Yes. The Sermon on the Mount was much more than a beautiful speech, a manual of conduct, a daring conference. He provided tools to transform *Homo sapiens*, this complex and beautiful species, which is also so violently and emotionally ill, into a healthy species, watered with a sustainable happiness. Many of us will keep on being positively haunted."

Unfortunately, the time of that round table in the open was over. The sun was setting when Marco closed it. The people in the audience complained; they were eager for knowledge. The theses of the most famous speech in history would be dissected in other debates. They would enrich mankind, regardless of ethnicity, skin color, culture and religion, and, above all, they would water the emotional landscape of each human being. It would be an unimaginable trip.

However, at the same time, they would penetrate the deepest layers of the intelligence of the man who shook history, they would suffer, and their lives would be at stake, as mysterious enemies sought to sabotage the most captivating debate that had ever come to light.

Review Request

Before you go, can I ask you for a quick favor?

Would you please leave this book an honest review on Amazon?

Your review won't take long, but it can help this book reach more readers like you.

Thank you for reading, and thank you so much for being part of the journey.

-Augusto

www.ingramcontent.com/pod-product-compliance
Lightning Source LLC
Chambersburg PA
CBHW021615270326
41931CB00008B/708

* 9 7 8 1 9 6 5 9 6 5 1 2 2 *